# GEORGE
# BEST

### WITH HARRY HARRIS

# *Hard Tackles*
# *and Dirty Baths*

## THE INSIDE STORY OF
## FOOTBALL'S GOLDEN ERA

EBURY
PRESS

Ebury Press
an imprint of Random House,
20 Vauxhall Bridge Road, London SW1V 2SA

Random House Australia (Pty) Limited
20 Alfred Street, Milsons Point, Sydney, New South Wales 2061, Australia

Random House New Zealand Limited
18 Poland Road, Glenfield, Auckland 10, New Zealand

Random House (Pty) Limited
Isle of Houghton, Corner of Boundary Road & Carse O'Gowrie, Houghton 2198, South Africa

The Random House Group Limited Reg. No. 954009

www.randomhouse.co.uk

Printed and bound in Great Britain by Bookmarque Ltd, Croydon, Surrey

A CIP catalogue record for this book is available from the British Library

Cover design by Two Associates
Cover images © Empics
Interior design by seagulls.net

All plate section images © Empics as marked.
All other images courtesy of the author.
Material quoted in Chapter 10 from *Clough: The Autobiography*
by Brian Clough and John Sadler, published by Partridge Press.
Reprinted by permission of The Random House Group Ltd.

9780091908768 (after Jan 2007)
ISBN 0 091908760

# CONTENTS

# FOREWORD

On 25 November, 2005 my best friend George died. It was the end of an extraordinary life, a fantastic career and a harrowing battle with the disease of alcoholism. Much has been written and said since George's death, and undoubtedly this will continue. While the vast majority of commentators paid handsome tribute and there was a genuine public outpouring of emotion, some of the media comments were more negative. It was my anticipation of this, perhaps, that prompted me to say, minutes after he had passed away, that he had gone "somewhere where nobody can hurt him".

I can only speak as I find. I was George's friend and manager (in that order) for years. I knew and loved a kind, decent and honest man. I know what I saw and recall countless incidents of stunning generosity. He gave his time and more to all kinds of charities, causes and to his public in general. If George had permitted me I would have asked the newspapers to run stories about this side of his life, but something tells me they wouldn't have been interested.

*Hard Tackles and Dirty Baths* is George's third book with Ebury Press and I can vouch for how much he enjoyed writing them, for football was his love and passion. Effectively, from the age of 17 he no longer owned his life, as he was sucked up into a whirlwind that finally laid him down last year. Writing *Blessed*, *Scoring at Half-Time* and this book allowed George to reflect on his life, times and sport like he never had before. He told me that he would like to be remembered for the football and nothing else, and although that may not be possible, this trilogy of books, I believe, does a great deal to put an accurate perspective on George Best's life and times.

Phil Hughes, 2006

# INTRODUCTION

As far as I am concerned, everything about the game of football during these golden years of the 60s and 70s had a different feel to it, a different attitude. That extra man in the dressing room, the so-called team spirit, really did exist in my playing days. Just look at the photograph on the cover of the book you are holding. There are two survivors from the Manchester United Munich air crash, three European Footballers of the Year and two World Cup winners, and there we all are, happy as can be, in a filthy, muddy tub, a couple raising their bottles of Brown Ale as we celebrate winning the league in 1967. Nowadays, of course, when they come in from training or after a game, there's a separate bath and shower unit for each star, no doubt with Armani dressing gowns and Gucci flip-flops, before leaving the ground in their six-figure cars to head home to their security-gated seven-figure mansions.

It might not sound too hygienic, steaming hot bodies all converging together in one huge tiled bath, the water quickly turning a murky shade of grey-black with the mud and dirt of a hard afternoon's toil on the field, but those communal baths of yesteryear were all meant to be about harmony and bonding. In fact, we prized the tiled bath at Old Trafford. The bath at the

Cliff training ground was concrete, and water was either ice cold or so boiling hot you couldn't even get in. All of the facilities were basic, but as players we put up with them. We didn't know any better, didn't expect anything grander, so it was accepted without complaint.

We threw our shirts into the centre of the dressing room, and they would be taken away to the wash room and returned to us for the next training session. There were no names on the back, no advertising logos, no fancy fabrics. These days, all the kit, boots and accessories are waiting for the players when they arrive for training. We would make sure we weren't late for training because all the gear was piled up in the middle of the dressing-room floor, and if you were unfortunate enough to be the last one in, you would have to put up with the left-overs, and that meant socks with holes in them, and plimsolls, or dabs as we called them for some unknown reason, instead of boots. And if your luck was really out, the dabs would be completely the wrong size.

The elevation of players from mere sportsmen to celebrity status was due to two major milestones in the history of the game, both of which began during the 60s: the advent of television coverage, and the removal of the maximum wage cap for players.

As Britain's population emerged from the impoverished post-war 50s into the brighter, optimistic 60s, with more cash in their pockets as disposable income soared, so the sport moved from being a source of local pride to becoming a global business with its money-making base firmly embedded in the new phenomena of television.

Television raised the public's awareness of the game. Committed fans already knew all about their local team, but suddenly a whole new generation – the newly coined teenage generation in particular – became hooked on the sport and its emerging personalities via programmes such as *Match of the Day*.

Kenneth Wolstenholme introduced the first-ever edition of *Match of the Day* on 22 August, 1964 with an audience of 20,000 viewers (less than half the attendance at the ground) tuning in to BBC2 to see Liverpool beat Arsenal 3–2. It was initially only broadcast in the London area, extending to the Birmingham area in December.

Less than two years later – on 30 July, 1966 – 32.3 million people (more than half of the entire population) watched the dramatic World Cup final. The surprising popularity of the television World Cup coverage ensured that by the 1966–67 season *Match of the Day* had a new slot on BBC1, and by the following year ITV had *The Big Match* on screen each Sunday afternoon. By the mid-70s, *Match of the Day* viewing figures averaged twelve million and by the end of the decade, the FA Cup Final could expect an audience of twenty million.

Of course, there was a downside to the explosion of TV coverage. The football authorities had been wary of the influence of the armchair fan, fearing that match attendance – and gate receipts – would fall rapidly. While there were huge gates at glamorous games from Old Trafford to White Hart Lane, there were serious concerns about less attractive fixtures lower down the divisions. As late as 1960, negotiations between the Football League and the Independent Television Authority had fallen through over fears that broadcasting a live game might have an adverse effect on people actually going to the games.

There was a highly cautious initial approach to the introduction of live games, but the broadcasting companies eventually did persuade the Football League that a highlights package would not be detrimental to gates up and down the country, and might even generate more interest in the game and attract a new generation of football followers.

Before television coverage, most teams' fan base was largely local. Seeing new teams, and new stars, quickly created a change of allegiance, often not connected with the area in which the fans lived. The glamour clubs attracted an even wider audience of fans; eventually, the fan base broadened from local to national, from national to international, as clubs began playing more in Europe. Manchester United know more about that than most. The club are still reaping the benefits of a worldwide renown that was borne out of the legendary, pioneering exploits of the Busby Babes in Europe. Today, we can watch virtually every game everywhere, at every level. I watch all the top football, particularly the Premiership, though I also love the football from Italy and Spain.

The lifting of the player's maximum wage was as big an influence on the game as the arrival of television, but it had a very different effect, swinging the balance of power away from the club towards the players.

Before 1960, some of the legends of the game ended their career impoverished. Tommy Lawton and Hughie Gallagher ended up on the dole, and Gallagher committed suicide by throwing himself under a train in 1957. In that year the

Professional Footballers' Association (the players' union) had a new chairman in Jimmy Hill, who led the campaign to remove the maximum wage cap, which stood at £20 a week, £17 during the close season. As player, manager and expert pundit, Hill has been involved in every area of the game. He is perhaps still most famous for the size of his chin, but it was where he stuck his nose that was more important to the game.

Hill became involved in football only because of the Army. When he was called up for national service he was a clerk in the Stock Exchange. But he played for the Army football team which, apart from Hill and one other player, consisted of professionals on an enforced sabbatical. After he was discharged from the Army, he was taken on at Brentford where he became the union rep. When he transferred to Fulham, he became the union man there and, eventually, the union's national chairman.

For years the Football League hardly condescended to meet with the players' representatives to discuss the wage cap, but in January 1961 the threat of a players' strike made the League take notice and in July the maximum wage was abolished. England captain Johnny Haynes became the first £100-a-week footballer and his Fulham chairman Tommy Trinder publicly declared that he was delighted to be able to properly reward his star.

The irony of this achievement by Jimmy Hill was that he never personally benefited from his campaign to end the £20-a-week maximum wage. While his team-mate Haynes saw his salary increase five-fold, Hill was forced by injury into premature retirement at the age of thirty-one, before his contract was updated.

Some figures in the game have recently suggested there should be a wage cap for today's footballers. I doubt you would ever persuade players to accept a situation that previous generations fought so hard to end. But I do wonder if the Football League would have capitulated, had it been able to foresee not just the astronomical sums now paid out to players but also the power this gave individual players.

# 1
## 1960–64

I was always determined to make my mark in this wonderful yet often so weird game of football. I had started my career at Manchester United in the ranks, the A and B teams, and thought I was lucky to be making such rapid progress when I graduated to the reserve side. But then not long after my seventeenth birthday, after only nine central league appearances, I became a full professional and stepped into the first team. I played against West Bromwich Albion at Old Trafford on 14 September, 1963 and I shall never forget it. I was at outside right and we won 1–0 with a goal from David Sadler. I dropped back into the reserves but just over three months later, on 28 December, I was brought in to play outside left, with another youngster, Willie Anderson, making his debut on the other wing.

Willie was even younger then me; he was just sixteen. Yet this was how the conveyor belt of talent operated at Old Trafford under manager Matt Busby. I managed to score in a 5–1 win over Burnley. Everyone was pretty pleased as the win was revenge for a 6–1 beating we'd received at Burnley just two days previously. Both Willie and I stayed in the side for our next game – an FA Cup debut in the third round at Southampton. Everyone keep asking me if I was nervous, particularly as our regular match-winner, Denis Law, wasn't playing. But I never seemed to suffer any nerves. We won 3–2 after a terrific fight back and I stayed in the side until the end of the season, contributing four goals in the league. Things just got better and better and after only twenty-one first-team games, I was honoured by Northern Ireland and won my first cap playing at outside right against Wales at Swansea.

I had travelled to Wembley the previous May with my father to watch United in the 1963 Cup Final. What an atmosphere. What an occasion. I instantly fell in love with the Cup Final and wanted to be part of it.

Manchester United were the outsiders against Leicester City, having finished a poor nineteenth in the First Division, while our opponents had finished fourth. But the excitement was gripping right from the start as United took control and reversed the odds. Within thirty minutes United took the lead when Denis Law cracked an unstoppable shot past Gordon Banks. Minutes later he almost made it two from an individual run that left three defenders trailing, and when he beat Banks his shot was cleared off the line. Fifteen minutes after the break United extended their lead when Banks could only parry a shot from Bobby Charlton and David Herd pounced on the loose ball to score. With ten minutes left, Ken Keyworth scored for Leicester with a diving header. That seemed only to sharpen

United's appetite, and a header from Law rebounded off the post. Then Banks fumbled a shot from Quixall and Herd was there once again to complete the scoring. How could so much exhilarating football fail to inspire?

My dad was there to check everything was okay with Matt Busby as I signed my professional forms for Manchester United. I had spent two years as an "amateur" when, in reality, I was an apprentice, but because of the rules of the day involving the Irish and Scottish Leagues, the club had to find me a regular job and I could train as an amateur only on Tuesdays and Thursdays. Of course, my "job" just happened to coincide with working at the training ground from 9am, where I was able to conveniently combine my duties with a touch of er ... training. There had been a big debate about the draining of talent from Scotland and Northern Ireland and they tried to make it more difficult for the English clubs to take the boys as apprentices, but there was always going to be a way round it. Before the club worked the fiddle with my job I did some actual work for the Manchester Ship Canal Company – making the tea and running messages.

Back then every young boy's head was turned by the glamour and thrill of football. Never mind playing; you dreamed of just being in the big grounds to watch your heroes. Growing up in Belfast, my grandfather lived just fifty yards from the main entrance to the Glentoran ground. In those days the local club would attract big crowds, and he or my dad would take me along. Children went in free if they were accompanied by an adult. Those who didn't have an adult to take them would wait at the turnstiles and ask a stranger to take them in. You'd be lifted over the turnstiles as the adult paid. Once you were in you would ask the other people in the packed stand to lift you up and you'd be carried above their heads down to the front so you could see the game.

After the match on a Saturday evening it would be a thrill waiting for the *Belfast Telegraph* to publish its football special, the Pink. It came out around an hour after the match had finished and you could buy it on the street corner. I would take it home, cut out the Glentoran match report and paste it into my scrapbook. Then, I would flip the paper over, and on the back were reports of the best of the English football, and of course at this time, the headlines belonged to my favourite team, Wolves. Even then kids liked to follow the successful team: they always appear more glamorous for that reason. I must have filled up half a dozen scrapbooks, and I wish I still had them. It was reading those reports of the Wolves games that got me hooked. I became aware of the great traditions of the Wolves team and their exploits domestically and internationally.

For me as a lad in Belfast, I was able to watch the glamour players in English football because one of my near neighbours possessed a television, a rarity in our street. Certainly my family were too poor to afford one. The neighbour was just a couple of doors away. I was just a kid at the time but I was around his house whenever there was a game on. I didn't care who was playing, I just loved watching. In those days it was in fact rare to see any football on television. *Match of the Day* hadn't started yet, and most matches broadcast were international football.

I was originally inspired by Wolves, because of the glamorous international ties they were involved in; playing a team from Moscow at that time was like playing a team from another planet. Wolves were one of the first to play under floodlights, and there was just an extra-special feeling about a game being played in the evening. It was sheer theatre.

I learned that it was on Monday, 13 December, 1954 under the floodlights at Molineux, home of the champions of England, that the idea of a European Cup, the most glamorous tournament in club football, was first conceived. It was on that foul, wintry night in the Black Country that Wolves defeated Honved, the dazzling Hungarian club side that included many players of the national team that had comprehensively thrashed England twice in the previous twelve months. Interest in the European game had reached new heights in Britain as a result of two humiliations suffered by the English side: 6–3 at Wembley in November 1953 and 7–1 in Budapest in the spring of 1954. Those results, and the manner in which they were achieved, had shattered once and for all the idea that the nation that gave the game to the world was still the dominant force. Under the inspirational management of Stan Cullis, Wolves staged a legendary fightback to win the match 3–2. And it was in response to the post-match euphoria that Gabriel Hanot, editor of the French sports paper *L'Equipe*, set about organising the first European club tournament. I had little clue then just how central this would be to my own footballing future.

Hanot had long campaigned for European competition at club level. When the British press proclaimed Wolves "champions of the world" following their victory over Honved, prefaced by the thrashing of Spartak Moscow – both friendlies – Hanot acted. The former France international wrote in *L'Equipe*: "Before we declare that Wolverhampton Wanderers is invincible, let them go to Moscow and Budapest. And there are other internationally renowned clubs: Milan and Real Madrid. The idea of a club World Championship, or at least a European one – larger, more meaningful than the Mitropa Cup and more original than a competition for national teams – should start. Let us take such a risk."

In September 1953 Cullis supervised the installation of floodlights at Molineux and arranged a series of high-profile friendly matches against continental opponents, who brought with them extravagant, exotic ball skills. Cullis ordered a special set of Wolves' famous old-gold shirts to be worn for floodlit matches. Manufactured in a satin material, they seemed to make the players glow in the dark. The matches provoked enormous interest through '53 and into the '54 season, mostly centred on the games scheduled for the end of the year against Spartak Moscow and Honved. Spartak arrived in November and were level at 0–0 after eighty evenly matched minutes before being steamrollered by the supremely fit Wolves forwards, who scored four times in the final ten minutes. That was impressive, but everyone knew that Honved represented the ultimate test.

Their team contained six of the players who had beaten England, including the fabulously talented Ferenc Puskas. The appalling winter weather had left the Molineux pitch sodden. Cunningly, Cullis, on the day of the match, summoned three apprentices to his office and ordered them to water the pitch, then to use the groundsman's heaviest roller to press the moisture into the surface. One of the teenage hopefuls who carried out his instructions was Ron Atkinson. Cullis's plan was certainly not immediately obvious when the game began at a heaving, expectant Molineux. Passing the ball silkily over the glistening surface, the Hungarians left Wolves looking bewildered and it was little surprise when Puskas aimed a free kick towards the head of Sandor Kocsis, who converted the chance. It was 2–0 after fourteen minutes when Kocsis sent Mathos clear to beat Bert Williams. Wolves trailed at the break and Cullis urged the team to believe that the game was salvageable. Wolves got the goal that they needed four minutes into the second half when Reg Leafe, the referee, rather harshly punished Kovaks for a foul on Hancocks and the same player converted the penalty. As Wolves swept forward, Honved's passing game was rendered impotent by the churning morass under their feet and the mud wore the Hungarians out. The equaliser that had begun to look inevitable came in the seventy-sixth minute when Roy Swinbourne, the centre forward, headed home a cross from Dennis Wilshaw. Two minutes later the pair combined again and Swinbourne provoked scenes of near hysteria with a thumping shot that put Wolves ahead. "There they are," Cullis said, gesturing at his mud-streaked, worn-out players, "the champions of the world". In the *News Chronicle*, Charles Buchan wrote: "Wolves struck another decisive blow for English football with as wonderful a second-half rally as I have seen in forty years." The *Daily Mirror*'s star columnist, Peter

Wilson, began his account on the front page: "I have never seen a greater thriller than this. And if I see many more as thrilling I may not live much longer anyway." I was just eight years old, but stories like these fired my mind.

Like many of the clubs that were big when I was growing up, Wolves are no longer a major player. These days the clubs that you'd expect to win the trophies can be counted on three fingers. One of the great things about the era I played in was the diversity of interest. You just never knew who, at the beginning of each season, would be in the ascendancy. There were teams which kept their form over time – Leeds, Liverpool, Everton, Chelsea and ourselves, certainly. But winners could come from almost anywhere – think of West Brom, Ipswich, Sunderland and Derby. You could be beaten 4–0 in one game and then beat the same team in the return fixture 5–0. I just don't think that happens today.

So who were the big teams of the eras in which I first pulled on my boots? The first great side of the 60s were undoubtedly Bill Nicholson's Tottenham Hotspur. Nicholson was a Yorkshireman with true grit and the original one-club man; Tottenham man and boy. He had played for Spurs in the 50s under the legendary Arthur Rowe and taken up Rowe's "push and run" philosophy as a manager, adapting it to his own style. For the uninitiated, "push and run" was the terminology used for a simple, yet highly effective, system of pass and move. The player releasing the ball did not stop, but kept going in order to find space to receive the ball, either from the player to whom he released it or from another team-mate in the passing move. The technique might appear simplicity itself, but it required speed of thought, and the ability to make a pass on the move and to receive the pass with a near-perfect first touch. It didn't work unless virtually the entire attacking area of the team possessed such skills. Nicholson was a perfectionist. In football that is never quite attained, but he wanted to come as near to it as humanly possible. Though Nicholson had assembled a formidable array of naturally skilful players at White Hart Lane, he further demanded an exceptional work-rate, bravery and commitment from each of them. Nicholson, starting in 1958, lifted Spurs from eighteenth in the First Division to the first league and cup double of the century in 1961. He did so by creating a team, as had Busby, that truly played the beautiful game. A man of unlavish lifestyle, living a conveniently short walk from the ground in a semi-detached house, he spent the club's money extravagantly but shrewdly: initially, Dave Mackay, Bill Brown in goal, John White, Cliff Jones and Jimmy Greaves, subsequently Mike England, Pat Jennings, Alan Mullery, Alan Gilzean, Terry Venables, Martin Chivers and Martin Peters.

Years later Martin Chivers recalled winning the UEFA Cup under Nicholson in 1972 and having to wait to open the champagne while his manager went to commiserate with the opposition, Wolves, for having been the better team. This was typical of the man. Bill Nicholson was always strict but fair, dogmatic but analytical, austere but honest, and always modest. Nicholson, who died aged eighty-five a few years ago, was also a man with a conviction.

He devoted a literal lifetime to Tottenham Hotspur: as £2-a-week apprentice painting the grandstand, as meticulous wing half denied more than a single England cap by the ever-present Billy Wright, as trophy-winning manager and, finally, as president. Just as with Matt Busby at Manchester United, Bill Shankly at Liverpool or Jock Stein at Celtic, Nicholson was the embryo of Spurs' greatness. First to arrive each day, last to leave, without Nicholson's nod no stone turned at White Hart Lane. With passing time, some players became uneasy with Nicholson's unswerving discipline and rigorous demands. He would respond: "The time to start worrying is when I'm no longer concerned." Nicholson earned universal affection because, during sixteen years as manager, he was devoid of self-acclaim in his pursuit of excellence and entertainment.

Perhaps his most crucial signing in the double-winning years was, like me, a mercurial, dribbling goalscorer. For a winger, Cliff Jones was brave in the air; you would have thought he had taken flight at the far post. Though not very big, he was able to outleap the tallest of centre halves. Jones was exceptional, above all, for his scoring potential, especially with his head. In eleven seasons with Tottenham he scored 134 goals in 309 matches; including a six-season spell – 1960–65 – of ninety-seven goals in 220 matches. For Wales, he scored thirteen in forty-one. A mere 5ft 8in, and built like a greyhound, he could truly be described as poetry in motion. What full backs mostly saw were his disappearing heels, though Bill Nicholson was once moved to say during Jones's early days at Tottenham, "The ball's round, it rolls: why don't you try passing it occasionally?" This was typical of Nicholson's bluff Yorkshire attitude, but he used such remarks as a challenge to his players to improve. Son of Ivor (West Bromwich) and nephew of Bryn (Wolves and Arsenal), both of them inside forwards, Cliff came from Swansea, an area that seemed to breed many footballers, in a similar way to the other coal-mining areas of the north-east and central Scotland.

Jones's passion and commitment were first imbibed from someone that I myself was indebted to: Jimmy Murphy, assistant to Matt Busby at Manchester United, who was also the Wales team manager at the time. His first cap, in 1954 aged nineteen, came against the Austrian 'Wunder Team'. The experience with Murphy was character-forming. "He was a motivator," Jones says. "His style was fixed bayonets, over-the-top, give them plenty of welly. He impressed on you that the greatest honour you could have was to play for Wales." Jones was also a modest man who never forgot his working-class roots. While a Swansea apprentice, on the insistence of his father, he also worked as a sheet-metal apprentice. Chaired off for his winning goal against England, he was back at the docks at 7.30 next morning. "Well done, lad," the foreman said, "and now there's your proper work."

Nicholson maintained the reality when Jones was transferred to Spurs for £25,000 in 1958, the then-highest figure for a winger. His first game was against Arsenal at Highbury. Arriving unrecognised from his national service depot in west London, he was refused entry by the commissionaire. Nicholson was summoned. "That's him," he said, pointing, and as an aside to Jones, "and by the way, you're late." Jones recounts his other favourite Nicholson idiosyncracy: after one particular pat on the back from Nicholson, he received the immediate rebuke, "Remember a pat on the back is only two feet away from a kick up the arse."

The immoveable rock at the back was Dave Mackay; the strong, silent type. Mackay was a legendary hard man among hard men. He never flinched from a tackle: believe me, I know. Bought in 1959 from Heart of Midlothian, Mackay signed on the spot for Nicholson, despite being a committed Hearts man because, as he explained, "I was impressed by his understatement, his modesty and his honesty."

After securing the league in 1961, Spurs met Leicester in the showpiece FA Cup Final. They won 2–0 against a Leicester side down to ten men, but it was a scrappy affair. Mackay recalled Nicholson's disappointment at his side's display: "We weren't thinking about how entertaining we could be," he said. "We knew it was for the double so we played a bit safe. I decided, like the others, to just sit back and let our forwards press on. But Bill wasn't happy. That was typical of the man. He always wanted to see a game of football and never liked to see his team winning if we played badly. He always wanted us to entertain."

Spurs should have actually won the "double double". The first team to achieve the double in successive seasons came thirty years later when Manchester United managed it in the 1990s. But Nicholson failed to win the league again because of just one team, an Ipswich side managed by one of the north London club's old boys, Alf Ramsey. Spurs lost 3–2 at Portman

Road and later in the season lost by the same score, playing the same way. As Nicholson pointed out, had they picked up just a couple of points against Ipswich, with a far superior goal difference, the title would have stayed at White Hart Lane.

Spurs did retain the FA Cup with a 3–1 win in the Wembley final over Burnley, with goals from Jimmy Greaves, Bobby Smith and a Danny Blanchflower penalty. The club fielded the same side that played in the previous final, with the exception of Greaves, who replaced Les Allen, and Terry Medwin, who was selected ahead of Terry Dyson.

Spurs fans had hoped to see such a fabulous side become the first British team to win the European Cup. But after a gallant effort, Spurs' European adventure was ended in controversial circumstances in the semi-final against Benfica. Even with the magnificent Eusebio in such phenomenal form, Spurs were convinced that refereeing decisions robbed the club of its rightful place in the final.

The north London club did, however, qualify the following year for the European Cup-Winners' Cup, which had only just been launched in 1960. And by this time it had a potent new weapon, which was to ensure, if it failed to become the first British club to land the biggest European prize, it would still make history as the first to land a European trophy.

Though Jimmy Greaves is most often associated with these glory years at Spurs, he was first a star with Chelsea. He joined the team straight from school, and he always makes a point of stressing that Chelsea was just as much a part of his life as Tottenham. Greaves had seven years at Chelsea and nine years at Tottenham. Greaves The Goal, as he was soon known, rose through the Chelsea ranks and commanded press attention even before his debut in 1957. In his first full season in the youth side he scored 114 goals. Chelsea had just won the league title for the first time in 1955, but the following season slumped to sixteenth. Then Greaves came along to help lessen the sense of frustration, scoring on his debut against Spurs on the opening day of the 1957–58 season, at the age of seventeen.

By the time he was twenty-one, Greaves had already collected a century of league goals, the youngest ever to do so. Greaves scored five goals in a game on three occasions, including all five at Preston in a 5–4 win in December 1959. He collected thirteen hat-tricks in all. He didn't stop scoring for the Blues until his final game at home to Nottingham Forest in 1961, when he scored four times. As the club knew he was leaving, he was made captain for the day and he was carried from the pitch on supporters' shoulders. He finally scored 127 goals in 167 games for the west London club. In his final season Greaves created a record of forty-one league goals which, of course, still stands today. He played only forty games.

Though he scored regularly for his new club, AC Milan, he did not like the move and despite Chelsea's attempts to buy him back, he arrived at Spurs to strengthen the double-winning side and become part of the club that made European history. Nicholson paid £99,999 to bring Greaves back from his one season in Italy, refusing to become the first manager to break the six-figure fee barrier. Nicholson didn't like the escalating fees and salaries, but more important, he didn't want

Greaves burdened with the tag of being the first £100,000 player. Even for a mere £1 Nicholson was determined to make a point.

Greaves and Denis Law (who had an equally unhappy time in Italy after leaving Manchester City to join Torino) were the phenomenal goalscorers of their generation. Greaves was the foremost goal poacher, slightly built with lightning-quick reflexes and rapid speed off the mark. Greaves remains the third highest goalscorer for the national side, behind Bobby Charlton with forty-nine goals and Gary Lineker's forty-eight. Greaves achieved forty-four, but he achieved this total with far fewer games than Lineker or Charlton. Greaves was a class act at international level, and was outstanding in European club football.

Spurs put out Rangers, Slovan Bratislava and OFK Belgrade en route to the Cup Winners' Cup final, where they met Atletico Madrid, beating them 5–1 with Greaves scoring two. A truly golden night.

The other great inspiration that night was the club captain and my fellow Ulsterman Danny Blanchflower. Who could fail to be inspired by a player and a man such as Danny Blanchflower? When Danny finally hung up his boots, on 5 April, 1964, at the age of thirty-eight, he'd played 382 games for Spurs and scored twenty-one goals. Bill Nicholson wanted the former skipper to succeed him after he quit in 1974, but the board had other ideas and, surprisingly, went for former Arsenal defender Terry Neill. Danny did finally become a manager in June 1976 when he took over Northern Ireland. He also took over as boss of Chelsea in December 1978, but there were severe financial troubles at the Bridge at that time and he failed to keep them in the First Division, so after nine months he resigned; that was Danny for you.

The Tottenham captain was also capped fifty-six times times by Northern Ireland. And for me it was such a thrill to watch Blanchflower star for Northern Ireland as well. My last game for Northern Ireland was during the spell that Danny was manager, and we drew 2–2 with Holland. He was certainly different. I often just didn't have a clue what he was talking about. I can recall that he once gave a team talk to tell us the five different ways you can take a penalty. I didn't know then there were five different ways, and I don't know even now that there are five ways to take a penalty. But, again, that was Danny for you. I lost interest after he explained method number three. Whatever one of the five ways I used, I seemed to have been pretty successful with it. But I really liked Danny because he was such a crazy Irishman.

My first live encounter with Nicholson's team was when, in their defence of the Cup-Winners' Cup, Spurs came to Old Trafford on 10 December, 1963. Though I was only watching from the stand that night, we beat them 4–1, winning the overall tie 4–3. Worse for Spurs was that Dave Mackay was carried off to hospital with a broken leg after only eight minutes. They battled bravely with ten men and remained ahead on aggregate until the last thirteen minutes. It was a night of high emotions, a game of tremendous action, yet despite the intensity was played sport-ingly throughout. Spurs, with a 2–0 lead from White Hart Lane, almost made it three when Smith put his point-blank header straight at Gaskell from Mackay's early cross. This was, in retrospect, the turning point – a minute later, David Herd pulled the all-important early goal back for United, flying in with a diving header. So when Mackay was carried off, Spurs' lead had been reduced to just one goal and, soon after the interval, Herd scored again to level the scores. This should have spelled the end for Spurs, but they immediately went on the attack as only a team under the charge of Nicholson could do. They broke through on the left with John White, who floated a perfect cross for Jimmy Greaves to score with a rare header. Spurs were back in front again. The team held out until Charlton latched on to a floated Crerand pass and smashed a volley home, and then, with only two minutes left, Bobby cracked in the winner.

For me, this Spurs team was a great side. As Nicholson said, prior to completing the double at Wembley against Leicester: "We've found the blend. With one or two stars a team should be good. With four or five, it should be something special." The following year Tottenham retained the FA Cup and its 1963 triumph in the Cup-Winners' Cup was followed by a third FA Cup triumph in 1967, the League Cup in 1971 and the UEFA Cup in 1972. Nicholson's last trophy, and his eighth as a manager, came with a second League Cup victory in 1973 before his departure a year later.

When England were beaten by Brazil 3–1 and failed to make the quarter-final of the 1962 World Cup finals in Chile, it marked the end of Walter Winterbottom's sixteen-year reign as England manger. His replacement was Alf Ramsey, fresh from working wonders at Ipswich. The East Anglia club had risen from the Third Division South to replace Spurs as English champions in just five years. Ramsey's team won the Division Two and Division One titles in successive seasons, only the fourth club to record that particular achievement. Ironically Ramsey had been schooled in the very same Spurs traditions, the Arthur Rowe "push and run" team where he played along-side Nicholson in the previous decade.

The Tractor Boys is a relatively new label for a club renowned for its friendly, humble environment in East Anglia. "Wonderful little Ipswich Town, the miracle team of all time" is how the *Football Post* described the club in April 1962 after a 2–0 home victory over Aston Villa confirmed Ramsey's team of unknowns as league champions. When Ramsey took over Ipswich in 1955 it was the youngest and probably financially poorest team in the league. Ramsey moulded Ted Phillips and John Elsworthy, already members of the team, into his key men and built round them. With no money for big signings, Ramsey had to spot cast-offs and make them believe in themselves. John Compton was an erratic left half with Chelsea, and Ramsey transformed him into a successful left back. Roy Stephenson was an inconsistent inside forward with Burnley, but at Ipswich he became a reliable outside right, thanks to Ramsey, who had actually played against him in the old days. Chelsea fans remembered Jimmy Leadbetter as a somewhat plodding inside left, but Ipswich followers know him as an outside left who kept defences constantly occupied. Ramsey converted Andy Nelson from an orthodox left half with West Ham to a tower of strength at centre half. I was intrigued by the

Ramsey methods and what he had to say at the time: "I never ask a man to do more than he has in him. My job is to get the best out of him. I had a plan, and I persevered with it. It was simply this – I picked the best team available and never asked the players to attempt anything beyond their powers. I concentrated on getting the maximum out of each man."

While Ramsey paid tribute to the players, the players owed so much to Ramsey. A typical example was Ray Crawford, the first Ipswich player ever to win an England cap, who expressed his eternal gratitude: "Mr Ramsey gave me confidence in myself. He understood my problems and provided the answer. I owe all my success to him." A tribute from a player discarded by Portsmouth and reluctant to join Ipswich in 1958. Crawford, a former office boy and building worker, earned the title of "Jungle Boy" on the strength of his service with the Royal Hampshires in Malaya, but Crawford modestly pooh-poohs the nickname: "I only did two patrols in the jungle and nothing happened." When Crawford joined Ipswich, Ramsey worked hard on his weak left foot until it became almost as deadly as his right, as his goals tally indicates.

The transformation was complete when he became known as "Thunderboots" Crawford. Ray was honoured to play for the Football League against the Irish in 1961. "I'm certainly glad I went to Ipswich," observed Crawford, by then the proud owner of a car, and worth four times the £6,000 Ipswich paid Portsmouth for him in 1958.

Ramsey believed his first job was with the players; office work was downgraded. Most days he would be out on the pitch in his tracksuit quietly coaching, giving the lads individual attention, and showing them that he believed in them. During Second Division days, everyone told Ramsey he needed a goalscorer. "I've got one, but he's injured. I'll wait till he's fit again," said Ramsey, referring to Ted Phillips. Phillips, possessor of perhaps the most powerful shot in football, came back and scored the goals that won promotion. Another very bright Ipswich character was Bill Baxter, a Scottish right half with a starry future although he cost only £400 plus £100 if he made good. He made good all right. He was only twenty-three, but had the coolness and confidence of an old-timer. Baxter said he owed it to his father, an engine driver from Granton, near Edinburgh. "He always said, 'Keep calm, keep playing and everything will come all right,' and I've always remembered his advice," said Baxter. "Keeping calm is a great asset. I see players who worry all the time. You can tell from the way they jump high into the air every time you tackle them."

Ramsey had no favourites but he was inclined to believe his left winger, thirty-three-year-old Jimmy Leadbetter, was a vital ingredient of the side. "I hope he plays as long as Stanley Matthews," said Ramsey hopefully. "He puts in more work, especially in tackles, than any other forward in the side. I think Crawford and Phillips will agree he is responsible for many of their goals." Promotion to the First Division in 1961 did not panic Ramsey even though cash was scarce and signings were few. There was only one signing of note – Scottish inside forward Douglas Moran for £12,000, an Ipswich record. When the club gained promotion a dazzling new concrete stand costing £35,000 was erected behind one of the goals and the supporters club said they would foot the bill. Their secretary, John Jacobs, noted the club only had £18,000 so he made an appeal to the town to show their appreciation of Ipswich by donating the rest. The appeal was directed mainly at the shops, hotels and restaurants who would benefit from the trade the club would bring to Ipswich. It should have been a huge success yet the appeal raised a miserly few hundred pounds.

Chairman Captain John Cobbold explained the apparent apathy: "Suffolk has no long tradition of soccer so the local people do not regard it with the passion and intensity you find in other towns. It takes a Suffolk man a long time to accept anything new because he is very reserved and conventional in his approach to life. You'll seldom find him roaring his head off during a goalscoring move, for instance, although he may appreciate it all right. It takes a long time for him to let his hair down."

John Elsworthy, the Ipswich town midfield mainstay, was dubbed "The greatest Welsh player never to be capped by his country". The cultured midfielder from Nantyderry played for Ipswich Town from 1949 until 1964, after signing as a seventeen-year-old for the princely sum of £25 on a contract paying him £7 per week during the playing season. Elsworthy's first taste of success came when Ipswich won the Third Division South title at the end of the 1953–54 season. The Town were only to survive one season in the higher division before finding themselves back in the Third. With relegation came change. Scott Duncan, who had managed Ipswich since 1937, stepped aside and was replaced by the thirty-five-year-old former Southampton, Spurs and England full back, Alf Ramsey. This appointment was the turning point for John.

Even now, at the age of seventy-three, the genial Welshman becomes excited when he talks about his former boss. "He was an incredible man. In those days we used to travel to away matches by train. The conversation among the players covered anything and everything. Alf would bury his head in his newspaper. When the conversation turned to football Alf would lower his paper and join in. He was only interested in football. During practice matches, if someone made a mistake, Alf would stop the game and explain the error in detail before allowing the players to continue. He was a marvellous man and it came as no surprise to us at Ipswich when, in later years, we heard the England players such as Bobby Charlton and Bobby Moore say how great he was."

He has no hesitation in naming the greatest game he ever played in. "January 1958, FA Cup fourth round versus Manchester United at Old Trafford. The conditions that day were absolutely awful and we fell behind to a goal from Bobby Charlton. We played brilliantly and Jimmy Leadbetter came close to equalising when his shot hit the post. Bobby got a second five minutes from time and that was that. There was a crowd of over 53,000 that day and they gave us a tremendous ovation as we left the field. That was the last time the Busby Babes played at Old Trafford. Less than two weeks later there was that terrible crash at Munich Airport and so many of their great players were killed. It was tragic and all of us at Ipswich were shattered. Duncan Edwards, Tommy Taylor, Roger Byrne,

Eddie Coleman and Mark Jones had all played against us and they all perished – it was so difficult to take in."

Ramsey had, by then, converted John into a left half, part of the strategy that, later on, the football world was to label "Ramsey's Wingless Wonders" on a far grander stage. Having won the Second Division title at the end of the 1960–61 season, Ipswich found itself, for the first time in its history, among the elite in the First Division. John recalled that the experts tipped them for relegation. "We started off with a draw at Bolton, followed by two defeats at the hands of Burnley and Manchester City but then Burnley came to Portman Road and we beat them 6–2," he recalls. "A large part of our success that season was down to the fact that we had very few injuries. We only used sixteen players and five of those played in five or less games. Ray Crawford scored thirty-three goals and Ted Phillips was only just behind with twenty-eight. We won the champion-ship on the last day of the season at Portman Road when we beat Aston Villa 2–0."

Ipswich won successive championships in the two top divi-sions and even now, forty years on, the feat has yet to be repeated. Alf Ramsey left to manage England in 1963 and at the beginning of the 1965–66 season, after 435 games for Ipswich, John decided to hang up his boots. John continues to live in Ipswich. He and his wife Ann are still avid Town supporters and can be seen in the directors' box at every home game. "When the blue of Ipswich is in your blood it never leaves it," he says.

The first Town player to be capped by England, joint top scorer in the First Division in the championship-winning season of 1962, was the club's record scorer, Ray Crawford. He recalled: "Me and big Ted Phillips just hit it off and the goals flowed. We were lucky in that we had great service from the likes of Jimmy Leadbetter and Roy Stephenson and we just seemed to have the knack of popping up in the right place at the right time. Scoring goals is what the game is all about in the end and if you have a couple of guys banging them in regularly, you have always got a chance of doing something."

Crawford's best goal was reserved for that final Aston Villa game. "I got the ball at the halfway line, beat the defender marking me and raced through to score," he said. "The keeper saved it, but I beat him to the rebound and scored from the six-yard line. I only ever scored from that range."

Ipswich found itself in the European Cup and beating AC Milan 2–1 at home when Crawford flicked the ball through the keeper's legs to score, although they had lost 3–0 away and went out. Crawford has no doubts about the influence of Ramsey: "Alf just had the ability to get the best out of players. He would call you aside and point out things on how to improve your game and nearly always he was proved right."

John Cobbold, then in his thirties, was the youngest chairman in the league, yet was also one of the nicest and wisest. He and his directors met rarely to discuss the club business. They let the manager manage and the professionals to run their club with minimum interference.

Ipswich boasted a fair sprinkling of blue blood on its board: a baron (Lord Cranworth), a baronet (Sir Charles Bunbury), the Prime Minister's nephew (John Cobbold), and an Old Harrovian

(Major A. D. Terry). It was John Cobbold's father, the late John Murray Cobbold, who founded Ipswich as a professional club. One day in 1935, brewery heir Cobbold senior stood watching the rain from his club window in Piccadilly. Beside him stood Sir Samuel Hill-Wood, then a director of Arsenal. Cobbold had intended to go racing, but Hill-Wood said: "You don't want to go to Kempton in this weather – come to Highbury with me instead." Cobbold did. He caught the 'football bug'. Arsenal was at the height of its fame in those days, and the enthusiasm and standard of play he saw at Highbury so thrilled Cobbold that he decided to take an interest in his local amateur club at Ipswich. Soon Ipswich were good enough to turn professional and enter the Southern League, and in their very first year they won the championship. Cobbold was so delighted that he said, "Fine, now I'll make Ipswich the Arsenal of East Anglia," and proceeded by signing Scott Duncan, one of the great managers of pre-war days, to perform the task.

Scott Duncan worked relentlessly to secure league status. He wrote to every league club personally, canvassing for support, and in 1938 he achieved his ambition – Ipswich were elected to the old Third Division South. To celebrate Ipswich landing the championship, Crawford, Phillips and the team were treated to a day out at Clacton and a plate of cockles. Dispensing largesse indiscriminately has never been the Ipswich style, though it's been said that the Cobbolds were said to have a crisis if they ran out of white wine in the boardroom.

While Ipswich were making their formidable rise in 1962, one of the most famous names in English football history suffered a sad exit. Accrington Stanley, among the league's founder members, had mounting debts and were forced to resign from the Fourth Division. This was another sign of the increasing polarisation between the haves and have-nots, a trend already present even then and, as we all know, continuing today with dramatic consequences. Exeter, the team who were to have been Accrington's next opponents, before they went broke, were also suffering crippling debts. There is a now-famous picture of Accrington's captain Bob Wilson posing next to a poster advertising the club's home game with Exeter for Saturday, 10 March at Peel Park Ground. But it was a game that would never take place.

Accrington went bust, out of business and out of football for good. While there was no way back for Accrington Stanley, it shows you how clubs can survive and how Exeter, recently once again dogged by financial scandal, came back to play Manchester United in the FA Cup and hold the mighty Premiership team to a draw at Old Trafford. Even in today's damagingly materialistic game, dreams can still come true.

Everton were the other club to make the running in the early 60s. The Toffees became a big hit and highly influential under the guidance of manager Harry Catterick. When Walter Smith parted company with Everton before the appointment of David Moyes he observed: "The Catterick dynasty is impossible to recreate in the modern era. There are only certain clubs that can maintain that sort of domination. Everton are a big club but they've probably become known as sellers rather than buyers." Under Catterick the club bought some of the best and most expensive players and became known as the "chequebook champions". An authoritarian manager, Harry Catterick took over Everton following the departure of Johnny Carey in 1961. Catterick was given a brief directly from chairman John Moores, who had made his fortune with Littlewoods department stores and football pools: get the club back to the top of the league again. Catterick set about transforming the club with a zeal that surprised their rivals.

He was another prolific former player; Catterick had played for Everton throughout the 1940s and early 1950s, scoring twenty-four goals in seventy-one matches. Older fans welcomed him back enthusiastically, hoping his talents on the pitch could continue off it. Confident in his own judgement, and unafraid of criticism, Catterick acquired a series of top-class players such as John Morrissey, Fred Pickering and Ray Wilson. Catterick elevated Everton to fourth place in the league during his first season, five points behind champions Ipswich. Poor away form and injuries to several key players cost the club a serious tilt at taking the championship. There was more steel and resolve in the team, a winning mentality had developed, and in Alex Young and Roy Vernon the manager brought together a top-flight forward partnership. Expectations were that a title might be a possibility for the first time since 1939.

The 1962–63 season began with Burnley, runners-up of the previous season's league and FA Cup. Playing away in the newly introduced strip with its hoop-necked shirt, Everton impressed with a 3–1 win. Just four days later 70,000 fans packed Goodison to see the team play Manchester United, with hopes still high for

Everton. The magical Young dominated the match, scoring twice, including one spectacular header over a United defender which, when it fell, he then hit sweetly and accurately into the net. Parker got the third goal.

On the day of the match against us, Catterick stunned not only club supporters but other local fans when he signed Johnny Morrissey from Liverpool for £10,000. Morrissey became only the fourth player ever to move from Anfield to Goodison. The move across Stanley Park was a real shock, as Morrissey had long been a devout Red, whose boyhood hero was Billy Liddell. Fans also asked why, when Catterick was meant to be building a side to challenge for the championship, he had splashed out so much for a player who had been kept out of first-team matches by Alan A'Court's continuing good form. Catterick's judgement of players, and his signings, were rarely questioned again as the acquisition of Morrissey turned out to be inspired.

When Everton met Catterick's former club, Sheffield Wednesday, in the next match, Vernon captured all the head-lines for his part in Everton's 4–1 win. Everton's return match against United at Old Trafford the following week turned out to be a real thriller. Keeper West kept United out of the net time and again, with Gabriel and Vernon hitting only the bar at the other end. The decider came in the seventy-eighth minute: Morrissey was fouled by Shay Brennan and Vernon converted the penalty to keep Everton's one hundred per cent record intact with a 1–0 win.

Everton continued to look impressive as the season got into full swing, though they lost the top spot following defeats at

Fulham and Leyton Orient. At the end of September, the club met Liverpool in front of a 73,000 derby crowd at Goodison Park for a dramatic needle match. Vernon's first-half penalty was equalised by a goal from Lewis.

The Toffees seemed set for success when Morrissey silenced the critics with his first goal for the club. Liverpool keeper Jim Furnell dropped the ball, and Morrissey ploughed it through the gap between Ron Yeats and Gordon Milne. Although Moran managed to stop the ball, the referee reckoned it had crossed the line. The Everton fans began to celebrate the seemingly inevitable victory but then, with only seconds to go, A'Court lofted the ball, Lewis got his head to it and Hunt converted it for the equaliser. Everton remained just a place off the top, after the 2–2 draw, with Liverpool already out of the reckoning. A goalless draw down south against Tottenham Hotspur on 1 December saw Everton regain the summit.

Then came the Big Freeze. The winter of 1962–3 was Britain's coldest since records began. Severe frosts and blizzard conditions caused the cancellation of virtually all league fixtures between 22 December and 12 February, though Everton did play two FA Cup ties at Barnsley and Swindon. It was during the enforced break that Catterick finally closed the deal to buy Tony Kay from his old club Sheffield Wednesday for £55,000. Everyone had expected Kay to follow Catterick to Everton, but the deal had taken eighteen months to broker, mainly because Wednesday weren't keen to sell. Kay was captain within the year, after Vernon gave up the job at the end of the season. Another new team member arriving at Goodison during the winter was Rangers winger Alex Scott, who was snapped up by Catterick in a last-minute raid just as Bill Nicholson at Tottenham thought he had the player in the Spurs bag. Scott – nicknamed 'Chico' by the Everton fans who thought he looked like a cut-out figure of a Mexican Indian being used in a television promotion of the time – was soon a firm favourite for his ability to scythe through the defence.

As play resumed at the end of February, Everton were behind Spurs and Leicester, though with a game in hand. Two decisive wins against Nottingham Forest and Ipswich Town buoyed the club's spirits after they crashed out of the fifth round of the FA Cup to West Ham. By 6 April Everton – still with that game in hand – were on forty-seven points, with Leicester and Spurs on forty-eight. Easter weekend saw a draw and then a win, against Birmingham, which brought Everton level with Spurs on points and games played, and just one behind Leicester's tally of fifty-one.

Spurs then arrived at Goodison for a virtual play-off for the title in front of a 67,500 crowd. After an early wide shot from a closely marked Greaves, Tony Kay played the ball to Vernon, who passed to Young, who leapt to it to put Everton in front. Everton held on to the slim lead to find themselves at the final whistle back at the top of the league for the first time since November.

A useful extra point was won from Everton's midweek draw with Arsenal, but the next game, against West Ham, got off to a depressing start with an own goal by Meagan after twenty minutes. But the team was keen to wipe out the bitter taste of its FA Cup exit against the London squad, and Young powered on with a ball to Vernon who equalised. Just before half time, Temple put Everton ahead, playing in only his second game of the season. Another Vernon goal, against Bolton on 4 May, maintained Everton's three-point lead over Spurs, with Leicester's hopes dashed after a defeat by West Bromwich Albion. Everton rammed home the message with a 4–0 win against West Brom a few days later.

Catterick's second season, and the dream of landing the title with panache, rested on the final game of the season against Fulham at Goodison. Everton dominated throughout the definitive fixture, winning 4–1, with a Vernon hat-trick and a single from Scott. After the final whistle it was the usual, relatively sedate celebrations compared to today's wild scenes. The players simply completed a lap of honour and when they left the field, the fans chanted their approval of club chairman Moores, the man they had, ironically, jeered at two years earlier after previous manager Carey's departure. Moores described it as "the happiest day of my life". Everton not only edged past Tottenham for the title, but effectively overtook the London club among the elite of this era. The spine of the side was strong, from keeper Gordon West, centre half Brian Labone and centre forward Alex Young, but essentially it was Carey's squad, topped up with a few key Catterick signings.

The winter freeze had played havoc with the fixture lists, with more than 400 games postponed, disrupting the season even more than the notoriously snow-bound winter of 1946–47. The pools companies initially suffered like everyone else, before coming up with a novel solution to the problem:

a "Pools Panel" made up of pundits who decided the outcome of postponed matches, allowing punters to still be able to have a flutter.

Everton would remain in the top six league contenders for the remainder of the decade but after the 1963 championship, three northern clubs dominated the domestic game: Leeds, Manchester United, but first and foremost, Liverpool.

Liverpool, Everton's city rivals, had had a miserable time in the 1950s, much of it spent in the Second Division. Manager Phil Taylor was sacked in November 1959 and a month later an unassuming Scotsman arrived. Forty-six-year-old Bill Shankly was persuaded to leave Huddersfield and take over at Anfield on a £2,500 salary. Over the next three years he let some players go, revitalised the careers of others and made some key signings. He snapped up Ron Yeats from Dundee United, Ian St John from Motherwell and Gordon Milne from Preston.

L iverpool stormed to the Second Division championship in 1961–62. The following season, 1962–63, was spent consolidating. The club had an equally slow start in 1963–64, but went on to take forty-seven points from the last thirty games to secure their sixth championship – the first since the late 40s. Other managers began to use tactical defensive methods to prevent the free flow of goals from teams like Liverpool. Yet their goal-scoring form was irresistible, particularly at Anfield, managing sixty goals in front of their home fans, an average of nearly three per game. Roger Hunt developed into a consistent goal-scoring machine, on this occasion hitting thirty-one of the team's ninety-two league goals.

While the measure of the best team in the country has always been winning the championship, the FA Cup provided the glamour, the thrills, the shocks, and sometimes a much-needed diversion from the routine of the league.

It had a charisma that somehow the league never quite provided. In my first FA Cup year, 1963–64, Oxford United, in only their second season since being elected to the league, beat Blackburn 3–1 to become the first Fourth Division side to reach the quarter-finals. Non-league Bedford Town won 2–1 at Second Division Newcastle in the third round.

The FA Cup Final was traditionally the last game of the season and always the most prestigious individual game of the year. Having had my appetite whetted by United's 1963 victory, it was a competition I longed to make it to the final of. But I agonisingly missed out in this first professional year. I also missed out on setting a record as the youngest player to that date to play in the final. We had made it to the semi-final but in the other semi-final Preston had a player, Howard Kendall, born 22 May, 1946 in Ryton, Tyne & Wear. In fact, we share the same birthday. Had we both got to the final they'd have been digging out the actual time of the birth to see who was the youngest! Preston did get to the final and Manchester United did not. And Howard, not me, became the youngest ever to play in a Wembley Cup Final. As it was, all I could think about was my first FA Cup semi-final defeat. It was a horrendous feeling. It had seemed that we were destined to reach the final and win it, considering that the semi-finalists were Swansea and Preston, who were drawn against each other, while we got West Ham. Naturally you think you are so close to the final you can touch it. It was a bad draw for the neutrals because everyone at the time wanted to see a Manchester United-West Ham final, which was the real glamour final, north versus south.

Forced instead to watch it like everyone else on TV, the black-and-white television coverage of the FA Cup Final crackled into life from the off. First Division West Ham were clear favourites against Second Division Preston. Twice Preston took the lead and twice the Hammers fought back, the second coming straight from the "what happened next?" archive. Geoff Hurst headed against the bar, and the ball rebounded away from goal, only to strike keeper Alan Kelly and roll back over the goal line. West Ham finally won, thanks to a last-minute goal by Ronnie Boyce. There were no post-match excuses or recriminations from Preston, just Kendall talking about how his "tummy tingled" with nerves. Everyone agreed it was the most exciting FA Cup Final since the Matthews match eleven years earlier.

The Hammers side included players of the calibre of Bobby Moore, Geoff Hurst, Martin Peters and Johnny Byrne. Wearing number seven in claret and blue that spring day was a twenty-six-year-old winger Peter Brabrook, born in Greenwich but raised in East Ham. He had moved from Chelsea a couple of seasons earlier and had quickly become a firm favourite in east

London. Now sixty-seven, Brabrook, who works for the club on a part-time basis, still vividly remembers that day: "I remember the build-up to the game. We had two weeks to think about it after the end of the league season. We were big odds-on favourites that day but Preston played better than us, in the first half especially. Twice we went behind and twice we pulled level. I can remember the clock ticking down and both teams straining for the winner. It looked like it was going into extra time." With less than three minutes left, Hurst galloped across the Wembley turf before releasing the ball to Brabrook on the right. "I had nothing left, nothing at all," he recalled. "The Wembley pitch was notorious for inducing cramp in those days and both my calves had seized up. They were like concrete. My socks were down around my ankles but I managed to push the ball in front of me and look up. There, in the middle, I saw Ronnie Boyce making a run into the box and unmarked. I managed to get a good contact and Boycey did the rest, heading home the winner."

It was with this final that future England great Hurst first came to prominence. West Ham's strikers in the mid-1980s, Tony Cottee and Frank McAvennie, were the best the club has ever had, rattling in fifty-four goals in 1985–86, but theirs was nothing like the sustained success of Hurst and "Budgie" Byrne, who scored 355 between them in the 60s, Hurst claiming a total of 248 goals for West Ham in 499 games. He was born in the Potteries in December 1941, the son of Charlie Hurst, who played for Oldham and Rochdale before winding down his career with non-league Chelmsford City.

Geoff grew up in Chelmsford, and joined West Ham straight from secondary modern school at sixteen. The Hammers were in the old Second Division at the time, but were promoted as champions in 1958. He made his debut, away to Nottingham Forest, in February 1960 at the age of eighteen, playing in the old left half position. Bobby Moore started there, too, and they actually vied for the position for a couple of seasons. But Moore was always the better half back, much more secure defensively. When Ron Greenwood replaced Ted Fenton as manager at Upton Park in March 1961, he was unimpressed with Hurst. "Geoff was a big, strong, ordinary wing half, happy going forward, but a terrible defender," said Greenwood. Hurst almost went to Crystal Palace in part-exchange for Johnny Byrne in March 1962, and it was the following season before his career took off at Upton Park. Hurst recalled: "At half back I was struggling for a place. Moore was quicker to grasp what he was being taught, partly because I had the distraction of cricket. Up until 1962 I was trying to make a career as a batsman with Essex." When Hurst broke into the West Ham team, in 1962–63, he quit cricket. When Greenwood asked him to play up front he initially wasn't keen, and only agreed because he thought it would be short-term. But Hurst just simply clicked in that new position and scored thirteen goals in twenty-seven appearances in the top division that first season. Remarkably, in 1962 he was still playing more cricket than football. But by 1963–64, Hurst had taken to the striker's role like a natural. "I was playing the position just about as well as I ever did," he said. Hurst recalled the Hammers' cup campaign: "We played well throughout the tournament but we didn't in the first half at Wembley. They were in front at the interval. I got the equaliser for 2–2, with a diving header which bounced down off the bar and over the line. A rehearsal or what? Then Boycey came out of a trapdoor in the box to get the decider from Peter Brabrook's cross and I'd gone from being second-choice left half at the start of one season to cup-winning striker the next."

There were some extraordinary one-offs during the 1963–64 season. England beat a Rest of the World XI 2–1 at Wembley on 23 October in a match to celebrate the centenary of the Football Association. A crowd of 100,000 turned out to see world stars such as Di Stefano, Puskas, Gento Raymond Kopa, Lev Yashin, Djalma Santos and Eusebio. The World XI team was allowed to use sixteen players. For England, Greaves was in exceptional form and the two Scots in the World XI, Law and Baxter, were thoroughly at home in such illustrious company. All the goals came in the last twenty minutes. Terry Paine shot England ahead after a Greaves effort was blocked. Then Law combined with Puskas and Di Stefano to put the World XI level. England went close when Bobby Charlton thundered a shot against the base of the post and Greaves scraped the bar. England finally produced the winner with seven minutes remaining. Goalkeeper Soskic, who had replaced Yashin for the second half, could not hold another Charlton thunderbolt, and Greaves, as ever, was at hand to crack the ball home.

North of the border, a crowd of nearly 121,000 at Hampden Park saw Rangers climax a record season with two goals in the last minute to beat Dundee 3–1 in the cup and clinch the domestic treble. Rangers were emulating their own treble feat of fifteen years earlier, the only other time it had been done until then. The only competition the team took part in but failed to win was the European Cup, having been trounced 6–0 by Real in Madrid.

Manchester City's Maine Road staged a benefit match and farewell appearance for Bert Trautmann, the former German soldier who was captured during the war and stayed on to capture hearts as the goalkeeper who played on after breaking his neck in the 1956 Cup Final. Bert captained a combined United-City team that beat an All-International XI 5–4. The 47,901 gate produced receipts of £9,155, a record for a British benefit match. The game ended four minutes early when the fans spilled on to the pitch and mobbed Bert, who had to be rescued by a posse of police while some fans who could not get near their hero swung on the crossbars.

People like to think everything was more gentlemanly and certainly less corrupt in those days, but scandal has never been too far away in football and one of the biggest ever occurred when three Sheffield Wednesday players, wing half Tony Kay, Peter Swan and David "Bronco" Layne were implicated in a match-rigging story broken in the *People* in April 1964. Kay, along with Layne and Swan, was found guilty of conspiring to throw a match against Ipswich in 1962, which they lost 2–0. Ironically, Kay had been voted Man of the Match by the same newspaper. Swan was also an England player, and had been to Chile as part of the 1962 World Cup squad. Investigations revealed that the problem was even more widespread than at first thought, with an ex-player named Jimmy Gauld the chief orchestrator of the scam.

On 27 May, the blackest day in football history, more than 300 died in Lima during riots after a Peruvian goal against Argentina was disallowed.

## 1963–64 ROLL OF HONOUR

*Champions:* Liverpool

*FA Cup:* West Ham

*League Cup:* Leicester City

*European Cup:* Inter Milan

*European Cup-Winners' Cup:* Sporting Lisbon

*Footballer of the Year:* Bobby Moore

*European Footballer of the Year:* Denis Law

# 2

## 1964-65

There was a determined mood in the Old Trafford camp at the start of this season. We had the FA Cup win under our belts and we'd performed better in the league, finishing second. This year we were aiming for first place. We had the players, we had the desire, and there was a growing sense that we were starting a season with a conviction to perform to our optimum on a consistent basis and to prove that we had the best team and the best individuals in the land. No one actually spoke about our aspirations of winning the league, or indeed our chances of pulling it off, but as the season unfolded through the winter, there was a deep focus that permeated the whole squad.

As a young lad starting my first full season, it was hard to gauge a "mood"; I was more wrapped up in how I would do, how I wanted to perform. But even at that embryonic stage of my career, there was no mistaking the unity and intensity among the senior players such as Denis Law, Bill Foulkes and Bobby

Charlton. The desire was there to end any under-performing. They knew they were a great side and wanted to prove it.

Even though I was the new kid, it wasn't long before I felt I was earning the respect of even the legends at the club. I forged plenty of friendships in that era that are still dear to me. Denis Law is still a great friend, perhaps even closer now than we were then. It's truly amazing that he and I are such great friends even now, considering that when I was a kid, he was a god. He was a real hero to the fans, especially the Stretford End at Old Trafford. Like me, he was no giant in build, but once he was on the pitch he would take on anyone, try any chance, no holds barred, and the fans loved him for it.

Suddenly finding myself playing with greats like Law was certainly the start of a learning curve. I had to come to terms with playing the man's game. It wasn't long before the opposition knew who I was and thought they knew how to stop me.

Most of the time I discovered that I would be kicked whenever I got the ball, or at least the defender would try to kick me if they could get near enough. It paid to be nimble, even on those atrocious pitches. As a winger I would usually be up against the full back, such as Paul Reaney at Leeds, though other sides would designate a man marker. Arsenal would usually put Peter Storey on me, while Chelsea had their hatchet man Chopper Harris at full back, so I was always up against him. Spurs believed in their football, and never usually assigned a man marker, they were one of the few sides that didn't, so I normally came up against their full back Cyril Knowles.

Every team had a hard man in the side – we had some

characters at Manchester, and some really hard men like Billy Foulkes and Nobby Stiles – but hard tackles were a common everyday occurrence on the training pitch, let alone in the games. At Manchester we'd sometimes train beside the rail track, in a small area covered with debris ranging from broken glass to bricks and stones, and yet we wouldn't hold back – we were kicking shit out of each other. Players would often finish the training sessions with a bloody nose. In fact if you didn't hand out the stick you were liable to be in trouble with the boss, Matt Busby. It was a tough sport; there was real physical contact and you had to get used to it in training to put up with it on the pitch because you could expect to be kicked, and often, during a game. So training was fierce, sometimes brutal, to replicate the sort of things you would have to put up with in the action for real.

On the pitch during games, we'd kick each other, and there were plenty of occasions when we would square up to each other. At times you'd thump the guy who deserved to be thumped. But it was all up front, all face-to-face; there was none of this deliberate elbowing, head-butting or revolting spitting you come across these days.

This, my first full season, coincided with the last season of the legendary Stanley Matthews' career. Matthews was chaired off by Lev Yashin and Ferenc Puskas at the end of his testimonial match on a Wednesday night at Stoke on 28 April when he retired at the age of fifty after a career spanning thirty-three years. Despite his age he was still full of tricks on the wing. It was incredible to believe that Matthews made his league debut for Stoke in March 1932 at the age of seventeen. It was a truly remarkable career for the player they called "Wizard of the Dribble". Sir Stanley was best known for his fourteen seasons with Blackpool, and most especially for the club's famous FA Cup Final win in 1953.

On 6 February, 1965 Matthews became the oldest active player in the history of first-class football when he helped Stoke City beat Fulham 5–1 at Stoke's Victoria Ground, five days after his fiftieth birthday; this was the final competitive match of his epic career. A hundred and fifty miles away, in north London, I was an eighteen-year-old wearing the number eleven as Manchester United took on Tottenham Hotspur. On that winter afternoon, less than two weeks after the death of Sir Winston Churchill, the era of Brylcreem and baggy shorts met the colourful new age of blondes and booze. We may have been born thirty-one years apart but we somehow appeared on the same day in the top division of the Football League. The fact that two distinct eras of the game, a mere generation apart, overlapped in this way was only possible because of the remarkable dedication and fitness of Matthews.

After returning to his hometown club, Stoke City, in 1961, he inspired the side's return to the First Division before injuries began to limit his appearances. Matthews had already told Stoke manager Tony Waddington that 1964–65 would be his final season, but on the day of his knighthood on New Year's Day 1965, he was not fit enough to be considered for selection. However, his knee injury was improving all the time and, before meeting the press to give his thoughts on his New Year Honour, he had already been for a run on Blackpool beach and had taken his customary cold shower (he had continued to live in the north-west after rejoining Stoke).

With his fiftieth birthday approaching, Matthews was the subject of considerable public interest. A BBC camera crew were following him around for a documentary – *Saturday Hero* – and, finally, he was able to play football, testing his fitness for Stoke reserves against Manchester United reserves at the Victoria Ground on 23 January. After coming through unscathed, there was a good chance that he would be called up for the following weekend's FA Cup fourth-round tie against Manchester United at the Victoria Ground. The match was already attracting considerable interest in the Potteries, but the possibility that Matthews would play elevated the mood still higher. Even the local bus strike would not deter any of the fans from making it to this historic event. The week was so cold layers of protective straw were needed and when they were removed from the pitch on Saturday morning, Waddington decreed it too hard for the limbs of his veteran right winger.

I did play, though, hitting the crossbar with a cross shot that was the nearest thing the match had to a goal. Had the weather been kinder in Stoke that week, we two wingers would have appeared in the same match and made an even more significant entry in the annals of football history. United won the replay, with Matthews again left out, and Stoke suffered injuries that forced Waddington to reshuffle his team for the game at home to Fulham three days later. At last he called on Matthews to wear the number seven shirt, in the process making him the oldest player to appear in the top flight of English football, a record that will surely stand for ever. Rodney Marsh, another name belonging to the new era, gave Fulham the lead but Dennis Viollet equalised and the moment the crowd had been waiting for came after seventy-three minutes when Matthews took centre stage with a breathtaking pass through the Fulham defence for John Ritchie to put Stoke ahead. Viollet added a third goal to ensure that the legendary Matthews' playing career ended with a win. Which was more than we had at White Hart Lane, where the gates had been locked with 58,639 inside. Our match was decided by a single goal from Ron Henry, the Tottenham full back, who ventured just inside our half, perhaps the most adventurous run of his defence-orientated career.

Matthews remained in the Stoke squad for the next weekend's game away to Nottingham Forest, but a cold ruled him out and Waddington never called upon him again. Matthews slipped into retirement, but has never been forgotten.

I never imagined I would play until I was fifty, but such was my enthusiasm and passion for football that I also never dreamt I would prematurely walk out on the game I adored. My head at that time was full of the glory – the quest for success, for medals, for achievement on the field. And off the field, it was snooker for relaxation, not, as everyone suspects, wild women and late nights.

I was still finding my feet and not a little on the shy side, but at least I'd stopped trying to avoid people. When I first arrived at Old Trafford I was so shy I used to walk the long way round to the dressing rooms to avoid meeting people. I suppose this was because everyone said I was too small and they probably had a point when you consider what my vital statistics were at the time – whoever heard of a professional footballer who stood not much over five feet in his socks and weighed a miserable eight stone wet through? That's all I could manage when I made the big trip to Manchester from my Belfast home when I was fifteen.

As my contribution to the side improved I felt more and more at home. I was "big" enough to even answer Denis Law back, and that was brave for me. When I first came into the side I hardly dared speak to him, and all that Law had said to me was, "How are you going, son?" accompanied, I might say, with a clip on the ear.

But I was lucky to start out alongside such a player. World class. Truly, not simply a figment of the media's imagination. I must say that my first reaction when I heard I was in the team was not so much one of worry as the feeling that with such skilful players around, I just couldn't go wrong.

Soon after I got established in the team, I found I was at outside left with Law my inside partner. Even in my first season, when I was on the right wing as all the forward places were being mixed and matched, Law was playing inside right. I think we hit it off quite quickly on the field, and off it for that matter, though we are very different people.

Denis Law was a livewire, always in a hurry, and despite his experience and achievements, he always got very nervous before a game. He also couldn't bear to watch the team if he was missing from a game and there was a lot at stake; he would rather sit it out in the dressing room. I was always asked at this time what it was like to play alongside Law. It was the easiest question to answer: it was a dream, a tremendous experience because he did things so much faster than most other players. If a pass from Denis Law failed to reach you it was odds on that you were not thinking fast enough to be in the right place for it. His lightning reflexes did get him into trouble at times. He had acted in the past out of instinct more than anything else, with dire consequences for himself, although we did remind him that his two suspensions did allow him to spend two Christmases in succession at home in Scotland!

His first sending-off was before I was in the team. The squad was on the coach on the way down to play Aston Villa. Law had been planning to make a quick getaway after the match to catch a plane home to Scotland for a romantic rendezvous with his fiancée. His team-mates told him he would never make it to the airport on time. He said: "Perhaps I'll get sent off." He did.

He and fellow Scot Paddy Crerand made a comic pair. They would spend hours in slanging matches, arguing about who was the ugliest player in football, though in my view they were among the contenders. Often they would wave from the team bus so enthusiastically that they confused innocent passers-by into thinking they must know them. Law also liked to pull Crerand's leg about the number of priests Pat seemed to know. As a devout Roman Catholic, Crerand often talked to priests after the match and I remember he once brought one who wanted to meet Denis Law in the dressing room. Law was intro-duced and said he was delighted to meet him because it made up a round hundred he had met that month!

Law was a showman on the pitch. His closest rival in those stakes was my fellow Irishman Derek Dougan of Leicester City. Northern Ireland played Scotland the previous season and Law and Dougan both crashed together and went sprawling. Being true professionals they both appealed for a free kick, but Law had met his match. The referee's decision went in Dougan's favour. Said Dougan to Law: "You might be a better player than me, but you are not a better actor."

Beneath all the joking, Denis Law was a deadly serious footballer. Above all else he wanted to win: it didn't matter if it was playing cards at the back of a bus or an FA Cup Final. He did not like to lose, and in the intensely competitive atmosphere of the game, it made him a good man to have on your side. Even in practice games, he liked to win. In training he might challenge you to, say, a series of three games at head tennis. But if he won the first two and therefore the rubber, he had no interest in playing out the third; he had won, and so off he went.

There was never a dull moment on or off the field with Law around. It's incredible to think that even someone with such immense talent had his critics, with the odd disillusioned, idiotic newspaper pundit suggesting at the season's conclusion that Law was no good. But at this crucial time there was no one more influential, as the statistics would bear out: he averaged a goal a game, with thirty league goals in his thirty games. The year before, his first after joining United from Torino, he played thirty-eight league games and scored twenty-three goals.

Law never complained, even when he was played when not

fully fit. This was deliberate because Matt Busby reckoned that the mere presence of Denis Law on the field always pulled a defender to mark him, so leaving more room for his team-mates.

It is fascinating to read up on all the facts and figures of the time in the *Manchester United Football Book* of the day, edited by my old friend David Meek, now retired but who then worked for the local evening paper in Manchester and produced the club's handbooks. He wrote: "United are still setting the pace and trends of soccer in this country, the only ground where big business can watch a match in £300-a-year 'opera' boxes complete with special lift and waiters with drinks and refreshments." Changes were happening both on and off the pitch at clubs up and down the country. But I'm sure David never imagined, and nor did I, that executive boxes would cost £10,000 a year, and at some clubs such as Chelsea, £1 million!

Leeds were one of the most improved teams of the moment, propelled to prominence by Don Revie. I bumped into Revie quite regularly and got on well with him, and he was always very complimentary towards me. This was his club's first season in the First Division and what an impact it made, in so many ways. Leeds could play breathtaking football with players such as Billy Bremner pulling the strings but it had real hard men like Norman Hunter, and even the side's so-called players of flair and vision, such as Johnny Giles, could put it about just as much.

When Giles joined Leeds United from Manchester United in 1963 the club were a Second Division side, but even at his cost of £35,000 – a hefty sum in those days – Leeds got a bargain.

Over the next twelve years Giles was a major influence in helping turn Revie's team into a force to rival Manchester United
and Liverpool. Giles was originally a winger, but at Leeds he
became a superbly skilled and creative midfield playmaker,
forming an almost telepathic partnership with the fiery
Bremner. In his first season at the club, Leeds won promotion
and during the next ten years Leeds were never out of the top
flight, never finishing lower than fourth in the table.

Leeds gained a reputation for their "professionalism" in
every sense of the word and in November, in this their first
season in the First Division, both they and Everton were ordered
off the Goodison Park pitch after thirty-eight minutes as the
referee tried to calm a heated atmosphere. It was ten minutes
before the match was able to resume.

Virtually all of Revie's Leeds team could look after themselves. Bremner and Giles were that unusual mixture of delicate
skills and hard-man tendencies. Despite beginning his career as
a winger, Bremner forged his reputation at the heart of the brilliant Leeds side of the late 60s and early 70s. Giles may have
been regarded as the skilful artist and canny ball player, but
Bremner's superb passing and incisive forward runs made him
a vital cog in the Elland Road machine. Bremner collected quite
a haul of runners-up medals during these years: Leeds finished
runners-up in the league on five occasions and were beaten FA
Cup finalists three times. But Leeds were determined to be
winners, and came so close on so many occasions.

West Ham also had a touch of steel, provided by Billy
Bonds, who gave the team a bit of backbone. The Hammers

played some stylish, fluent football that at times made us all sit up and take notice. The previous season's FA Cup winners, West Ham, and the reigning champions Liverpool, were the teams that we knew we had to beat to bring the championship to Old Trafford, while Leeds United were the side that everyone began to fear.

From the very start of this season, there seemed no clear favourite for the title. The beauty of the game in those days was that usually four different teams were on the winners' board. You can't believe that would happen much these days. But there were plenty of good teams around, each one had ample flair and inventiveness, and the football was far more competitive in the sense that several teams had a capability to be champions. The fact that the silverware had more of a chance of being shared around added to the excitement that the game generated throughout the country. In real terms there were many great teams competing for the honours all the way through the league, not just among an elite group as there is today.

For so long, Chelsea thought they would be champions. Chelsea had last won the league under manager Ted Drake in 1955, but this season the club thought they had cracked it again, at long last, and led the way until Tommy Docherty took a hard line with eight of the team's stars after they broke team rules about pre-match drinking.

The players included, surprisingly, John Hollins – who had a goody-two-shoes reputation later in his career with Arsenal and as a manager – and even more surprisingly, George Graham and, perhaps unsurprisingly, Terry Venables, who had never got on with the Doc. They had broken the Doc's rules and escaped from their team hotel by shimmying down the fire escape, to walk to a nearby drinking hole. When they sneaked back later they were confronted by train tickets home waiting on their beds. The Doc brought back five of his rebels but the effect was devastating as the team lost its final game of the season 3–1 and blew its biggest chance of winning the championship. Chelsea actually ended up third after the "sending home" incident.

It was hilarious, years later, to listen to Niall Quinn recalling how much hard-man George Graham had come down on him during their time together at Highbury when Graham was a disciplinarian manager. Niall said he hadn't had a clue that his tough boss was one of the troublemakers who had been sent home, and had he known might have given his boss some stick back.

Chelsea, drawn against Liverpool in the semis, also blew it in the FA Cup. Docherty's young side seemed to have that special "it" and were tipped to be the team of the 60s. With Venables at the fulcrum and Ron Harris as the enforcer, the team were cocky and full of cor-blimey arrogance, the embodiment of flash London boys on the move, ready to deal with the unsophisticated from the north. Yet they never quite made it.

This was also a defining period for Bill Shankly's champions. Liverpool had never won the FA Cup and that failure hung heavy on the club and the fans. Everton, with their two successes, were always able to lord it over their neighbours because of their lack of success at Wembley. Liverpool had been forced to play a European Cup play-off match against FC

Cologne in Rotterdam on the previous Wednesday, which went to extra time and was settled finally by the toss of a coin. Shankly's side arrived fatigued at Villa Park and were expected to get the runaround from Venables and co. Yet this team of outstanding youngsters, often criticised for running too much, were reduced to looking like old men. The pragmatic Liverpool team outplayed the King's Road kids. After John Mortimore had a first-half goal disallowed, Liverpool took control. Peter Thompson roasted Marvin Hinton and Albert Murray, cut inside and smashed a left-foot shot past Peter Bonetti. Ian St John gave Ron Harris the runaround until a frustrated and angry Harris brought the Liverpool forward down in the penalty area and Willie Stevenson made it two from the spot.

Liverpool were off to Wembley. Though Chelsea won the League Cup, Docherty's momentum was stalling. Liverpool had followed up their championship season a disappointing seventh in the table and were looking to make up for it with the FA Cup.

The final between Leeds and Liverpool ended goalless after ninety minutes and went to extra time. Liverpool scored first through Hunt, Bremner equalised, then St John headed in an Ian Callaghan cross for the winner. The real hero though was Liverpool's Gerry Byrne, who played for most of the match with a broken collarbone following an early clash with Bobby Collins.

Seventy-two hours later, on Tuesday, 4 May, there was more glory to come for Liverpool. Kick-off for the European Cup semi-final, the first leg against Inter Milan, was 7.30pm at the Anfield ground, but at 5.30pm the gates had to be locked. The atmosphere was electric thanks to the 25,000 supporters singing their hearts out on the Kop. Shankly knew that this was a massive advantage. But Shankly wanted more, much more. He sent out Gerry Byrne and Gordon Milne to parade the trophy the fans had waited so long to see. Liverpool pulled off a remarkable 3–1 win over Helenio Herrera's much-admired team. There was, however, little Shankly could do about the poor refereeing in the second leg. Three controversial goals by the Italians in the San Siro turned the tie in their favour. The ball was kicked out of keeper Tommy Lawrence's hands for one of Inter's goals. Such incidents led Shankly to speculate that the officials might have been bribed.

But some European silverware was brought back to England. West Ham beat Munich 1860 2–0 at Wembley to win the European Cup-Winners' Cup, only the second British team to lift a European trophy.

My first full season playing for Manchester United taught me a lot about the way hopes can change as the season goes on. That first flush of anticipation and expectancy almost deserted us after a poor start in terms of results. I didn't think we were playing that badly, and we were scoring right from the start, but the opening three games illustrated that we needed to tighten up at the back.

The big kick-off was a big let-down: a 2–2 draw with West Bromwich Albion at Old Trafford on 22 August, with goals from Charlton and Law. Two days later we lost 3–1 against West Ham and then drew again at Leicester 2–2. I scored my first league goal of the season when we had our immediate return game with West Ham at Old Trafford on 2 September, winning 3–1. Our mood lifted further with a 2–1 win at Fulham and a respectable 3–3 draw at Everton. We had actually only won two of our opening six games – but had scored thirteen goals. We were the great entertainers with a strike force the envy of the league. But we had to find a higher level of consistency if we wanted to challenge for the title.

Our next game was a 3–0 win over Nottingham Forest at Old Trafford and that initiated a formidable run of fourteen games, of which we won thirteen. It included a sensational win over Aston Villa, 7–0 on 24 October at Old Trafford, with Denis Law in unstoppable form with four goals. I notched three goals myself during that impressive spell, in a 2–1 home win over Everton, in a 2–0 win at Stamford Bridge and at home to Blackburn when we won 3–0.

The end of our winning streak, came, inevitably, against our main challengers. The rivalry between Leeds United and Manchester United was reaching new heights around this time. Leeds beat us 1–0 on our own pitch on 5 December, and that was a body blow which took us time to recover from. In fact we went on a poor run of only one win in eight games. Finally, we shook ourselves out of the depression at losing to Leeds by winning 1–0 at Sheffield United when I got the winning goal. We then set off on another good run, but the doubts crept back in when we lost 1–0 at Sunderland. It was now or never to put ourselves in with a chance of pipping Leeds for the title. And we responded with three straight wins, all at home, and a glut of goals to enhance our goal difference over Leeds. We won 3–0 against Wolves, 4–0 against Chelsea and then beat Fulham 4–1.

A 1–0 defeat at Sheffield Wednesday was little more than a hiccup as we then set off on another of our incredible runs – we won seven on the trot starting with an impressive 2–0 home win over Blackpool. Among our best performances and results was an incredible 5–0 win at Blackburn, while I scored a couple in a 4–2 win at Birmingham City. We beat Liverpool 3–0 and I scored again against Arsenal at Old Trafford in the 3–1 victory that finally gave us the championship.

We were beaten by Leeds in the FA Cup semi-final in a replay. The match having ended goalless at Hillsborough, Leeds finally finished us off 1–0 at the City Ground, Nottingham. We also reached the semi-finals of the Inter-Cities Fairs Cup, but we wanted the championship most of all, obviously, and it was so satisfying beating Leeds so narrowly.

Both Uniteds finished with identical records in our forty-two games – won twenty-five, drawn nine and lost seven – but we were the joint top scorers with eighty-nine, conceding thirty-nine, while Leeds had scored eighty-three, but conceded fifty-two, leaving us with a superior goal difference. I'd contributed ten goals myself.

I had played in all but one of the forty-two games, and in fact, it was one of the most consistent line-ups of all time; virtu-ally the first eleven played the entire season with just a handful of enforced changes, using just eighteen players in total. The team was basically Pat Dunne in goal, Shay Brennan and Tony Dunne (no relation) the full backs, Bill Foulkes at centre half, with Nobby Stiles in defence, Paddy Crerand in midfield, John Connelly on one wing, Bobby Charlton, plus Denis, myself (I wore the number eleven all season) and David Herd in attack.

It was a season of high-scoring games all round, with Spurs beating Wolves 7–4, Manchester United beating Aston Villa 7–0, and a 5–5 draw between Blackburn Rovers and Birmingham City. Goals were the life blood of the game, and of course, they still are, but the way that goals are now celebrated has altered dramatically. In the 60s there were no stage-managed, choreographed or even wild off-the-cuff goal celebrations. There were no sixteen somersaults, no running to the corner flag to do the latest dance, no stripping off and throwing your shirt to the crowd. When we scored a goal it was a manly handshake, perhaps a show of emotion by putting your arm around the goalscorer, but there wasn't even a peck on the cheek, let alone a proper smacker.

So winning the title was an inwardly wonderful experience, but outwardly there weren't the wild scenes of jubilation and celebrations you might get now – no quarter of a million thronging the streets of Manchester to witness the open-top bus parade and the civic reception at the town hall. It was our job to score goals and to win trophies. Yes, there was a wonderful sense of achievement, a glow of satisfaction individually and collectively, but not a lot of fuss.

No, it was parade the trophy, back to the dressing room for the ritual drinking of champagne from the trophy or the cup, and then off home or maybe for a meal out to celebrate.

# 1964–65 ROLL OF HONOUR

*Champions:* Manchester United

*FA Cup:* Liverpool

*League Cup:* Chelsea

*European Cup:* Inter Milan

*European Cup-Winners' Cup:* West Ham

*Footballer of the Year:* Bobby Collins

*European Footballer of the Year:* Eusebio

# 3

# 1965-66

I was completely gobsmacked by the way Bill Shankly had begun the Reds Revolution domestically, but now we were all in awe as Shanks started to make an impact in Europe. Liverpool made it all the way to the final of the Cup-Winners' Cup in 1966, following a titanic struggle with Celtic in the semis, and that was one of the first major European ties that really captured my imagination.

Passions were aroused to a far greater extent when such "Battles of Britain" were fought out by players who had such a great affiliation to their teams, in an age when there were hardly any foreign stars, and "imports" were those from Scotland, Wales and Ireland. In the first leg at Celtic Park, a crowd of 80,000 saw Celtic win 1–0 with a goal from Bobby Lennox, a result that prompted a green-and-white invasion of Merseyside for the second leg just five days later, bringing the city centre to a virtual standstill. This was a formidable Celtic side, one year away from becoming the first British winners of the European

61

Cup, but they capitulated to second-half goals from Tommy Smith and Geoff Strong. The injured Strong hobbled into the penalty area to head the winner. Liverpool went on to face Borussia Dortmund at Hampden Park in the final, the Germans eventually winning 2–1 in extra time.

Back in the league, Liverpool took over at the top on 27 November and were never in much danger of losing control of the title, although the team, as FA Cup holders, went out at home to Chelsea in the third round. It turned out to be a disappointment the club would work relentlessly to overcome. Liverpool were always more motivated after an adverse result.

Ron Yeats was the pillar of that Liverpool era and will forever remain an Anfield legend. Bill Shankly paid Dundee United £30,000 for Yeats in 1961, made him club captain and assembled a team around him which would rise from the old Second Division to become a world power. Having signed centre forward Ian St John two days earlier, Shanks saw the towering centre half Yeats as the final piece of his jigsaw, and invited a group of newspaper reporters into the changing room to cast their eyes over his latest acquisition. "I've just signed a colossus. Come in and walk round him…" "And it's a bit embarrassing being called a colossus," recalled Yeats, "when you've just stepped out of the shower and are bollock naked at the time."

For a man who captained Liverpool to some of their greatest triumphs in the 60s, Yeats was awarded a paltry two international caps, partly due to the consistency of the Old Firm's Billy McNeill and Ron McKinnon, but mostly because of an unwritten tradition that required successive Scotland managers to select a home-based player over an "Anglo" whenever possible. Indeed, Yeats's second, and last, international appearance in 1966 was at number nine when the Scottish team travelled to Italy for a World Cup qualifying tie with a squad ravaged by injury and missing an entire forward line in Jimmy Johnstone, Alan Gilzean, Denis Law, Neil Martin and Willie Henderson, not to mention Jim Baxter. And so part-time manager Jock Stein was forced into a radical change of tactics. "Jock had seen me mark the Italian playmaker Sandro Mazzola out of the game when Liverpool met Inter Milan in the semi-finals of the European Cup earlier that season," explains Yeats. "Jock asked me to follow Mazzola all over the pitch, never to let him out of my sight. 'If he goes to the toilet,' Jock told me, 'I want you to go to the toilet with him.' That's why I'm the only centre forward in history to have kicked off then run backwards.

"I didn't have a bad game, and neither did Mazzola for that matter. He never got a kick of the ball and nor did I – we simply cancelled each other out. I felt sorry for Mazzola, who was a good, good player, because even if he drifted out to the corner flag in the hope of getting the ball, there I was, grinning at him. No wonder he got madder and madder as the game went on. But without all our best players, Scotland never really had a chance. I think the general feeling among us was 'just let's keep the score down'. Italy were a great team and even without Mazzola they had Gianni Rivera pulling the strings. It was also the most intimidating atmosphere in which I've played with only a moat separating you from 60,000 mad Neapolitans. We had a couple of little chances but, in truth, we did well to lose 3–0. I felt sorry for Jock because he'd had no time to prepare."

Stein resigned to concentrate his managerial skills on Celtic and Yeats returned to Anfield, his brief international career over. "My one other appearance, the season before against Wales, in Cardiff, had been equally miserable. 'The good news,' manager Ian McColl told me, 'is that you won't be up against John Charles because he's playing centre half too.' It didn't matter: big John scored anyway and we lost 3–2. I'm glad I got the chance to play for my country but it never really bothered me that I only won two caps. Nothing could beat playing for Bill Shankly and Liverpool. Jock Stein was obviously a great coach and tactician, but although Shanks was no coach, when he delivered one of his monologues, the hairs on the back of your neck stood up. You couldn't get to the opposition quick enough."

Yeats's affection for Shankly remains undiminished all these years after the great man's death. Under Shankly, Yeats inspired the club to promotion in his first season (after eight forlorn years in the Second Division), won two championship medals and became the first Liverpool captain to collect the FA Cup. Yeats is still at Anfield as a senior scout. "As far as I can see, no manager has loved his club more than Shanks. Sir Alex Ferguson might be the only one who stands comparison and I'd love to spend a week with Fergie to see how he prepares his players for a big game. Like Shanks, Alex can get players to play for him. Jock Stein did the same at Celtic where he had a few great players but a lot of workers, too. It was a wonderful honour to be Shanks's captain for ten years."

One of his favourite Shankly memories is the manager's often-repeated observation that with "my colossus at centre half, we could play Arthur Askey in goal". "Maybe that's why big Tommy Lawrence, who was our goalkeeper, was scared to death of him," Yeats said. "After our final tactic talk on a Friday – during which Shanks could talk for an hour and a half without pause, no problem – he would pick one of the first team to compete with him in a penalty challenge, with the loser donating a tenner to charity. Comes my turn: me, who had never taken a penalty in my life, and Shanks, who was a lovely kicker of the ball. Slots home his first two against Tommy with all the players crowded around the back of the goal crying with laughter. Shanks scuffed his third attempt and Tommy managed to get a hand to it. Before Tommy could get to his feet, Shanks – who hated losing at anything – was standing over him, glaring down. 'I was lucky there, boss.' 'Aye, you were lucky, you fat t\*\*\*,' came the reply.

"My turn: first one top corner, second one I close my eyes and ball goes right as Tommy goes left. Number three I hit the best left-foot shot of my life, top corner just beyond Tommy's fingertips. Shanks, who hadn't lost in over a year, stood over Tommy's body. 'Not so lucky that time, eh, Tommy? But I'll tell you what' – and Shanks never swore – 'if it had been a \*\*\*\*\*\*\* meat pie you'd have caught it!'"

Yeats had a confrontation with Tony Hateley, signed from Chelsea for £100,000 and sent to Coventry less than two years later at a loss. "Shanks didn't know he was a naturally funny man. 'Big man, I don't know why I signed you: you can't kick a ball, you can't pass a ball, you can't shoot...' Big Tony lost his head at this point: 'I'll give you that, boss, but you have to admit I'm great in the air.' 'I'll grant you that, son, but so was Douglas Bader and he had two better legs than you'll ever have.'"

Under the manager's shrewd guidance, Liverpool tied up the title ten days before the end of the league campaign by beating Chelsea 2–1 at Anfield. Liverpool finished six points clear of Leeds, who were ahead of Burnley on goal average. We finished fourth – never really recovering from a poor start of only one win in five. Busby had even briefly dropped me, reminding me that no one has a divine right to a starting place.

The Shankly era was taking a firm grip with Liverpool's third major trophy in three years. This title equalled Arsenal's record of seven league titles. Shankly landed the championship with the remarkable total of only fourteen players, virtually twelve as two players made only four appearances between them, one of them in the last match, a draw at Nottingham Forest when the team had eased off. A well-balanced side with a strong defence, in which Tommy Smith and skipper Ron Yeats served as twin stoppers, Liverpool conceded only thirty-four goals. Roger Hunt was top scorer for the fifth season running, with thirty league goals, and he and Ian St John enjoyed excellent service from wingers Peter Thompson and Ian Callaghan, the latter ever-present, as he was in the title-winning side of two years earlier.

*Match of the Day* was at Anfield to see Liverpool seal the title in April against Chelsea. At the final whistle the crowd chanted

"We want Shankly" and he reluctantly walked out to accept their applause. Kenneth Wolstenholme remarked that "not one person from the Spion Kop has invaded the pitch and that should go down as an example to all other supporters".

As the big prize went to Liverpool and we finished fourth, Matt Busby was thinking hard about how to revive his team with £100,000 to spend after the money-spinning previous season. Busby had celebrated his twentieth anniversary as manager of Manchester United in October. Louis Edwards was a shy, retiring kind of chairman, who had an enormously successful meat-manufacturing business and chain of butcher's shops. No Roman Abramoviches or Mohamed Al Fayeds were around in those days. Unlike the modern-day chairmen, Edwards was not a media man, and stayed very much in the background, so it shocked the press contingent that on the flight back from a first-leg European Cup match against Helsinki he chose to break the red-hot story that he and his fellow directors has decided to reward their manager on his anniversary with 500 £1 shares, an unprecedented gesture. Unfortunately all the writers who were following Manchester United in Europe were 30,000 feet in the air and unable to contact their newspapers, although one tricky bugger managed to persuade the pilot to radio his story through! It was certainly worthy of a champagne celebration for the princely sum of five bob (25p) a quarter-bottle on the BEA flight.

It was estimated that the shares' true value was £12,000 so it was a big deal at that time and made all the headlines once the journalists got off the plane and rushed to the phones to file their stories to their newspapers.

The players also paid their own tribute to Busby, presenting him with a valuable cut-glass vase which had been on exhibition as the finest example of glass from Czechoslovakia. Bill Foulkes made the presentation because Denis Law just didn't like those kind of things. When we asked him as team skipper to present Busby with our grand gesture, he turned to Bill Foulkes and said: "You do it, please, Bill. You have been here almost as long as the Boss, and anyway, you know me, I'd only drop it."

It's worth recording at this point how it all began in 1945 when Busby was finishing his national service and realising that his career as a professional player was also at the end of the road. He was about to return to Liverpool, his last club before becoming a physical-training sergeant major, as coach, when he was called by James Gibson, then chairman of Manchester United. In that interview the thirty-six-year-old Busby probably won his first important managerial battle. The United chairman offered a three-year contract; Busby emerged with one for five, no mean achievement from James Gibson, who was accustomed to running the club his way. Yet Busby knew he needed at least five years to transform the club. He faced a depressing prospect when he took charge of the team. The Old Trafford ground had been blitzed out of business and the club had an overdraft at the bank of £15,000. Home games were being played at neighbouring Maine Road and several of the players were still away on duty in the services.

Busby had seen many, many changes since then, in the game and at Manchester United in particular. By 1965 Manchester United were raking in huge profits, while Manchester City were wondering where their next week's wages were coming from. One club was in the running for league and cup and enjoying European triumphs, while the other was struggling in the bottom half of the Second Division after relegation.

In United's 1965 championship season, when they also had a run to the semi-final of the FA Cup and the semi-final of the Inter-Cities Fairs Cup, the club took in gate receipts of £348,766. Manchester City, though, had receipts of just over £48,000. Some of the profits disappeared on wages: United's wage bill soared to £131,216. City, despite not being a successful club, were paying wages totalling £60,000 including bonuses.

When I first signed for United, my contract stipulated a payment of £4 a week, but it rose sharply to £25 or £30 a week based on bonuses. This might not sound like much, but it was a fortune to a kid like me. The biggest bonus was based on attendances at Old Trafford. For every 1,000 over 35,000, there would be a bonus, and there were 54,000 for my first game against West Brom. Every home game was a sell-out, so I was raking in the crowd bonuses. There was also a bonus for being in the top six, and there were win and draw bonuses.

Just as today, the money helps to buy the best players. In September 1958 Matt Busby had splashed out a record fee of £45,000 to bring Albert Quixall to Old Trafford. Unfortunately Quixall never quite lived up to his transfer tag. Busby went out and paid another record £115,000 to bring Denis Law back to

Britain from Italy in the summer of 1962 and fees like £43,000 for Pat Crerand and £56,000 for John Connelly were still big, big money in the early 60s.

Other teams saw renewed and significant levels of investment too. Everton enjoyed loans from pools tycoon John Moores, Leeds United were boosted financially by Harry Reynolds and Hull City were given shares worth nearly £250,000 by Harry Needler. Bill Harrison gave a £65,000 loan when he became chairman of Walsall, while Derrick Robins secretly gave Coventry City £75,000 when he gained control. Wealthy Stafford Heginbotham bought out Bradford City, while another prosperous, outspoken and controversial young man, Ken Bates, pulled Oldham Athletic out of the red. Millionaire Clifford Coombs bought control of Birmingham City and provided a loan of £75,000, interest free. Rich men were providing nearly a million pounds between them to gain control of the clubs they had targeted for a variety of reasons; for some it was still a hobby, an act of faith, but increasingly, in other cases, there was the deep suspicion they were in it to turn a fast buck. Ken Bates, of course, remains in the game at Leeds after his long association with Chelsea. I love characters like Ken. The game needs them. And, of course, as my lawyers have asked me to point out, I would not, ever, include Ken as an owner out to turn a fast buck!

Manchester United, in contrast, were generating their wealth through success on the pitch, but that is always the hardest part.

One mitigating factor in our failure to defend the league title was our presence in two cups. By April United had reached the semi-finals of both the FA Cup and the European Cup, and Busby deliberately eased his interest in the league by resting a number of players before these crucial ties. He did not, however, go to the lengths that Everton – who we had drawn in our semi – had. They fielded virtually a reserve team against Leeds at Elland Road the Saturday before we were due to meet on neutral ground at Burnden Park. They were fined £2,000, but couldn't care less. With Everton's hopes of the championship long-since extinguished and aspirations for European qualification all but over, the club's attention was all focused on the cup. Everton won with a single Colin Harvey goal beating Harry Gregg with only twelve minutes to go. Though Law had an effort cleared off the line in the last three minutes, Harvey's was the goal that sent Everton back to Wembley, after an interval of thirty-three years, at our expense. I was destined yet again to fall before the final.

In the final, Everton were to meet their manager's former club Sheffield Wednesday, on 14 May. I was never a great "watcher", but if the FA Cup Final was on and I was near a television, then I would make an exception.

Outsiders Sheffield Wednesday almost had the FA Cup in their grasp at Wembley but defensive errors in the last half-hour allowed Everton to complete a thrilling comeback. The Everton hero, with two goals, was new signing from Plymouth Argyle Mike Trebilcock, a surprise replacement for the more experienced Fred Pickering. Catterick had a reputation for pulling surprises, but no one had expected this. Pickering was an established England international who had sixty-eight goals in 107 Everton matches under his belt. Everton, who had reached Wembley without conceding a goal in seven matches, found themselves one down after just four minutes' play. Centre forward Jim McCalliog, a Chelsea discard and the brains behind the constantly switching Wednesday attack, fired in a shot that was deflected past the helpless Gordon West. Wednesday went another goal ahead after fifty-seven minutes through Dave Ford.

The Everton fans, many of whom had travelled all night to get to the match in the capital, were stunned. But in the next minute, Trebilcock flashed a half-volley past Springett to make it 2–1. Five minutes later, a poorly headed clearance by Wednesday's inexperienced centre half Sam Ellis, a stand-in for the injured Vic Mobley, let Trebilcock in for another chance, which he accepted. Everton's third goal was a personal tragedy for another defender, Gerry Young, who failed to control a harmless-looking punt and left Temple with a clear run on goal, and the winger slipped the ball past Springett for a dramatic winner.

In the last minutes of the match, Trebilcock almost made it a hat-trick after Young picked up the ball again and unselfishly passed it to him. However, instead of taking a straight shot, Trebilcock tried to take the ball round the keeper. Fortunately the game had already been won: referee Jack Taylor blew the final whistle and fans in both Wembley and on Merseyside began celebrating wildly. It had been a dramatic turn-around. Catterick's gamble on playing newcomer Trebilcock instead of the seasoned Pickering had paid off. Catterick later described the Cup Final triumph as, "The thrill of my footballing life. That was my greatest moment. The cup hadn't been to Everton for many years and it was wonderful to bring it back to Merseyside and receive the acclaim of the crowds as we returned to the city." The players were awarded gold medals by the club at a post-match dinner, where fellow guests were the surviving members of the 1933 FA Cup-winning side.

The reasons for our failure to land any of the big prizes was a subject of enormous debate.

Matt Busby was annoyed at the way the international calendar fell in World Cup year, making it even more difficult with the number of players required for international duty. If I was looking for personal excuses, it was a season plagued towards the end for me by a serious injury.

I had been hurt in the sixth round of the FA Cup at Preston on 26 March, tackled and brought down from behind, twisting my right knee. I managed only one game all season after that. The problem was diagnosed pretty quickly as the dreaded cartilage. Our physio Ted Dalton must have known it straight away and if I hadn't been such a key player I would have been carted off to the operating table. But with so many vital games coming up, there was no way the club wanted me out. The club publicly claimed it was light ligament damage and privately decided to rest the knee and hope for the best.

Every day I went to the training ground for hours of treatment. One of the options was to play on until it got so bad that there was no choice but to operate and remove it. Taking out cartilages was commonplace, and even in those days of limited medical techniques for sporting injuries, it was not the kind of injury that threatened a player's career. However, it wasn't pleasant either. After surgery of this kind you would have to wait for weeks for the wound to heal and you'd be limping around on crutches with the leg immobilised in plaster. Of course, it's vastly different with today's modern techniques, and in particular keyhole surgery, which means that the cartilage can be removed without opening up the knee. You can be back playing, as good as new, within a couple of weeks.

Footballers are vulnerable psychologically and it will always go through a player's mind that he might not be quite as good when he comes back from such an injury. But I was reassured by the specialists that a cartilage removal, if it came to it, was a routine injury and that, in fact, the knee joint didn't actually need the cartilage, which kind of alleviated any fears.

The club probably don't know to this day that I was not convinced about the treatment I was getting. Our physio-cum-trainer Ted Dalton was a nice enough chap, but didn't exactly instil the greatest confidence in me. One day when he was looking at the knee to see how it was getting on and asked me how it felt, I became a touch concerned because he was looking at the wrong leg. That made up my mind that I needed to go elsewhere to have a second opinion in the hope of speeding up my recovery rate.

I flew off to Belfast to see the Glentoran physio, Bobby McGregor, who was also the man the Northern Ireland team entrusted with their injured players. I had a great deal more faith in Bobby. It was against club policy to seek alternative treatment and they would have been livid had they found out, but they never did. When I was flat out on the treatment table, Bobby gave me a piece of wood and told me to put it in my mouth and bite hard on it if I felt any pain.

He then put his fingers to the back of my knee and with a great deal of skill, speed and strength readjusted my ligaments. He was right about the pain, though, and I nearly bit right through his piece of wood. After a summer of rest I would be ready for the new season.

It had taken Busby eight years to build another Manchester United capable of first winning the championship and then taking on the cream of Europe again, so it was a strange irony that when we reached the last four of the European Cup we had to fly to Belgrade, the scene of the last match in the European Cup, against Red Star, played by the old team before the crash. The knee was still painful, but Busby took the risk and played me in Belgrade. The gamble failed and we lost 2–0 to a solid Partizan side. Despite the strapped-up knee I did my best. Denis Law might have scored from my cross but the ball bounced off his body on to the bar. I didn't play again after the match in Belgrade and in the second leg United could only win 1–0 with a goal from Nobby Stiles, but it was not enough and it was the end of the European trail.

The most wonderful memories from this campaign came, of course, from the round before against Benfica when I was still fighting fit. The Portuguese press nicknamed me "El Beatle" as I played one of my greatest individual games.

Benfica with their talisman Eusebio were the team that had wrestled the distinction of being the most powerful side in Europe from Real Madrid and Inter Milan. The first leg at Old Trafford on 2 February didn't begin very well, with Jose Augusto opening the scoring after half an hour. However David Herd equalised six minutes later and by the interval Denis Law had put us into the lead. Hopes soared when Bill Foulkes moved up from centre half to make it 3–1 in the fifty-eighth minute with one of his rare goals, only his third in fourteen seasons at Old Trafford. But the exquisite Eusebio again outwitted our defence to set up a goal for the towering Torres to make it 3–2. The Portuguese players walked off with smiles on their faces; they fully expected to go through.

So we went to Lisbon with a slender one-goal lead for the second leg against the Portuguese champions who had a formidable home record in Europe. Up against the likes of Eusebio, Coluna and Germano, we had our work cut out to gain the draw needed to get through to the semis. The tension was fabulous, just the way I like it. The roads to the stadium were jammed and even the famous Italian referee Lo Bello was delayed. Perhaps it was the ref getting to the ground a touch late or, more likely, the drawn-out presentation of the European Footballer of the Year award on the pitch just before kick-off to Eusebio – whatever the reasons, we were kept hanging about waiting to start.

Then there was the unfortunate incident inside our dressing room. The shattering of a mirror, broken by Pat Crerand.

Footballers are a superstitious lot and Denis Law even came to the game wearing a scruffy shirt which made him look like a tramp, but which he regarded as lucky to wear on big match days. Law looked thoughtfully at the broken mirror. Busby told us to play a holding game for the first twenty minutes, but after the game joked that "Best must have had cotton wool in his ears".

Perhaps it was all the tension in the build-up that sharpened our game, but I took on Benfica's defence and put United two up inside the first twelve minutes. The first was a header from a Dunne free kick, which stunned the crowd to silence. For the second I set off on a run before sliding the ball past their keeper, Costa Pereira. Left winger John Connelly scored a third to put us 6–2 up on aggregate. Nobby had a stranglehold on the normally unstoppable Eusebio and their only consolation was a Brennan back pass that beat his own keeper.

Denis Law put Paddy through for the fourth, and Bobby Charlton went on one of his majestic solo runs from his own half before slamming the ball wide of the keeper. The final tally was 5–1. What a night, and in Benfica's own Stadium of Light. It was one of the finest team performances by an English side away from home in European competition. Reading the club's handbook, David Meek wrote at the time: "It was nineteen-year-old Best, the youngest player in the side, who expressed the steadiness of nerves and stamped his genius on the game. Experienced stars have wilted as the rockets shoot into the air and they are greeted by an 80,000 continental crowd. But the unruffled George stayed so cool and confident that he scored twice and had a hand in another with John Connelly to give United three goals in the first quarter of an hour." Who am I to argue?

After a night of such glory it was a pity that the season finished without any tangible success. Matt told the press afterwards that "this was our finest hour". I might have been the hero but I also had to suffer a frightening experience when a man with a knife came at me along the tunnel as we left the field. Fortunately, he only wanted to hack off a lock of my hair as a memento. Another Portuguese fan presented me with a canary, which had to be given to the coach driver at the airport because of quarantine restrictions.

We came back down to earth when we flew straight to London for a match with Chelsea, only to lose 2–0. But our defence of the league title was long gone. That's why, after the glory against Benfica, our semi-final exit in the European Cup was so hard to take. Busby was also very sensitive to critics' suggestions that he allowed players like myself to play off the cuff. He insisted there was a method to his game, but he also said at the time: "When a team has international players like Denis Law, Bobby Charlton and George Best in the attack they have their own ideas and it is a waste of talent to subject them to a list of dos and don'ts."

A writer in the West Bromwich Albion programme summed up the whole situation nicely: "This season United have gone flat out for the grand treble of European Cup, FA Cup and league championship. In the final run in, it is now clear that they have to watch three other sides take the trophies they have fought so hard to collect for themselves. A disappointment perhaps, but what an achievement in itself. After all, they were only a coat of paint away from the final of the European Cup, a single goal from the final of the FA Cup and they are still around the leaders of the league. Perhaps United think they have failed. No, we in English soccer are proud of them."

This also illustrates the affection felt for United in those days. It's strange to think how that affection vanished over the years and has been replaced by "Stand Up If You Hate Man U", with so many fans jealous of the club's successes. In this year, the nation seemed to be proud of the team. However, love or loathe Manchester United, they remain one of the world's most watchable teams, and in this season, they were hardly ever off *Match of the Day*.

Goals were the story of this season and in the first seven programmes of *Match of the Day* the cameras covered Nottingham Forest beating West Ham 5–0, Arsenal's 6–2 defeat of Sheffield United, Leicester City losing 5–0 at home to Manchester United and then Tottenham's 5–1 win over us. At White Hart Lane, Jimmy Greaves scored one of his greatest solo goals for Spurs as he accelerated past four players to score, whilst at the other end there was a classic long-range goal from Bobby Charlton. Two months later the teams met again at Old Trafford. Greaves was missing with hepatitis and the score was reversed, us winning 5–1 with Charlton on target again, this time with a right-footed volley from outside the box. Spurs were also involved in another remarkable high-scoring home game in March when they went 5–1 up against Aston Villa before Tony Hateley scored four times to level the match at 5–5.

David Herd scored plenty of goals for us, yet he was another who was targeted for a great deal of criticism. Denis Law recalled at the time: "A policeman stopped David Herd for speeding last season. He flagged his car down and then walked in that majestic way that only policeman have up to his driving window to ask all the usual particulars. 'What's your name?' went the conversation. 'David Herd,' replied our centre forward. 'You mean David Herd the footballer?' asked the policeman. 'Yes,' said David. 'Oh', said the policeman. 'I see you can't drive either.'" Amusing as this was, too often he was made to carry the can by the fans when things were not going right for Manchester United. In the year we'd won the championship, I was top scorer with twenty-eight league goals, but where would we have been without David's twenty, and his twenty the season before, and his nineteen this season?

It's interesting to look back to comments made by Denis Law that year aimed at yours truly: "It is an essential part of the game to recognise the style of one's team-mates and work to make the best of it. Take young George Best, for instance. I should think that at some time or other, all of us in the team have screamed at him for going on himself instead of passing. Yet in honest reflection, we would not try to change him because his long tricky runs are an important part of his game. He had a couple of fantastic games in December. He scored twice in a 3–2 win at Sunderland and came back to delight the fans at Old Trafford four days later when we beat Everton. And who could forget the way he took Lisbon by storm with his two goals and thrilling display in our 5–1 European Cup win against Benfica in March? George has fantastic ability and even showed it at fifteen when he first joined the club and looked like a skinned rabbit. I remember Harry Gregg being impressed before he even knew the lad's name, because Best the unknown made a monkey out of Harry.

"It happened when Harry got caught up in a little five-a-side match with some of the youngsters down at the Cliff, our reserve training ground. A situation cropped up where Harry was left facing one player who was bringing the ball up to him. An experienced goalkeeper like Harry Gregg can usually fool a junior into shooting where he wants. But Harry ended up diving one way while the youngster calmly slotted the ball home on his other side. Harry thought to himself, 'Well, it can happen to anyone, the kid was lucky.' This kid, however, was George Best and a few minutes later a similar situation arose and once again Harry Gregg went the wrong way. After that, he could not find out the name of the youngster fast enough and I remember he came back from the Cliff full of praise for a lad the rest of us did not really know. We did not have long to wait, for George shot to the top and everyone at Old Trafford knows about his talent now. The year we won the championship was only his first full season in the first team, yet what a wonderful contribution he made, scoring ten goals from outside left, which is a fair tally for a winger. What one admires about George is that it is pure skill that brings him success. He is not big and he is an individualist."

Actually there was one trophy for United: Bobby Charlton became only the second Englishman to receive the European Footballer of the Year award, the first being Stanley Matthews in 1956. But any report of the 1966 season will only stand out for what occurred at the end of it. Something that also involved Bobby ... England winning the World Cup.

You know how everyone says they can remember precisely where they were when Kennedy was killed, or the Second World War ended, or the Berlin Wall came down, or even the moment frozen in the minds of all Manchester United people, the day of the Munich air crash? But I don't remember any of them. I suppose the moments that really live in the memory are the ones when you are actually there. Everyone says they can remember exactly where they were when Geoff Hurst completed his hat-trick at Wembley. But I can't.

It is perhaps the question I am asked the most: "How do you feel that you never played in the World Cup finals?" When England won the World Cup in '66, it was a massive day for English football and I was delighted for them, but it never occurred to me at the time that it would become one of my big regrets. It's only something you can fully appreciate when you reflect on it. The love of my life was Manchester United and I only really had one thing on my mind in those days and that was playing for the club I loved. I was tingling with excitement at the prospects ahead, and it wasn't long before I was in the side winning league titles and playing alongside two European Footballers of the Year in Denis Law and Bobby Charlton, and some other pretty useful players like Paddy Crerand, Nobby Stiles and Alex Stepney.

Alf Ramsey was perhaps the man most responsible for bring-ing the World Cup home. Ramsey transferred the team ethic he'd built at Ipswich to the England set-up and called Moore "my right-hand man, my lieutenant in the field". England's start in the World Cup campaign was inauspicious as I remember it, a goalless draw with Uruguay. Despite accumu-lating sixteen corners and managing fifteen shots on goal, England failed to score. England had a solid, organised look about them. Nobby Stiles was the defensive anchor in front of a solid back four. Ramsey did have wingers in his squad, plenty of them, in Callaghan, John Connelly and Terry Paine, but as the tournament progressed he opted to dispense with them. Ramsey thought that with strikers of the calibre of Jimmy Greaves he would be able to break down the opposition. But progress to the knock-out sector was unspectacular: the lifeless, goalless draw against Uruguay was followed by 2–0 wins over Mexico and France.

The quarter-final clash with Argentina was an explosive affair, quite out of character after what had passed before. The turning point came when Argentine captain Antonio Rattin was ordered off for verbally abusing the German referee after he had been booked. There was a long delay as Rattin refused to leave the field. Ramsey branded the Argentine players "animals" and his remark nearly caused a diplomatic incident. Ramsey had also refused to allow his players to swap shirts with their opponents.

The brutality that Ramsey had seen with the South American team was not an isolated incident, as elsewhere in the tournament there were some ugly moments. Pele had come in for some very rough treatment as Brazil failed to make it beyond the group stages.

Geoff Hurst scored the game's only goal against Argentina, a deft glancing header thirteen minutes from time.

The semi-final against Portugal was a sedate and sportsmanlike game compared to the game with the Argentineans. In a fast, free-flowing game Bobby Charlton scored twice but it was a nervous finish as the masterly Eusebio pulled one back from the penalty spot.

When Geoff Hurst left the field after England had beaten Portugal in the semi-final on that Tuesday night, he did not know if he would be playing in the final. He has often said that he was certain that Alf Ramsey would bring back Jimmy Greaves, whose injury in the qualifying match against France had unexpectedly opened the door for the West Ham striker. Hurst was glad to be in the squad of twenty-two and he must have felt confident after the Portugal match: he had played well and laid on the pass for Bobby Charlton to give England a 2–0 lead, eventually winning 2–1. But Greaves was one of the game's greatest all-time strikers and despite a dip in form and his injury it seemed inconceivable that Ramsey would leave him out once he was fit. Greaves was the country's most prolific striker, with forty-three goals in fifty-one appearances. Astonishingly, there was little media coverage of the issue. It was all so low-key in comparison to the deluge of media outlets that there are today. Hurst was not even interviewed after the Portugal match.

Ramsey was not a great one for team meetings. He liked talking one-on-one. Just before a match he would go up to each player and say a few words, just remind them what they had to do. Alf liked to keep it simple. On the day after England won the World Cup, ATV held a lunch for the players and wives at Pinewood Studios. Some journalists approached Ramsey, cautiously as usual, and asked whether they could have a few words on England's victory. He said: "Not bloody likely. It is my day off." Ramsey was in the identical mould to Nicholson, Shankly and Busby: they never courted media attention, they found it intrusive, and could live without it.

Ramsey was a players' manager. He would not tell the press anything he had not already told the players. He was a strict disciplinarian and made it clear that anybody who stepped out of line was out. There was no drinking allowed and, for the entire month of the World Cup, the players did not see their wives, except for one occasion for half an hour in the main reception area of the hotel. The wives were not even invited for the dinner on the Saturday night, at the Royal Garden Hotel.

On the day of the final itself, some of the players went for a stroll in Golders Green and did some shopping. There was no satellite television, no agents, no concentration of sponsorship. The England players were used to promote a Barracuda raincoat and they had a choice of blue or white. The match fee was £60 and the players received £300 a game for wearing Adidas boots.

Just before the tournament, Hurst was earning £45 a week, which had risen to £90 during the World Cup, and reached £140 the following season. But money was not that important to the players in those days and most believed in sharing everything equally.

Alf Ramsey had one of his rare team gatherings and told the players that the FA had given them a bonus of £22,000 for winning the World Cup. He said it would be paid pro rata to the number of games each had played. But immediately the senior players, led by Bobby Moore, Charlton, Ray Wilson and Greaves, said they would share the money equally. So each received £1,000. Otherwise, having played only three games, Hurst would have got a lot less!

Ramsey liked his players to go to the pictures together. For the month of the World Cup there was a lot of free time and Ramsey used it to indulge his love of films. His favourites were westerns and, even if in a foreign language, all the players had to sit through the movie. If you left before it finished Ramsey would get very angry. He would say to Harold Shepherdson, one of the trainers from Middlesbrough, "I think we'll go to the pictures," and they would follow. Then they would have to return and discuss the movie with Ramsey. Once the players voted against going to see Michael Caine in *Funeral in Berlin*, as some of them had seen it. But Ramsey, who always liked to get his own way on the choice of movie, just said: "Right, you have voted to see Michael Caine." The lads were not pleased so, as the movie started and the villain, called Dolby, appeared on the screen for the first time, Ray Wilson shouted out: "Dolby has done it." Alf was visibly angered but didn't say a word.

When Ramsey made up his mind to play Hurst in the final instead of Greaves, all he said to Hurst was: "Do not tell anyone you are playing." But there was an even bigger secret to keep: Moore had tonsillitis and might have missed the final. He wasn't the only one – Jack Charlton also came perilously close to missing out too, with Wolves' centre half Ron Flowers standing by to take his place. Flowers woke up that morning of the World Cup final pencilled in on Ramsey's final team list. Jack Charlton went to bed the night before with a heavy cold. Ron Flowers recalled: "Alf said to me that I'd better be ready, because I was playing." But that morning Big Jack took a fitness test and passed. Flowers said: "I missed out. I was very pleased for Jack, because my international career was pretty much over and he was first choice. The authorities only struck eleven medals so none of the reserves got anything at all."

Between the semi-final and the final the players did a little light training, either with Shepherdson or Les Cocker of Leeds United, and half an hour of five-a-side football at the Wembley FC ground. At the hotel they played cards for an old penny a point: it's a tried and tested means of relaxing and killing time before games.

On the day of the final, with management beginning to understand the merits of better nutrition, steaks were out and Welsh rarebit, tea and rice pudding was on the menu.

Alf Ramsey gave the players a team talk and, in their grey suits, they set off for Wembley. There was just a single cameraman outside the hotel and fifteen or twenty curious onlookers. Imagine how many photographers will be lying in wait for the England team when they play in Germany in 2006. At Wembley, Ramsey gave Hurst his final instructions: "Get to the near post;

it unsettles the defence." England's own defence was upper-most in Ramsey's mind. He knew the Germans carried a goal threat and was worried about the fitness of key defenders.

Gordon Banks had not conceded a goal in the competition until the semi-final against Portugal and then it was a late penalty. West Germany had beaten Uruguay in the other quarter-finals when the South Americans were reduced to nine men.

The Germans shocked Banks – and the whole country – when Helmut Haller opened the scoring after just thirteen minutes, capitalising on a weak clearance from full back Ray Wilson. But within minutes the teams were level as Bobby Moore flighted a free kick on to the head of his West Ham team-mate and Hurst powered the ball past Tilkowski. The third of the Hammers contingent, Martin Peters, put England ahead for the first time with less than fifteen minutes to go. The midfield player, whom Ramsey had described as "ten years ahead of his time", scored from close range after a Hurst shot was blocked. A West Germany free kick in the last minute somehow found its way through a crowded box and Wolfgang Weber squeezed the ball in at the far post. It meant that extra time would be played for the first time since 1934, which was also the last occasion that the host nation had won the tournament.

The period between the end of normal time and extra time is crucial for the manager to make a few important points. Ramsey was brilliant. Alf could find the words when he wanted to and did so at full-time. The Germans had equalised in the dying seconds of normal play and the England players slumped to the Wembley turf feeling very dispirited. Ramsey came and said: "You have beaten them once, now go out and do it again. Look at them. They are tired, they are sitting down. Now get up; do not show them you are tired."

England were full of running in extra time, none more so than twenty-one-year-old Alan Ball, and it was his right-wing cross ten minutes into extra time that led to the most controversial moment in World Cup history. Hurst controlled the ball, turned quick as a flash, and as he was off-balance he still managed to let fly, only to see his shot hit the underside of the bar. It bounced down and was cleared, but had the ball crossed the line? The referee consulted his Russian linesman who was in no doubt that it had.

Then in the very last minute Hurst scored the goal that made it 4–2 and it was all over. But Hurst was unsure whether the goal had counted or not and had, therefore, not ensured he captured the match ball. By the time he got back to the dressing room the German, Helmut Haller, who had scored the first goal, had got the ball, and Hurst did not see it until 1996 in an extraordinary media hype engineering by the tabloids. Of course the Germans haven't forgiven Geoff Hurst to this day they still claim the ball never crossed the line.

Geoff Hurst was knighted in 1998 and remains the only man ever to score a hat-trick in a World Cup final. Wolstenholme's commentary remark when Hurst struck his third goal – "They think it's all over – it is now" – is almost as famous as Hurst scoring the goal. With the aid of new technology it has been suggested that Hurst was fortunate not to have his second goal ruled out, but at the time no one was even thinking about the controversy which has never gone away – and perhaps never will. Nothing could detract from the scenes of jubilation at Wembley on 30 July, 1966. England were the World Cup winners.

Hurst recalled: "I made my debut for England against Germany in February 1966, winning 1–0 – Nobby Stiles scored – and then came the World Cup final. When you win a match like that there is first of all relief and then bedlam. My most distinct memory is of Bobby Moore as he walked up the steps to collect the World Cup from the Queen. I was just behind him and as we reached the royal box, Moore noticed the Queen was wearing white gloves and he wiped his muddy hands on the red carpet draped over the parapet. I thought it was strange but that was Moore, immaculate as always. He did not want to put dirt on the Queen's gloves. That walk was another thing that made Wembley special. In other stadiums they organise the giving of medals in the centre of the pitch on a makeshift podium. But at Wembley you walked between supporters who patted your head or back as you went up to collect your medals and then the spectators on the other side got a chance to congratulate you as you walked down with the medals. I knew fans who had waited forty years to get such a chance. Wembley gave it to you straight after the match. All that was part of the Wembley magic." These are memories that will never leave a footballer.

Sir Bobby Charlton recalled: "What I remember about the 1966 World Cup final was that I ran around for the whole match and really contributed very little because my orders from Alf Ramsey were to stick to Franz Beckenbauer. His manager had told him the same. We didn't contribute much to the game and I thought that was a pretty good deal from England's point of view. My team could do without me more than Germany could do without him. Everyone talks about the third goal but I thought we were the better team and I don't lose much sleep over that." His brother Jack Charlton commented recently: "There is not a day that goes by when I don't think back to what it felt like to lift the World Cup."

Alan Ball soaked up the wonder of the occasion, made all the more special because it was at Wembley. As the new Wembley prepares to open you can forgive Alan for reminiscing about the old stadium: "You never experience anything like it, walking from the deep-down dungeon of the dressing room, the climb in half-darkness up the fifty-yard slope unable to see anything, just hearing the buzz. And then suddenly you were out there, the picture unfolded: the colour, the banners, the sea of people, the noise, the band, the geometric lines of the pitch still thirty yards away from you. Perfect! From the first time, the emotion stayed with me for years. I must have played there thirty-odd times and the sensation never got less; always that fantastic feeling of pride." Alan Ball's performance on that momentous day, tearing down England's right wing, can never be eradicated from the memory of not just the player himself but also the fans who witnessed it.

The reputation of the '66 team seems to grow with every successive English failure to land the trophy. "Oh aye, you're praying every time that they'll win it so that they don't have to keep wheeling us out," said Ball. "No, you would love them to do it again, course you would, you're proud of your country. They've got a very talented squad and next year they've got a real chance. Forty years on from us, that would be marvellous."

In 1966 Ball was an unexpected addition to Alf Ramsey's squad. He played for Blackpool, a club unlikely ever to provide another England international. Yet Ramsey simply could not ignore the claims of the flame-haired terrier-like midfielder. "There were twenty-seven of us went to Lilleshall a month before the tournament. We knew after five days being assessed that only twenty-two of us would be picked," Ball recalls. "I looked at it another way: five weren't going to be there on the biggest stage, a World Cup in England. It wasn't going to be me. That week I was unbearable: I wanted to be first at training, the first in the sprints, best in five-a-side. There was always a mountain to climb and me dad was behind me all the way, pushing me up it. 'What do I do, Dad?' 'Get in that squad.' 'What's next, Dad?' 'Get in the team.' 'After that, Dad?' 'Win it.'"

His fearsome drive came not just from his father, Alan Ball senior. It stemmed also from bitter memories of rejection. "At fourteen, Wolves told me I was too small," he remembers. "Then, at sixteen, I was rejected from Bolton – imagine that, my home-town team – for being too small, too weak, frail. I was never going to let that happen to me again. That was the reason I was what I was: I was frightened, terrified of failure."

And yet, at his finest moment, Ball barely grasped the momentousness of the occasion. While Nobby Stiles was dancing around Wembley with that distinctive toothless grin and Bobby Charlton was convulsed in tears, Ball was almost bemused. His no-nonsense approach manifested itself at the end of normal time before the potentially draining extra time. "At the end of the game I saw all the older players so emotional and drained, and there was me thinking, 'Come on, we can win this whenever we want.' It's only as time goes on you realise the enormity of what we achieved. At the time? Nah."

That night, along with Stiles, Geoff Hurst and Martin Peters, Ball celebrated in London's West End.

"We went to the Playboy club, for whatever reason I can't imagine," he recalled. "Then we finished up at Danny La Rue's club, with Ronnie Corbett as the cabaret, and they treated us terrific. It was just fabulous." At his side was his girlfriend Lesley, who two years later became his wife. "Course she was with us. She was the first person I looked for. We were a team; course she came."

One man, though, found it hard to join in the celebrations and I don't think anyone should blame him: Jimmy Greaves. His expression exposed his bitterness even at the very moment England succeeded. Jimmy did his best, putting his arm around Alan Ball, but he was wearing his suit and tie, and deep down looking a forlorn figure. He sloped away, missing out on the after-match celebrations and it was, perhaps, the saddest day of his footballing career. Greaves was a genius, and as a fellow professional who has suffered the lows as well as the highs, I know precisely how he was feeling. But while it was an all-time low for Greaves, it was an all-time high for his replacement. Every fact of Geoff Hurst's life and career has been written about since that day.

As well as his hat-trick, Hurst also has the distinction of being the only first-class cricketer to win a World Cup medal. He batted for Essex against Lancashire in 1962. Between 1959 and 1972 he made over 400 league appearances for the Hammers, helping them to win the FA Cup in 1964 and the European Cup-Winners' Cup the following year. In 1972 he moved to Stoke City, then after a period at West Bromwich Albion he went into management and helped with the national squad. His managerial career didn't last long with Chelsea, but he became a successful businessman.

The golden boy of football at the time, though, was certainly his West Ham team-mate Bobby Moore. Essex boy Moore was another, like Charlton, who can be described as a "gentleman footballer". Moore joined the Hammers in 1958 at the age of seventeen and was one of those who showed incredible loyalty, playing 545 games for the east London club. There were far more one-club men in those days, rattling up huge numbers of appearances without ever cashing in on a move. Moore, in fact, did move on, which in itself was a huge surprise at the time. He led his beloved club to their first-ever FA Cup Final win, over Preston North End, in 1964 and the European Cup-Winners' Cup the following season with a 2–0 victory over Munich 1860, so the World Cup was a hat-trick of his own at Wembley. After a record eighteen outings for England's youth team, Moore joined the senior side in 1962. He played in that year's World Cup in Chile when England lost to Brazil in the quarter-finals. A year later, with Ramsey in charge, Moore became England's youngest-ever captain and, of course, carried off the Jules Rimet trophy. Four years later he captained the defending champions in Mexico, where he had one of his most memorable games in the group-stage match against Brazil. Moore and Pele embraced at the end of the game, which Brazil won 1–0. That picture is one of the most vivid images of world football: the greatest defender and the greatest forward in World Cup action, the pair of them full of mutual respect and admiration.

In the 70s, after a series of disagreements with manager Ron Greenwood, Moore left West Ham to join Fulham and helped the team to reach the 1975 FA Cup Final. Like myself, he ended his playing days in the United States. Ever since Ron Greenwood sent Bobby Moore, Geoff Hurst and Martin Peters from Upton Park to win the World Cup, the London club has become known as the Academy of Football. Buckingham Palace has elevated two of their players to the rank of knight: Sir Geoff Hurst and Sir Trevor Brooking. They may never have won the championship, but the Hammers have acquired a reputation for a certain style while producing a constant supply of dazzling young players. According to Greenwood's philosophy: "The crowds at West Ham have never been rewarded by results but they keep turning up because of the good football they see. Other clubs will suffer from the old bugbear that results count more than anything. This has been the ruination of English soccer."

# 1965–66 ROLL OF HONOUR

*Champions:* Liverpool

*FA Cup:* Everton

*League Cup:* West Bromwich Albion

*European Cup:* Real Madrid

*European Cup-Winners' Cup:* Borussia Dortmund

*Footballer of the Year:* Bobby Charlton

*European Footballer of the Year:* Bobby Charlton

# 4

# 1966–67

Everyone, including myself, awaited the reaction to England winning the World Cup. There was an air of anticipation. A feeling of pride permeated the entire game. Increased crowds, greater television coverage, more media attention.

Post-World Cup the focus, naturally enough, was at Upton Park. Just three weeks after Bobby Moore lifted the Jules Rimet trophy at Wembley, the three West Ham heroes were back on parade with an inevitable tumultuous welcome. Even the opposition fans from London rivals Chelsea cheered them on. But goals from John Hollins and Charlie Cooke secured a surprise 2–1 away win as Chelsea made a bright start to a season in which they felt that their team of outstanding individuals could make a challenge for the championship.

There was most definitely a belief that a title challenge could come from the south, but not from White Hart Lane, for a change. Perhaps it would be west London, maybe even east London. The Hammers had won the FA Cup, then the Cup-

Winners' Cup the following year and got to the semi-finals in 1966, with a team that had underachieved in the league.

"We were more of a cup team," Hurst said. "We didn't have the players, or play the sort of football, to grind out a result; we believed in attacking, win or lose. We were out to put bums on seats. We weren't a team to scrap and battle. I had thirteen great years at the club, and I was able to fulfil my ambitions with England." He felt he played better the year following the World Cup, when he scored forty-one goals. "That's the season I'd pick out ... I was runner-up to Jack Charlton for Footballer of the Year. The confidence that came from the World Cup helped no end and I was at my peak – still young enough to run through a brick wall but old enough, mentally, to know what I was doing."

But London had to watch out. Matt Busby was getting his act together at Old Trafford. This was to be a thrilling season for me and the rest of the players. Everton too were a force. They had just signed that little bundle of non-stop World Cup energy Alan Ball for £110,000, the first six-figure transfer between English clubs. "To play on Merseyside at that time, what an arena," Ball said. "The music, the fashion, the football – it was like being at the centre of the universe. I thought, 'There's nothing better than this.'" On the wall of his study there is a snap of Ball celebrating a goal alongside Howard Kendall and Colin Harvey. Kendall, Ball and Harvey, the Merseyside rivals to Law, Best and Charlton. Evertonians will argue they were football's holy trinity of the 60s.

So would the championship land on Merseyside or would West Ham have the impetus from its World Cup trio? Perhaps

Leeds would be the dominant force, or would it be the swagger from down the King's Road? The big news of the opening day of the season was that the Busby Babes had made another fine start as we beat West Brom 5–3 with two from Law and one from myself. We then beat Everton 2–1 at Goodison. The following week brought us back down to earth when we lost 3–1 at Elland Road, although I scored the only goal of mine that *Match of the Day* managed to capture on camera that season. That was a shame, because I started to get into a goalscoring groove. After wins against Everton (at Old Trafford) and Newcastle, the team lost again when goals from Alan Gilzean and Jimmy Greaves cancelled out Denis Law's opener. After securing a derby victory against City with a single Law goal, we demolished Burnley 4–1. I scored two in a 2–2 draw with Liverpool and then enjoyed an epic encounter the following week with West Brom at the Hawthorns when a David Herd hat-trick ensured a fantastic 4–3 win with all seven goals coming in the first half.

It was a season packed with exciting games as well as our own. Derek Dougan scored a memorable hat-trick for Wolves in a 4–0 win over Hull, but Bobby Tambling managed one with his left foot and three with his right in Chelsea's 6–2 win over Aston Villa. Chelsea also drew 5–5 with Spurs, although Sheffield Wednesday scored the most goals in a single game, putting seven past Burnley.

United were making a huge impact on the title race with the classic formula of winning at home and drawing away. This was the pattern from Christmas. The sequence started with a 1–0 win at Old Trafford against Spurs on 14 January. The following week at Maine Road we drew 1–1 with Manchester City and then never looked back.

Denis Law was on fire with fifteen league goals before Christmas, but he was at his regal best when Scotland went to Wembley to put one over the World Cup winners. On 15 April, 1967, you would have thought Scotland had became football champions of the world. They faced England in a crucial European Championship qualifier, and won 3–2, becoming the first team to beat the reigning world champions. So, of course, in the eyes of their supporters at least, Scotland were the best team in the world.

Today's Premier League may be dominated by some of the best talent from around the world, but in the 60s the Scots were predominantly the "foreign" stars of English football. The Scotland win over England was a perfect showcase of the ability of the Scottish exiles in the English game, and with players of such enormous talent they enhanced it. These days, the Scottish game is virtually wiped clean of emerging new talent and there are precious few big-name Scottish stars in the Premiership.

The Scotland Wembley win was inspired by Jim Baxter, who was at his mercurial best that day. I just loved watching Baxter perform: he had style and grace and was a match winner. Jim could have been one of the all-time greats, and should certainly have won more than thirty-four caps. Baxter had the lot, and treated the Wembley crowd to an audacious demonstration of his skills, most notably taunting England by juggling the ball as if performing tricks.

It was Denis Law though who put the Scots ahead after twenty-seven minutes, and it remained that way until the seventy-eighth minute, when Bobby Lennox made it 2–0. England responded in the most positive fashion and stormed forward, pulling a goal back through Jack Charlton in the eighty-fourth minute. Jim McCalliog, who was making his international debut, scored Scotland's third with just three minutes remaining. Geoff Hurst pulled one back, but Scotland were not to be denied their famous win. It is two decades ago since the annual Home International series was terminated, and nearly forty years since Jim Baxter's outrageous showmanship against England, but the Scots have never forgotten. There would never be another day for Scotland that Law would enjoy so much. He wasn't alone, of course: everyone in that Scotland team that day were heroes. None more so than captain that day John Greig, synonymous with Rangers, for whom he played 857 games and scored 120 goals. As a player, he was capped forty-four times, won the treble three times and was captain when Rangers beat Moscow Dynamo to win the Cup-Winners' Cup in 1972.

The defence contained some individual brilliance, such as central defender Frank McLintock, who started his career at Leicester before going on to enjoy tremendous success at Arsenal. There were few classier full backs than Eddie McCreadie, who joined Chelsea in 1962 from East Stirling for £5,000 and played until 1973, making more than 300 appearances. He won twenty-three caps. McCreadie also managed Chelsea from 1975–77. Centre half Ronnie McKinnon was a rock at the heart of the Rangers defence, playing 473 times for the

Glasgow club. He had the misfortune to be at his prime at the same time as Billy McNeill, captain of Celtic, and, as a result, played just nine times for Scotland.

Other "Anglo" Scots, too, lost out on their fair share of caps during these years. Goalkeeper Ronnie Simpson, who won the FA Cup with Newcastle in 1952 and 1955, was a veteran of thirty-six when he starred for the Scottish champions Celtic in the 1967 European Cup final against Inter Milan. It is a travesty that he won only five caps.

It's hard to believe now, more than forty years on, that the Scotland selectors would regularly omit one of the most dynamic British players in history, on account of his playing career in England. Dave Mackay was a power-house of a man and player, one of the most influential club captains of his generation. He started his career with Heart of Midlothian, then joined Spurs in 1959 and became their inspirational half back. In 1965 Mackay had broken his left leg twice within ten months, something which, particularly in those days, would have ended the career of a player with less resolve and guts. He battled back to play for eight more years. In a ten-year international career, between 1957 and 1966, Mackay played a mere twenty-two times for his country. Yet Sir Alex Ferguson has stated: "Davie should have been Scotland's captain for fifteen years."

There were some Anglos too good to ignore, though. Arguably the most famous player ever to don the dark blue shirt was, of course, my friend Denis Law. Law made his international debut when he was just eighteen, the youngest Scot to be capped since 1899. He went on to win fifty-five caps and scored thirty goals for his country – a national record he still shares with Kenny Dalglish.

If there was a player who epitomised the never-say-die spirit of Scottish football, it was Billy Bremner. He made his debut against Spain in 1965 and was at his peak in the 1974 World Cup finals in West Germany, when Scotland were knocked out only on goal difference having not lost a game. He won fifty-four caps before being suspended by the Scottish FA after an incident in a bar in Copenhagen.

I am convinced that the England-beating side of 1967 must rank as one of the all-time greatest Scottish sides when you consider it also possessed Tommy Gemmell at left back. Tommy was a world-class defender who had a knack of scoring crucial goals for Celtic. He hit eight in Europe, including the equaliser in the 1967 European Cup final. After a decade of success at Celtic, he and manager Jock Stein fell out, and Gemmell was transferred to Nottingham Forest.

This game was the highlight of Jim McCalliog's international career. It doesn't get much better than scoring against England at Wembley as a twenty-year-old on your debut. After that he won just a paltry five caps, the last coming in a 2–0 defeat in Portugal in 1971, though he did go on to join Southampton, with whom he won the FA Cup in 1976.

It was an extraordinary season all round, north of the border, where Jock Stein led Celtic to an unprecedented year of success, winning all three Scottish titles and then becoming the first British team to win the European Cup – the "Lisbon Lions" defeating Italian giants Inter Milan 2–1 in the final in the Portuguese capital. It was a triumph for attacking football over the ultra-defensive Italian style that had been threatening to suffocate the game on the continent at this time. Former captain Jock Stein had worked wonders since taking charge at Parkhead two years earlier. First he transformed the ailing club into the best team in Scotland, and now they proved themselves truly kings of Europe.

No British side had even reached the final before, but Celtic went into the match brimming with confidence, having cleaned up at home with their first domestic treble. Now it was the grand slam. But the 12,000 fans who travelled to Portugal to lend their vociferous support were briefly silenced after only eight minutes when Mazzola converted a penalty. That was the signal for Inter to retreat into their typically Italian defensive shell and for the rest of the game it was Celtic's attack against the formidable defence. Tricky right winger Jimmy Johnstone proceeded to give Burgnich a trying time, and Bobby Murdoch put himself majestically in control of the midfield. But Celtic's greatest threat was their overlapping backs Jim Craig and particularly Tommy Gemmell on the left. With Giuliano Sarti performing heroics in goal, and Bertie Auld and Gemmell both hitting the bar, it was well into the second half before Celtic broke the Italians down. Gemmell fed Murdoch, who switched play to the right. Craig cut the ball back across field for the advancing Gemmell to hammer it past Sarti from twenty-five yards. Six minutes from time, the heroic Gemmell moved up again on the left and squared the ball to Murdoch, who drove the ball low into the crowded penalty area. As Sarti moved to cover it, Steve Chambers deflected it past him for the winner. That was Celtic's 200th goal of the season in sixty-four games, and it was some conclusion to their historic season. Above all, they had won the battle for the attacking game.

Over at Rangers came the Scottish Cup shock of the century. It was a game of "Jock The Giantkiller" at Shielfield Park where a jubilant, if incredulous, record 13,365 crowd saw Berwick Rangers knock out mighty Glasgow Rangers in the first round. The Berwick hero was Jock Wallace, their goalkeeper-manager, who kept the marauding Rangers forwards at bay with a string of spectacular saves after Sammy Reid had put Berwick ahead in the thirty-second minute. Berwick, the only club in the Scottish League whose ground is in England, had never finished higher than number eight in Division Two. It was arguably the most sensational result in the history of Scottish football. Rangers, though, did make it to the final of the Cup-Winners' Cup but just failed to make it a Scottish double in Europe, losing 1–0 to Bayern Munich in extra time.

Back on the domestic scene, I was fascinated to see how the league was trying to maintain interest in its less-regarded cup competition. This was the year in which the League Cup was revamped, with ninety clubs taking part. Only Liverpool and Everton opted out. The final was held at Wembley for the first time and in a dramatic match QPR of Division Three shocked favourites and holders West Brom by winning 3–2. It was an outstanding season for the west London club, later promoted as Division Three champions.

By the end of a season, the League Cup final is often overtaken by more momentous events. Naturally classed as the second-rate cup competition, the League Cup became more popular in different guises. From the Milk Cup to the Littlewoods Cup, Rumbelows Cup, Coca-Cola Cup and Worthington Cup, it currently masquerades as the Carling Cup. But it's a pity that it's looked down on, because the league competition has tended to produce more intriguing confrontations and sometimes less predictable outcomes.

Critics have rarely warmed to the League Cup, which meanders through the first half of the season making few major headlines. Even when York City won the opening leg of a second-round tie 3–0 at Old Trafford ten years ago the result was put down to Manchester United's lack of interest. Nevertheless, a scan through the finals of the past forty-five years does the League Cup credit. Some games have been truly awful – witness the two draws shared by Aston Villa and Everton in 1977 before Villa won an entertaining second replay 3–2 – but more than a few have produced as much quality and excitement as the perceived superior FA Cup Finals.

That 1967 Wembley League Cup final remains the pick of the bunch. Rodney Marsh was at his impudent best as Alec Stock's Queens Park Rangers, then on its way out of the Third Division, came back from 2–0 down to win a 3–2 thriller against the West Bromwich Albion of Jeff Astle, John Kaye and Bobby Hope.

Two years later another rising Third Division side, Swindon

Town, were inspired by Don Rogers as they won 3–1 against an Arsenal team two seasons away from Highbury's most momentous season. Stoke City supporters of a certain age will recall with affection the 2–1 triumph over Chelsea in 1972, which brought the veteran George Eastham a winner's medal.

Chelsea made it to Wembley in 1967 for the showcase FA Cup Final, having lost at the semi-final stage in the two previous seasons. Playing Spurs, it was the first all-London final, with all the inevitable hype, but there have been many better finals. Neither side lived up to the occasion, although Spurs showed more guile and co-ordination. With goals from Jimmy Robertson and Frank Saul, Chelsea were beaten 2–1, with Bobby Tambling scoring four minutes from time. It was the third time in seven seasons that Spurs had won the FA Cup. Spurs had developed into a club with a reputation for excelling in the cup competitions, where their emphasis on flair prevailed, whereas they couldn't sustain such high standards over the long period of a championship campaign.

Tottenham Hotspur had been in the process of rebuilding the team. Bill Nicholson had brought in Alan Gilzean, Pat Jennings, Cyril Knowles, Alan Mullery and Terry Venables to add new energy to the side. Like most of Nicholson's purchases, they gelled well as Spurs went unbeaten in the league from mid-January to rise to third in the First Division and then into that final against Chelsea. The majority of Nicholson's sojourns into the transfer market proved successful but Venables was one of the exceptions, as he failed to win over the demanding Spurs supporters.

The new Spurs had some brilliant individual players, including Pat Jennings, who learnt his catching skills playing Gaelic football before joining Watford in 1963. A season later he was plucked from the Third Division for £27,000 by Nicholson and spent thirteen years at White Hart Lane, winning the UEFA Cup, FA Cup and two League Cups. In 1977 he joined Arsenal, where he won the FA Cup in 1979. He earned 119 caps for Northern Ireland and, when he retired, became a goalkeeping coach at Spurs.

Centre half had always proved to be a problem position for Nicholson for many of his later years, but during this period he had one of the best in Welsh international Mike England.

Spurs paid £95,000 to secure the towering, dominant stopper from Blackburn Rovers at the start of the season. By the end of his first winter he was repaying Tottenham's investment with a commanding performance in the final. England was a rock in the defence for eight seasons and won forty-four caps for Wales. He went on to become manager of Wales and masterminded a 1–0 win against England in 1984 in the last Home International tournament.

Spurs had one of the great characters and indeed hard men of this era playing at left back: Cyril Knowles, a player I would often come up against whenever we played Spurs. He joined Spurs from Middlesbrough after being rejected by Manchester United and Blackpool, but it was in north London that his career took off. Spurs bought him in May 1964. He won four England caps, but a knee injury forced him to retire in 1976. He was immortalised by the song "Nice One, Cyril".

One of Nicholson's most astute signings was when he captured Alan Mullery, a fiercely hard-working midfielder who joined from Fulham in March 1964. Mullery was an inspirational figure. He won thirty-five England caps and in 1972 returned to Fulham. Joe Kinnear was another of Nicholson's youngsters, a fleet-footed Irish right back whose career was dogged by injuries. He signed for Spurs in 1963 and played more than 250 times until moving to Brighton in 1975. Kinnear won twenty-six caps for the Republic of Ireland.

Nicholson loved his wingers: Jimmy Robertson was a nippy flank player signed from St Mirren in 1964. The nineteen-year-old Scot made an impressive start with his ability to run at defenders. A provider rather than a finisher, he did, however, score in the final with a half-volley from the edge of the area. After 177 appearances for the club and one cap for Scotland, he was one of the few who moved across north London to Arsenal in 1968.

But the most striking aspect of this new Spurs side were the "G-men", strike partners Greaves and Gilzean. Gilzean, who was artful in the air, grabbed the attention of Tottenham by helping Dundee win the Scottish league title in 1962 and two seasons later scored fifty-two goals. He linked up with Greaves and their striking partnership proved productive. To supplement their attack there was Frank Saul, an apprentice who made his reserve debut at fifteen and turned out for the first team in 1960 aged seventeen. Although he never lived up to his promise, Saul enjoyed his best spell at the club in 1967, with vital goals in the cup run, including one in the final.

Terry Venables was a successful Chelsea apprentice who joined Spurs in 1966 for £80,000, and although he helped Tottenham beat his former club in the Cup Final, he never attained the standards he had shown at Stamford Bridge, where he had played 237 first-team games and won two England caps. The Spurs fans never took to the flashy Venables, and he became victim to White Hart Lane's notorious boo-boys. After 115 league games for Spurs he moved to QPR in 1969, then Crystal Palace, where he became manager. Venables' popularity with Spurs fans only materialised when he joined the club as manager from Barcelona.

Whatever the ups and downs elsewhere, this was a phenomenal season for Manchester United. No one was winning with as much flair and attacking football. The club's attendances were at record levels, not only at Old Trafford but everywhere the team went. Not everyone loved Manchester United, even in those days, but everyone wanted to see us. Matt Busby had brought together some talented players who were compelling to watch. And, of course, Manchester United were back in search of the holy grail, the European Cup. Ten years earlier Busby had first led the club into Europe in this competition, defying the Football League to do so. He defied the football authorities because he was sure that the game in this country could not afford to remain insular and cut off from new ideas and concepts, as they had been for so long.

Players' salaries at Old Trafford were soaring, while the game was gripped by the controversy over players' signing-on fees. Cliff Lloyd, the players' union leader at the time, finally thrashed out a compromise agreement, that there should be a ten per cent levy on transfer fees, half to go to the player and the other half to go on his behalf to the Football League's Provident Fund, to provide an end-of-career payment, tax free, to players earning below £2,000 a year. But there would be no payments to a player who asked for a transfer, unless he could convince the league there were reasonable grounds for a move.

There had been big-name players on the move in the summer: Ball, Mike England, Wyn Davies, all influenced by the whisper that Jim Baxter had been paid anything between £5,000 and £10,000 as a signing-on bonus, but Busby refused to budge on his principles and wouldn't sign anyone demanding such a payment. Busby's view was that his United players were all highly paid anyway at £4,000 a year.

We were now near-perfect right the way through the team. Alex Stepney was, to my mind, the best keeper in the country at this stage. At centre half we had Bill Foulkes, who was really the archetypal old-fashioned stopper, good in the air, not so clever on the ground, a player who would rarely cross the halfway line and who does his job to perfection, simply winning the ball in the air. In midfield there were few more creative and combative than Paddy Crerand, while Bobby Charlton and Denis Law were at their peak, performing to their best, and I was on pretty good form myself. If Best, Law, Charlton didn't frighten defences, we had an up-and-coming striker in Brian Kidd, who on his debut went up against Mike England, the

Spurs and Welsh centre half rated the best in the business. Brian gave him a torrid time.

There were some unsung heroes too, like our full backs Shay Brennan and Tony Dunne. With a front line of Law, Best, Charlton it was easy to see who would grab all the headlines with our goalscoring exploits, but it was players like Brennan and Dunne who made the team such a formidable force. Irrespective of the era in which the game is played, the team is made up of certain players who don't stand out, yet without them the team wouldn't function. Shay began as a left winger but ended up playing right back, with a rather effective guy taking over on the left wing – Bobby Charlton. Tony was the opposite of Ashley Cole, who is gifted going forward but suspect in defence, as he was immaculate defensively but you wouldn't really want him to cross the halfway line. I am glad I never played against him, because he was just so quick and defensively he was simply brilliant. When you talk of hard men you think of players like Nobby Stiles but Foulkes was hard in the sense that he just got on with it, injured, in pain, no matter what.

A measure of just how powerful each player had become within the team unit was how many gifted young players came through but failed to make it. Ian Moyr was a promising Scottish winger, who got himself injured in training, and I replaced him for only my second game against Burnley. Jimmy Ryan, who is now one of the assistant coaches at the club, was another of a bunch of truly talented players; Phil Chisnall was another, a gifted inside forward who was always on the verge and who would have got in to most other First Division clubs but failed to become a regular at Old Trafford. When you think that the club could afford to ditch Johnny Giles! My dad, not a bad judge, went to the 1963 Cup Final and came away singing the praises of Giles, and couldn't understand why he left after such a magnificent match.

John Aston would often get booed by the home fans – supporters always need a target and at this time it was poor John for us – yet he was a good honest player who suffered from being in a team full of stars, and because he was compared to the bigger names. All of these players had helped bring the team to its winning run in that '67 season. It became fashionable in this era for fans to find a scapegoat, and just as Spurs supporters targeted Venables, it was so sad to witness John Aston's treatment by our own supporters, particularly as this was such a successful period.

At the turn of the year we were locked in a three-horse race jockeying for top place with Liverpool, while Nottingham Forest were the dark horses, rising swiftly after a powerful winning streak. Forest got to within a point of us at one stage and our meeting on 11 February was inevitably crucial. They came to Old Trafford with 62,727 inside and the gates locked. It took United until five minutes from the end to crack them, but the scoring maestro, Law, banged in the winner. That was the beginning of the end for Johnny Carey's team, and sweet revenge for our first encounter of the season with Forest in October, when they beat us 4–1. It was our heaviest defeat of the season, that saw us slip to eighth place, our lowest position that year. We were dubbed the "Busby Boobies" by one acidic football writer at that point.

By mid-March we were just ahead of Liverpool on goal average and our contest against them on 25 March would be decisive – the challengers United against the reigning champions, in the lions' den at Anfield. As it turned out no one scored, but the point was a great result for United and a bad one for Bill Shankly's team, who slowly slid out of the picture.

Bobby Charlton had an outstanding second half to the season playing in a more forward role and Busby compensated for the absence of the injured Herd in attack by switching Stiles up front and bringing David Sadler from the forward line to partner Foulkes at centre half. All these changes gave us more bite – notably Stiles! Stiles took to playing with his "plate" in because he considered that his fierce toothless appearances as seen on television during the World Cup frightened referees. It also got him into a lot of trouble. While all the focus of attention centred on our star-studded attack, Busby was shrewd enough to know he had to strengthen the defence. In September Alex Stepney had arrived from Chelsea for £55,000, United's only signing of the season. "Without him I don't think we would have won the championship," was Busby's verdict.

We took the title with a game to spare, and quite a few goals. (I scored twenty-eight goals that year.) We beat West Ham 6–1 at Upton Park with a scorching display of determined football and our biggest win of the season. Nobby Stiles said afterwards: "Just after we had scored our sixth goal I trotted over to Bill Foulkes and said, 'Congratulations, Bill, on your fourth championship medal,' but all he did was give me a rollicking and tell me to concentrate on the game." It was Stiles's determination that started the scoring. The little devil went for goal and pressurised the West Ham defence; the ball spun loose across the goal for Bobby Charlton to streak through a gap between two players and hammer home a goal after only two minutes. Pat Crerand, Bill Foulkes and myself added goals to put us four up in the first twenty-five minutes. Denis Law scored twice in the second half, one from the penalty spot, to make it a final to remember.

Looking back at the club books, there were a few quotes about winning the title, one from myself: "If the championship was decided on home games we would win it every season. This time our away games made the difference. We got into the right frame of mind." Manchester United paraded the league championship trophy at the final home game of the season, after a goalless draw with Stoke. We finished four points ahead of both Nottingham Forest and Spurs.

There can be no greater satisfaction or test of a team's true greatness than winning this title.

Manchester United had won it in 1952, 1956, 1957 and 1965, and this latest title represented a personal triumph for Busby, who by now had been at the United helm for twenty-one years and had steered the club through all of its post-war honours. With championship wins in 1908 and 1911, United now could boast a total of seven titles, to equal the record jointly held at that time by Arsenal and Liverpool.

## 1966–67 ROLL OF HONOUR

*Champions:* Manchester United

*FA Cup:* Spurs

*League Cup:* QPR

*European Cup:* Celtic

*Cup-Winners' Cup:* Bayern Munich

*Footballer of the Year:* Jack Charlton

*European Footballer of the Year:* Florian Albert

(Ferencváros and Hungary)

# 5

# 1967–68

It was a unique season for me and for Manchester United. It all started in bizarre circumstances at Wembley and was destined to end in the same stadium with the most glorious moment of my career.

The season's traditional curtain-raiser was the FA Charity Shield, when the winners of the league championship and the FA Cup play each other for the season's first silverware. At this time it carried far more kudos than it does today. The *Radio Times* noted that the BBC2 transmission of highlights from Tottenham Hotspur versus Manchester United in the Charity Shield on 12 August would be screened in colour from some transmitters – the first time in Britain that a soccer match had been shown in colour. Who could forget that? It was extraordinary, and would be the prelude to an exhilarating season for all concerned at Old Trafford.

The Charity Shield match was spectacular for another reason – the twenty-two-year-old Tottenham Hotspur goalkeeper,

Pat Jennings, scoring against us after just eight minutes. I shared many marvellous experiences with Big Pat as a room-mate during internationals with Northern Ireland. I knew Pat had exceptionally large hands, useful for a goalkeeper, but he also possessed one of the biggest kicks I have ever seen from a keeper. He certainly put one of those phenomenal kicks to exceptional use. When he unleashed this gigantic kick down-field, no one could have guessed what would happen next: it bounced straight over the head of our keeper, Alex Stepney. That was some start for Spurs.

The Wembley match ended 3–3 and included two tremendous left-foot shots from Bobby Charlton. One of them impressed Kenneth Wolstenholme so much he said, "Oh, that was a goal good enough to win the league, the Cup, the Charity Shield, the World Cup and even the Grand National."

We lost our opening league game in defence of our title to Everton 3–1 at Goodison Park with two goals from Alan Ball. Also on the team sheet that day was Alex Young, who was known to Everton supporters as the "Golden Vision" and was the subject in 1968 of a highly watchable BBC film written by Ken Loach.

Manchester United were still the team everyone wanted to see. We followed the loss at Goodison with a mixed run of wins and draws, then found our form again starting in late September with a 3–1 win over Spurs at Old Trafford in which I bagged two. This was followed directly by a sweet win over City in the Maine Road derby game with Charlton getting both. Yet City were developing into an exciting side with Mike Summerbee, Colin Bell and Francis Lee.

Indeed, as we concentrated on our quest to win the European Cup it was becoming increasingly hard to keep our nearest challengers, Manchester City and Leeds, at bay in the league. To retain the championship was something we desperately wanted to achieve, but winning the European Cup was that much more special, more significant, and drove us on even more.

Every player who walked through the doors at Old Trafford after Munich knew of the importance of Matt Busby's quest to win the European Cup. Footballers thrive on ambition and challenges, but it went far beyond this. It was a mission, a crusade. No one sat around discussing it, but we knew of the ghosts of Munich and sometime, somewhere, those ghosts had to be exorcised.

For players like Charlton and Foulkes I could detect that it was present in their very existence, as they had been on board that Elizabethan airliner that crashed on its third attempt to take off from a snowbound Munich airport on 6 February, 1958 on their way home from a European Cup quarter-final in Belgrade. Even putting aside all emotion, simply playing in Europe, notably on the biggest stage of them all, was an exhilarating experience for me and many others. Getting on a plane for foreign fields was exciting, but for those veterans of Munich it must have brought back memory flashes. Charlton, a survivor, had then been one of the youngest of the young Busby players, but at thirty he was now the elder statesman. Despite looking older, he played with the same sort of enthusiasm and high level of fitness.

Having failed to reach the final in 1966, this was United's fourth European Cup campaign, and you could sense from players like Bobby Charlton that Busby might have considered quitting if he hadn't finally got his just rewards. United were regarded as an international club side, supported by the public on a tide of patriotic fervour, which had continued since the World Cup win. The country desperately wanted Manchester United to deliver the European Cup to these shores. It was a great feeling for myself and the rest of the players as we embarked on our campaign.

My first taste of an abroad match was in Malta. Thousands of locals dressed in red and white cheered furiously as we arrived. Manchester United flags and banners were everywhere, with players' names – including mine – painted on huge sheets. I thought it was like one of those welcomes the Beatles used to get when they came back to England from an American tour. I think we got an even bigger welcome than the Queen when she visited the island a few weeks later. We were there for the second leg of our first-round tie against the island's Hibernians Valletta team: we had already beaten them 4–0 at Old Trafford. Given such an enthusiastic welcome by the locals, it hardly felt like much of an intimidating away tie. The home fans were delighted that their part-timers were hosting such a big-name club from world football. The Maltese were of course pro-British and they loved United: they even had their own United supporters club. They cheered us all the way to the hotel, following us in cars and buses. We had to force our way through the crowds to get into the hotel. The Maltese team were coached by a priest, Father Hilary Tagliaferro, who always took his place on the touchline dressed in his full habit.

Fortunately for us there was no divine intervention – in fact they suffered all the bad luck. In the first leg, seventeen-year-old winger Francis Mifsud went missing when he got lost going to get an ice cream when the team were watching an Arsenal match at Highbury. The police were called in to help find him. It turned out that Mifsud couldn't remember the name of his hotel in London, but he at least showed some initiative, as he travelled north on his own and met up with his team-mates there. But the occasion, in front of 43,000 at Old Trafford, was too much for the small island team. David Sadler headed in the first after just twelve minutes. Law then cracked in an unstoppable thirty-yarder. Sadler made it three in the second half, aided by myself with a little dribble, then Law finished off the scoring.

Father Tagliaferro might have been delighted to have kept the score down to four in the first leg, but far more important to us was a comfortable winning start when so often mistakes can be made because of complacency.

We performed a professional job in the heat and dust of the Maltese stadium, though the rolled sand, gravel and lime pitch didn't do much for Law's suspect knee. It was, in fact, a tough away assignment and ended, disappointingly for the fans, in a goalless draw.

As the home season got into full swing, we were doing well. By November we were top of the league, having just beaten Liverpool 2–1 at Anfield, where I scored both goals. But then we had to travel to Yugoslavia for our draw against some really tough opponents, FK Sarajevo, Yugoslav champions and losing cup finalists. We were fully aware that FK Sarajevo had been eliminated in the semi-finals against Partizan Belgrade in 1966, and so they merited our respect.

For almost ten years, since the Munich air disaster, every Manchester United team had travelled to Europe matches by train. This time Busby put Munich out of mind and ordered a special charter plane for the journey. We flew to Dubrovnik and then went on by coach to Sarajevo. It was an arduous six-hour, 200-mile journey. Players loathe such monotonous trips and this sure was tedious and slow, often on tricky, winding roads meandering up and down the mountains with a sheer drop to one side. Just to enhance the feeling of weariness, it was dark before we got there.

Worse than the journey, though, was the knowledge that some of our most-needed team-mates would not be playing. Denis Law had been banned for six weeks after being sent off against Arsenal in a league match. Busby's pleas to the FA to get him released for the European Cup had failed. Stiles was also missing with a knee injury: he'd had the cartilage removed a few days before the tie. And poor David Herd was still recovering from a broken leg.

In came Scottish youth international Francis Burns to replace out-of-form Brennan. Fellow Scot John Fitzpatrick replaced Nobby Stiles, with winger John Aston standing in for Law.

From the kick-off Kidd, Burns and myself were victims of some brutal, crude tackles. You could immediately tell they weren't interested in football, merely concentrating on intimidating us. It certainly helped when they went down to ten men as one of their players went off injured before half-time, but the match ended goalless with Busby proud of us for refusing to rise to the bait, despite the constant provocation.

Fitzpatrick was suspended for the return leg, so that necessitated more Busby changes. Burns moved into midfield while Brennan regained his place at full back for the Old Trafford match. After only ten minutes Brennan and Crerand broke out of defence, Kidd crossed to me, and I managed to head it goalwards. The keeper palmed the ball straight out to Aston, who gave us the lead. "Yet always Best remained the centrepiece of the chessboard," wrote Geoffrey Green of *The Times*. "He was the knight and the bishop as he slanted on varying angles..." Geoffrey was a fabulous writer, and I suppose he must have been impressed by the fact that I made the opening goal and then rattled the upright a couple of times. He continued by describing me as "a player full of fantasy; a player who lent magic to what might have been whimsy. He may have been provocative as he goaded some of the Yugoslav players with gesture. But Best now lives the life of a marked man, and these days has to suffer much." I certainly did, but who could have put it better?

Unfortunately, even though Busby preached that if you lose your heads you lose the game, I had taken too much from the Sarajevo team in both matches and I lashed out at their keeper, Mustic. Thankfully, I missed him, and the ref missed the whole thing anyway. But Mustic made a great act of it and complained that he had been hit in the face. Then the whole team lost their heads. Prljaca came looking for me on a couple of occasions and finally his kick was so blatant that he was sent off, and I got the best form of revenge – I scored from the resulting free kick. The Sarajevo players were furious, but pulled themselves together for one last crack at saving the match, with Salih Delalic heading in a cross three minutes from the end. But it was too late for a comeback. After we'd left the pitch, Crerand and Mustic started fighting in the tunnel. Busby was hit in the face as he tried to calm everyone down. Whatever the circumstances, we were through to the quarter-finals, drawn against Poland's Gornik Zabrze: yet another uninviting trek into Eastern Europe.

Spurs had given the Polish team an 8–1 thrashing in 1961 at White Hart Lane, winning 10–3 on aggregate, but in the previous round the Poles had beaten the favourites Dynamo Kiev, who had knocked out title holders Celtic. Busby had been on his usual "spying" missions and he returned full of admiration for the Polish team. Denis Law, though, was still suffering from knee problems and the day before the first leg he had severe pain during training and was given a pain-killing jab by the club doctor. Law didn't realise that he was allergic to the pain-killer he'd been given. After he got home that afternoon, his leg blew up like a balloon; he just managed to crawl to the phone to tell Busby what had happened. His knee was in such a bad condition he couldn't make it to the game, let alone pass a fitness test. Jim Ryan was given the daunting task of deputising for Law in front of a 64,000 crowd. Gornik were tough and resilient opponents. It wasn't until the sixty-first minute that we got a breakthrough and I am pleased to say I had a hand in the goal. I took the ball round Latocha, who had been marking me tightly throughout, lost it, then regained it and hit the shot, which deflected off Florenski past Kostka, who had been outstanding with save after save. The relief and excitement generated by the fans was extraordinary, especially behind the goal where they had a habit of cascading down the terraces, something that can never happen at the highest level now because there are no more terraces. I felt we would have to settle for a one-goal win when, with just a minute remaining, Kostka punched a free kick out and the ball landed at Ryan's feet. It was a mis-hit, but Kidd cut off the ball and back-heeled it through a crowd of players, wrong-footing the keeper as it trickled over the line. The United players formed a guard of honour to the tunnel as we came off, the crowd applauding the Polish team. Players and fans often had a far more sporting approach to the game in those days.

We lost 3–1 at home to Chelsea just ten days before the Gornik return match. Law was still out of the reckoning, but at least he managed to get out of hospital before his wife left for Scotland for the birth of their third child.

Busby had been to watch Gornik play again, and came back worried by the bad weather and dreadful winter playing conditions. He was worried, too, by Law's continuing problems and tried a quiet bid for West Ham's England hat-trick hero, Geoff Hurst, as we were leaving for Poland. Busby left a message for West Ham manager Ron Greenwood: "£200,000 for Geoff Hurst, yes or no? Please telephone or telegram your answer to Katowice. Busby." Greenwood was shocked, and famously cabled a crisp reply: "No. Greenwood."

But Busby was by then focused on the task facing us in the depths of the Polish winter. The tie had been switched from the Gornik stadium to the massive Slaski stadium in Chorzow, near Katowice, right in the heart of the coal-mining area of Upper Silesia. Again, we had to go by charter plane to Krakow, then endure an uncomfortable two-hour coach journey. It was below freezing as we drove through a blizzard. The worst fears about the weather conditions were confirmed: their football season had only just restarted after the mid-winter break and it was pretty bleak. We were comfortable inside the Katowice hotel, but it wasn't great leaving for even an hour's training at the stadium. Snow fell for two days solid before the tie, and three inches of snow lay on the pitch. Busby was so worried, he approached Italian referee Concetto Lo Bello to consider post-ponement, but when Lo Bello inspected the pitch he declared it playable. As a distraction some of us went to visit Auschwitz. Busby didn't come with us: he still had to finalise the team.

David Herd, his leg fracture now healed, was back in the front line even though his match sharpness was suspect, having been out for some time. John Fitzpatrick was brought in to midfield to protect the two-goal lead as a priority, and David Sadler replaced Foulkes, who was recovering from torn liga-ments and didn't want to play in such tricky conditions. Most of the players seemed worried about this, but I considered it to be a challenge to my skills to play on such a tricky surface.

The excitement generated by the European Cup tie was so intense that, despite it being twenty degrees below, an incredible 105,000 Polish fans were at the game, and another 100,000 had also applied for tickets. It was so cold that even the Polish players turned out in polo-necks, tights and gloves. Of course, in those days we didn't play with gloves or tights – we would have been laughed at – so we were in our normal nylon shirts. Nothing stopped the biting cold anyway.

The tie was always going to be tricky but it was made even tougher when Dunne took a knock just before half-time, which left him virtually a passenger for the second half. Even more worrying, the ref came into our dressing room at half-time to warn us that he wouldn't tolerate time-wasting, and turned his attentions to Stepney, saying that he would penalise him if he kept the ball more than four seconds. That's exactly what happened when, just twenty minutes before the end, Stepney was looking to throw the ball when the ref penalised him for time-wasting. Gornik were awarded the indirect free kick virtually on the penalty spot. All of us lined up shoulder to shoulder on the goal line. Kuchta's shot was blocked, but a minute later Kuchta found Lubanski, who smashed it in off the bar; the first goal against us on the Continent in this competition.

It could have been far worse had we conceded a second. On balance I felt this was one of our best-ever performances, given all the unwelcome circumstances. "I think this is our year," Busby was reported as saying afterwards. "It is the one thing the club wants to win and the one thing I want to win. It's good to be back and feel the warmth of a dream still living on … that the Reds will win the European Cup."

The other semi-finalists were Juventus, Benfica and Real Madrid. We would have liked to meet the Spaniards in the final, but they paired us with the mighty Real; not quite as mighty as they used to be, but still determined to protect their wonderful reputation. If we could win this one, we would then be favourites, and if we could topple Real, I believed we would win the European Cup.

Real had won the premier European crown six times, including the first five in a row, and had also reached the final twice more. This semi-final was our first match since Real Madrid had beaten the pre-Munich United 5–3 on aggregate in the 1957 European Cup semi-final, and the clash had captured the imagination of the entire country. More than any other club, Real Madrid stood for all that was good about European football.

As the Real team prepared for the journey north, we were facing other problems in Manchester. I had taken a bad kick on the ankle and Bobby Charlton was even more of a question mark after ricking his back in the league tussle with Sheffield United. We had lost our edge in the league, losing 2–0 to Coventry on returning from the Gornik match, and had lost two home games against Manchester City, 3–1, and Liverpool, 2–1. Law by now had turned to an osteopath for further treatment, but there was one thing for him to celebrate: he had a new son, Robert. Law did play in the Sheffield match, scoring the opener in the first five minutes. We were still top with fifty-four points, with Leeds a point behind with a game in hand and Manchester City four points behind with a game in hand, but minds quickly switched from the championship to the European Cup.

Real had just won the Spanish title, despite being without star forward Amancio Amaro Vareloa, who was suspended after being sent off in the match against Sparta Prague. In the frenzied build-up to the opening tie, the Spanish side's ageing superstar Gento said he didn't mind if United won the first leg, provided it was only 1–0, as he was confident of winning overall.

Busby wasn't happy when Law arrived with his knee heavily strapped, but as it was nearing the end of the season the manager opted to take a risk and play him. Both myself and Charlton were also passed fit. Charlton, playing for England, had tormented the Spanish national team the previous month and the Spaniards had christened him *"El Monstruo del Futbol Ingles"*... The Monster of English Football. A useful team-mate to have for this European clash.

Old Trafford was packed for the match, but it soon became obvious that Real were on the defensive and we'd have to make all the running if we wanted goals. On the half-hour Aston pulled a perfect pass to me and I hit it straight away into the roof of the net from fifteen yards. Many years later, Alex Stepney described it as one of the best goals I'd ever scored. We tried to get a second but it was tough and there was little excitement in the dressing room, even though we had won. We all wondered whether the lead would be enough.

Before the second leg we had a tough climb in the home championship title race. We'd crashed to a 6–3 away defeat to FA Cup finalists West Bromwich Albion, while Manchester City's 2–0 home win against Everton moved them above us on goal average. We fought back in our match against Newcastle

United, beating them 6–0 at Old Trafford. I managed a hat-trick that Saturday, which saw us level with City on fifty-six points but still second on goal average, though we had one game to play. Leeds had been a point behind with a game in hand but blew their chances, losing their unbeaten home record in their last home match, 2–1 to Liverpool.

We could only hold on to the title if we got a better result against Sunderland at Old Trafford on the very last day of the season than City could achieve against Newcastle at St James's Park. We lost 2–1 and City won 4–3. *Match of the Day*'s cameras were, naturally, at Old Trafford to see the defending champions, when strikes from Colin Suggett and George Mulhall denied us the vital win, despite one of my goals. City's win at Newcastle left them two points ahead of us.

It was gutting to have conceded the title having gone all the way to the last week with a chance of winning it again. But it wasn't quite as dramatic a climax as, perhaps, that would be today. In this era, the title was a far more open affair. It was hardly ever won by April, as it has been on occasions more recently, and often went to the last week of the season. To win the title you have to be exceptional because there were sixteen teams out of the twenty-two who were good sides. You would have to be a terrific side to warrant becoming champions, and you would need to have an amazing season. You just didn't have easy games in those days. More often than not you couldn't guarantee that one team would beat another. Now, something like seventy per cent of the games are more or less predictable. Of course, on any given day a bottom team might upset one from

ABOVE: Captain Noel Cantwell looks after Bobby and the Cup after Manchester United's win over Leicester in the 1963 final, with Paddy Crerand modelling new headwear for the afternoon, and Tony Dunne, Albert Quixall and David Herd looking on.

RIGHT: Bobby Moore and an ecstatic Ken Brown milk the occasion (and poor Johnny Byrne, holding the Cup) after West Ham's 1964 FA Cup Final victory over Preston.

"A nice new car for my retirement" – the legendary Stanley Matthews at the end of his career in 1965 when, aged 50, he was still playing at the top level with Stoke City. He and I came so close to playing each other, but it just wasn't to be.

Two of the greatest managers ever to grace the English game, and what contrasting personalities – Don Revie of Leeds and Bill Shankly of Liverpool lead out their teams for the 1965 FA Cup Final.

Liverpool triumphed 2–1 on the day. Geoff Strong and Wilf Stevenson lift their captain Ron Yeats shoulder-high to salute the fans with Peter Thompson, Ian St John, Gerry Byrne and Ian Callaghan.

ABOVE: A lap of honour with the League trophy for the Old Trafford faithful after we clinched the title in 1965 – this would seem a distant memory next season where the unthinkable happened and United finished with no silverware.

LEFT: Revenge is sweet – a 5–1 win in 1966 against Spurs, who'd beaten us by the same score earlier in the season. No wonder Denis, David Herd and I look so pleased with ourselves.

OPPOSITE: Denis congratulates Benfica's Eusebio on his European Player of the Year award before the second leg of our European Cup quarter-final in Lisbon in 1966. The night belonged to us though, as I ran in two of our five goals in another thrilling 5–1 win that saw us through to the semis.

ABOVE: Good boy! Boxing star Henry Cooper gives David Corbett and his dog Pickles their reward of £1,000 and as many bones as Pickles could eat after he discovered the stolen Jules Rimet trophy in Corbett's garden in Spring 1966.

RIGHT: Kenneth Wolstenholme, just weeks before his legendary "They think it's all over" commentary, slices wide at BBC TV's World Cup launch.

© EMPICS

Norman Wisdom jumps on the World Cup bandwagon with
Jimmy Greaves during a visit by the England squad to Pinewood
Studios on 12 July, 1966. England had been rather more sluggish
the previous day with a goalless draw against Uruguay in their
opening match. As the squad toured the studios, West Germany
were thumping the Swiss 5–0 at Hillsborough in their opener.

A quiet game of cards for semi-finalists England at their training camp in July, 1966. Looks like Bobby's lost his money already and is helping Ron Springett!

England manager Alf Ramsey, sports minister Denis Howell and Prime Minister Harold Wilson at a reception in London for the World Cup semi-finalists and FIFA officials. Looks like Alf is searching in his jacket for his Final XI to show the PM…

An iconic image of an English footballing icon. Bobby Moore, perhaps the most famous man ever to wear the red and white of England, holds the Jules Rimet aloft at Wembley on 30 July, 1966.

Looking at this foolhardy stunt, you wouldn't have guessed
Dave Mackay had broken his leg twice in two seasons! Seeming
relatively unconcerned about this are Spurs team-mates Cliff
Jones, Ron Henry and Jimmy Greaves.

Two Scottish giants head-to-head – Jock Stein, manager of Celtic,
greets his counterpart Bill Shankly of Liverpool at the airport,
ahead of Celtic's 1–0 Cup-winners' Cup semi-final win at Parkhead.
Liverpool clinched the reverse 2–0 at Anfield to win the tie, after
a last-minute Celtic equaliser was controversially disallowed.

Bill Nicholson may have been a Yorkshireman, but he lived and
breathed Tottenham Hotspur as a player and manager. Here he
is schooling his charges Saul, Kinnear, Venables and my mate
Pat Jennings before the 1967 Cup Final.

ABOVE: Jim Baxter, Scotland's talisman in their 3–2 win at Wembley in April, 1967, is hugged by jubilant fans proclaiming the Scots "World Champions", as they become the first side to defeat England since their World Cup Final win.

RIGHT: A great day for Celtic – Billy McNeill lifts the European Cup in triumph after the "Lisbon Lions" beat Inter Milan 2–1 in the 1967 final.

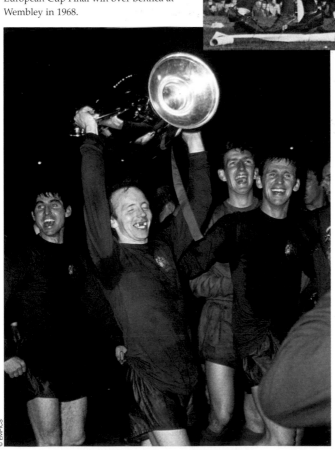

RIGHT: Law, Best and Charlton – three names to strike fear into the hearts of sides throughout Europe in 1968.

BELOW: Nobby Stiles can't contain his joy (or teeth!) as he celebrates our brilliant European Cup Final win over Benfica at Wembley in 1968.

© EMPICS

RIGHT: Sir Matt holds the cup at a reception with the Mayor for thousands of delirious fans from the red half of Manchester.

BELOW: A none-too-subtle vote of confidence from the United faithful, who recognised Matt Busby's achievements through the difficult years after the Munich disaster to the glory of 1968.

OPPOSITE: First my idol, later my very good friend, Denis Law, always on-hand with advice both in our playing days and today. Here he's doing his best to escape the attention of Everton's Brian Labone in 1968.

Jack and Bobby Charlton may have been brothers, but two more different players you couldn't have found in the game – Jack, the bluff, hard-working defensive lynchpin of Revie's Leeds, and Bobby, our softly spoken flair forward. Here, they take a break from training together with England in the mid-sixties.

the top, but it happened far more frequently in the 60s and 70s. That's why a number of titles were actually decided on the slenderest of margins, goal difference.

Another big difference was the lack of animosity between the managers. While Sir Alex would be at the throat of his Arsenal counterpart Arsène Wenger, Busby was quick to congratulate City on their championship triumph.

But we were just four days away from facing Real Madrid for a place in the European final. We knew the only way to trump City winning the title was to go on and win the European Cup. Even so, it was a great achievement for City, and rather than envy we would be the first to congratulate them.

When City persuaded old pro Joe Mercer to come out of semi-retirement to take the helm in 1965 they were at their lowest ebb, having finished eleventh in Division Two. In his first week, Mercer signed Malcolm Allison as coach and assistant manager and in their first season together they took City back to Division One. Mercer's shrewd buys included Francis Lee for £65,000, Colin Bell at £45,000, and Mike Summerbee at £35,000, but it was local product Neil Young who led the scoring with nineteen goals. Veteran Tony Book, a bargain at £13,500, made an inspirational captain. Full back Book was well known to Allison, who managed him at his previous clubs, Bath and Plymouth. City had a cracking team, not merely Summerbee, Lee, Bell (who people referred to as City's "Best, Law and Charlton"), but also the likes of Marsh, and Doyle.

One of the architects of City's championship was Francis Lee, who made his first-team debut for Bolton as a fearless sixteen-year-old and, playing alongside his mentor, the great Nat Lofthouse, scored in a victory over Manchester City at Burnden Park. Naturally, it took him a little time to establish himself in the team, but once he became a regular, he finished as leading scorer in five successive seasons and, in 1964–65, scored sixteen goals in a phenomenal spell of fourteen games. However, Bolton's relegation from the top flight in 1964 – and their failure to make a rapid return – convinced Lee that his future lay elsewhere and he made a number of high-profile transfer requests in an effort to secure a move to a stage that he felt suited his talents better. After scoring eight goals in the first seven league games of 1967–68, he bade farewell to Bolton in a League Cup victory over Liverpool, and joined Manchester City after totting up 210 games, and 106 goals for Bolton. His decision to move on was vindicated instantly by the fact that he pocketed a championship winner's medal at the end of the season.

This was certainly some season to be in Manchester. I had become friendly with City's Mike Summerbee when he first joined the club in the mid-60s. Mike was a Swindon boy but we had so much in common and we holidayed together with a crowd of us in Spain on a number of occasions. Eventually Mike and I opened a boutique together; our business partnership has been well documented. I was also best man at his wedding; he was married long before I managed it. While we played the game in a much more sporting spirit, there was one notable exception: the derby.

The Manchester derby had always been an intense affair. All week the hatred was building up – yes, pure hatred – and not only from the fans, but also the players. I suppose there was a far greater feeling of rivalry because it was mostly local boys playing each other, whereas now there are so many foreigners in the team that that level of intensity would be harder to reach. On the City side they were blue through and through; captain Mike Doyle, for instance, really did hate Manchester United with a passion and was never backward in coming forward to let everyone know just how he felt.

When the fixtures came out, that's the one you looked for. You held the dates in your head all season. City-United, United-City, and everyone knew how much was involved. It was a kind of hysteria. I mean, I broke Glyn Pardoe's leg one match. Total accident. That wasn't my game at all. But everyone was very pumped up. Most of the lads understood there was no intent when Glyn got hurt but Mike Doyle went crazy and I ended up getting booked.

My favourite football photograph of all time was when we played City in 1964. I'd just made the first team but I was also in the youth team. We were in the FA Youth Cup semi-final, two legs, first one at Old Trafford. We beat them 3–2, but they were confident they'd come through in the end. Then we played the second one at Maine Road. A chance came up at their end and I steamed in hard. Mike Doyle slid in with me and the ball went skidding in off his foot. Anyway, this great shot was in the *Manchester Evening News*. It shows the ball in the net, him on his arse and me leaning on a post, laughing at him. I love it, love it – listen to me, I sound like Kevin Keegan.

Then there was the derby in November 1971 which ended

3–3, when Sammy McIlroy scored his first United goal against City and I promised him champagne, and brought it in on the Monday morning. They were invariably exciting, attacking games because Joe Mercer and Malcolm Allison had the same philosophy as Matt Busby – there was no such thing as defence, you just went for it, took the chances and the best team won.

I met up with Mike Summerbee recently and he recalled: "In that particular era, United were far better than us individually but collectively we were in a different league." Mike's right: as we went through a spell in the 70s when we just couldn't beat City, it was amazing. Mike and I, though, were really good friends and we would always try our best to diffuse the tension and potential animosity leading up to the derby games. In the build-up to the games we would be in constant touch, plotting and planning some novel way of starting these games. Mostly it was humorous charades we would play out in the first minute: he would come over and kick me and I would kick him back, or he would put the ball through my legs and then I'd put it through his legs. Once that little giggle was out of the way he would kick shit out of me and I would try to do the same. Nobody really knew what we were up to, but we would be laughing as we did it.

There is a lack of fun in the modern game, I think. It's taken far too seriously and there are few characters left who can inter-act with the fans and with each other on the pitch. It used to be played with a smile. Even the most fearsome, committed char-acters seemed to be more fun in those days. There was no more committed player than little Alan Ball, but he could lighten up when he wanted to and would sit on the ball, taking the mickey after the fans tried to give him some stick. Players would stop and have a chat with the supporters before they took a corner or a throw-in; the whole game seemed to be played in a more sporting way with a rapport with the fans. There seemed to be more humour among the fans too. If they targeted me and chanted some personal comment, it would usually make me laugh. The empathy has gone between fan and player. You could say it's the astonishing amounts the players now earn, but we were high earners in our time too. It's always the prerogative of the old pro to discuss whether the game was better then than it is now. It is impossible to make such comparisons because it's so different. However, I prefer the game the way it was.

The main event of the season finally arrived: the formidable task of trying to defend our solitary-goal lead in Real Madrid's Bernabeau stadium. Stepney had played in the Bernabeau with the England team in a European Nations Cup match in front of 125,000 people as England won 2–0. Good omen. Busby attended the other semi-final where Benfica won 2–0 against Juventus and returned more convinced than ever that the winners of the United-Real tie would win the European Cup.

Law was nowhere near fit, so Kidd was to play up front next to me. Billy Foulkes was recalled for his twenty-ninth of United's thirty-two European Cup ties, which came as a surprise to him as he still had his knee strapped too. But he was the sole survivor from the Busby team that lost in the same stadium in their first European Cup semi-final. Foulkes had been in at the start of Busby's obsessional pursuit of the European Cup. This was going to be his last chance to win it, and he knew it.

Stiles was assigned to mark returning danger man Amancio. It was always a delicate balancing act with Nobby: his astute man-marking techniques were vital, but there was always the danger he'd get on the wrong side of referees. Which is just what happened, after only two minutes. Stiles was in trouble for a bruising tackle when Amancio came up behind him and threw a punch. Stiles struck back and Amancio fell to the ground. His performance was greeted with howls of protest from the 30,000 United fans among the 120,000 crowd. Amancio stayed down for as long as he could, surrounded by angry Real officials and photographers. It was the usual tactic of trying to influence the referee, and also stir up the passions of their fans.

We held out until half an hour. The ball went out and the ref gave a goal kick but then noticed the linesman had flagged a foul by Aston. The ref awarded a free kick. Amancio lofted the ball to Pirri, who headed it straight past Stepney. The aggregate score was level. This was the crucial point of the tie. Ten minutes later an error from Brennan allowed the veteran Gento to cut in, speed past him and crack in a fierce low drive to beat the advancing Stepney.

Now it was time for United to attack and when Dunne hit a forty-yard lob into the area, Zoco kicked wildly at the ball – into his own goal. That goal gave us all the encouragement we needed. Sometimes you need the ball to break your way; a touch of luck.

Just three minutes before half-time, Stiles was booked for another foul on Amancio, who responded by squirming clear of Stiles to receive a pass and, without pausing, turned and struck the ball, which found its way past defenders and Stepney. We were trailing 3–2 on aggregate by half-time.

I'd had a stinker of a match so far. The guy marking me was Sanchis. I could beat him, but he always got back goalside. Sanchis was only a kid but he was one of the best defenders I've ever played against.

We waited for Busby in the dressing room, expecting a right rollicking, and we would have deserved it, because we were facing defeat. Busby walked in after about ten minutes. He seemed very calm. Finally, he spoke: "Come on, keep going," he said. The referee's whistle blew outside the dressing-room door. It was time for us to go out, for the defining half of our lives. Busby reached the door first, and said, "Hold it." It had not gone well, he told us, but there were forty-five minutes left, and Real were looking tired. They were sprinters, they weren't good at the long haul. "Don't give up hope. Remember the score isn't 3–1 for Madrid, because George scored at Old Trafford. You're only 3–2 down overall at the moment; there's just a single goal in it. Time to attack. We've been playing a defensive game and we don't play it very well, do we? Attack and we should be all right. Keep calm and come at them, come out to meet them. You've done well to get so far, so don't worry. Don't fear defeat. Go at them."

We were taken aback by Busby's final instructions. We had struggled to get a kick and he ordered attack. I mean, there's this old bugger who'd give his left arm to win the sodding cup and we're screwing it up for him and he tells us to keep on playing football. Now, that was a little bit special. But before the second half started, the referee was determined to maintain control.

The referee ordered Stiles and Amancio to him. He smashed his fist down into the palm of his hand and said to Amancio: "Stiles no hit you." He told them to get on with the game. The Spanish players were strutting down the tunnel, looking confident, but Busby's reasoning had been absolutely right: just one goal would put us right back in it, and it would also be a massive jolt for Real, so we knew what we had to do, and we were all fired up with our confidence and faith suitably returned.

We went out and staged a courageous recovery. Charlton, playing deep, got us a free kick. Crerand scooped the ball to the edge of the area, I headed it up to Sadler and the ball bounced between keeper Betancort and the defence. They all left it for each other, allowing Sadler to whisk in and side-foot it just inside the post, to even up the tie with fifteen minutes left.

Then came something really unexpected. Crerand was preparing to take a throw, when Foulkes made a surprise dash out of defence. His sudden move forward was a distraction as Crerand threw the ball to me. For once, Sanchis wasn't right on me, so I got past him and also beat Zoco. All this time they were screaming from the bench for Foulkes to get back, but he kept going. I was on the ball ready to cross, and the only red shirt in the area belonged to our centre half who should have been protecting our goal! The defence tried to cover my run, but I pulled back a low centre and when I realised who it was on the end of it, I thought it would be wasted. I was shocked when he calmly side-footed the perfect pass into the far corner of the net. Unbelievable. I couldn't have done better myself. Busby and Murphy hugged on the touchline; Law leaped from his seat near them and smashed his hand into a metal roof support but probably didn't even feel it. Of all people to turn in one of his rare goals for the winner. The crowd were stunned, but United were in the final at last and on our way to Wembley.

Busby wrote later: "The sight of Big Bill tearing down the pitch and then connecting with George Best's cross will be a memory I shall cherish to the end of my days. That, indeed, was going at them!" Of course I preferred to score myself, but an assist was still something for which you could gain great satis-faction and it was appreciated as much then as it is now.

At the final whistle Charlton broke down on the ground, just as he had done when England won the World Cup; he could sense we had virtually won the European Cup. Busby was hugging us all, the fans were on the pitch, the officials were in tears. There were even more emotional scenes in the dressing room. David Sadler and I had walked straight off the pitch and sat on the floor of the showers and let the water run over us without taking our kit off. Outside the local fans turned ugly, and when we returned to our coach there was some trouble. Stiles was struck by an empty wine bottle as he bent down to retrieve his glasses, which had fallen off. He was lifted on to the bus unconscious. When he came to a few seconds later he was shouting: "Let me get at him." Several players held him back, as blood poured from the wound and the doctor declared his shirt was ruined. "It cost £6," he said.

During the game we'd had tomatoes thrown at us and even a shoe. The Spanish fans spat and screamed at us as we left. Hundreds of our fans who had made the trip came to the Fenix Hotel to celebrate. Later, the players hit the town to celebrate, but Bobby Charlton had to be left behind as he felt drained, too exhausted physically and mentally. Some of us, like Crerand, Law and Stepney went to a nightclub called Stone's. It was packed with United fans; it was a great night and we were delighted to share our triumph with the supporters.

When Denis Law woke next morning he discovered that he'd broken a bone in his right hand after the collision with the dugout roof. And Amancio was being gracious in defeat. "One could not help but feel pleased for Señor Busby's sake," he was reported as saying. Manchester United were going to be the first English team to appear in the final, and now we believed that we were destined to win.

When we arrived back in Manchester, some of the players and myself flew straight to London for the Professional Footballers' Association Player of the Year awards. I was the winner. I had already scored twenty-eight league goals, finishing joint top scorer in Division One, and felt in top form going into the European Final. Benfica's Brazilian manager had no doubt about the danger man, as he was quoted as saying: "Of the United players, the one I especially admire is Best. He is what we say 'Muito Bon'."

The player we had to watch out for was Eusebio, the Black Pearl. As European Footballer of the Year in 1965 and runner-up in 1962 and 1966, the Mozambique star inspired a generation of players from the Third World countries.

Benfica defended the European Cup in 1962, meeting Real in the final. Benfica won 5–3 with Eusebio scoring twice. Eusebio was on the losing side in two more European Cup finals, against both of the Milan clubs, AC and Inter, in 1963 and 1965. He had been European Footballer of the Year in 1966 and top scorer in the Portuguese league for the previous three seasons. Stiles had marked him well enough in the World Cup semi-finals, so was naturally given the same job in the European Cup final. But it wasn't just a question of keeping tabs on Eusebio: Benfica had other talented players too. Jose Augusto was still an exceptional forward, Simoes a quick left winger, Mario Coluna a very experienced wing half, and at 6ft 4in, aptly named Jose Torres was, of course, useful in the air. Any team with a record of four European Cup finals in five years were phenomenal and had to be respected.

Having put Benfica to the sword 5–1 in the European Cup quarter-finals in Lisbon in 1966, we were clear favourites. But as the final approached, the realisation set in that Benfica were going to be a tough nut to crack. Since that European Cup quarter-final triumph, which I felt had been one of my best games in Lisbon, we had played them in a post-season tour of America and Australia in the summer of 1967, after we had won the championship title, and they beat us 3–1 in Los Angeles.

We went to a sixteenth-century country hotel, Great Fosters in Surrey, to prepare for the Wembley final. We travelled by train, as just about everybody connected with the club made their way south. Great Fosters had become a hotel in 1930 and had had some notable guests, including Charlie Chaplin, Orson Welles and Vivien Leigh. But while the setting was idyllic, there wasn't an awful lot to do after training, besides listening to Busby discuss the opposition. Father Hilary Tagliaferro, the manager of Malta's Hibernians, helped us in the build-up with his vast knowledge of the Benfica players. But the pressure intensified the closer we got to the big night.

Players vary considerably in their degree of "butterflies" in the stomach. Everyone commented at the time about how relaxed I looked. I didn't suffer from nerves, but this was such a big occasion, it meant so much to the club, to Matt Busby, and to everyone connected to the club, that even my team-mates thought I would at last be struck down by an attack of the jitters. You'd see other players in the dressing room before the game, with butterflies, some of them being physically sick. But I used to go out and have a cup of tea with my pals. I'd be out there maybe ten minutes before kick-off. Fans would be walking past, saying, "You injured?" and I'd say, "No, no, I'm playing." They'd send somebody out to get me. I'd go and take my suit off, put my gear on and run out. I never warmed up or anything. No one cared then. It worked all right.

But I could always find a novel way to relax. And there was a particular young lady called Sue who knew precisely how to relax "Bestie" all right. I had first got to know Sue's aunt, and met Sue for the first time when she was just sixteen.

Well, back to the build-up to the European Cup final, and Sue was a little older now and would tear down the motorway from Manchester in her E-type Jag to Great Fosters. Of course, it was tough keeping it a secret from everyone, especially the lads and the back room staff whose job it was to check on the players and make sure we were all tucked up in bed at the appropriate time.

Well, I seemed to be tucked up in bed at the most inappropriate time, after training in the afternoons. Players liked to take an afternoon nap, but sleeping wasn't something I had in mind when I went to bed in the afternoon! Unfortunately, Sue was spotted. Fortunately, not by anyone inside the camp. It was a member of the press who caught me out.

Now, the media was a vastly different animal in those days. Invariably each newspaper had one football correspondent, and he would be assigned to the big game, and that was it. No paparazzi, no newshounds, no extra sports quotes man with little to do but dig up the scandal. At best there was sometimes a columnist on hand to write the colour pieces, but he probably wouldn't turn up until the actual event. As for the football correspondents, they were from the "old school" of journalism. They were trustworthy in the main, and you could even go out for a drink with them, and no matter what happened it would be kept private and confidential. So I begged the journalist who spotted us at it, and he kept our confidence. No one ever knew. For me it was a vital part of the preparation. Relaxation is the best way to describe it.

A couple of the lads took up an invitation from racehorse owner Robert Sangster to watch the Derby at his home; anything to take our minds off the final. But, sorry, no nerves for me. Instead I felt pretty confident, and kept on telling people I would score a hat-trick, although I never really imagined that I would.

I'd already got my own personal double – just before the final, I was named by the football writers as their Footballer of the Year, which partnered my PFA Player of the Year title. At just twenty-one, I was the youngest to ever receive the FWA award.

Come the day of the final, we had a meal and made the journey from Egham in Surrey to Wembley by coach. Wives, parents and players with any connection to Munich were at Wembley, invited by the club. Charlton was to be captain: Law was in hospital again.

Together with Bobby Charlton, I felt I enjoyed one of my best ever games in our unfamiliar strip of royal blue. We changed because our usual strip was almost identical to Benfica's. I was trying to break them down with some individual play, but not everyone agreed that it was working. Charlton, for instance, was sceptical, as he said at the time: "I think the game was disappointing from his point of view. George loved the big stage and you could hardly get a bigger stage than the European Cup final. I could see in everything he did that he wanted to use it as a platform for a great virtuoso performance, but it didn't quite happen. There were reasons for that. Benfica defended well, and it was a hot, humid night. The conditions weren't right for individualist stuff; you had to pass the ball around and share the load because the heat sapped your energy, and that didn't really work for George."

First, Cruz tried to stop me, then it was Humberto's turn, and he got himself booked for his troubles. Eusebio struck the bar, and although Aston was getting plenty of joy on the other flank, it was a thoughtful dressing room at half-time as Busby set to work trying to lift us during the ten-minute break.

I was marked even closer at the start of the second half but perhaps that provided more space for others. After fifty-three minutes Sadler's near-post cross was niftily headed by Bobby Charlton. Though hardly renowned for his heading prowess, it was perfect, straight across goal into the far post. It was his first headed goal for years.

With Benfica now committed to attack, I got the ball in the net but it was ruled offside. I also got more space and fewer tackles probably because one defender had already been booked and because fatigue was setting in later in the contest. Getting past three defenders, my shot brought a fine save from Henrique. "Best, with a shrug of the hips and a twinkle of the toes, made a mockery of any preconceived plans to mark him," was the verdict from the *Guardian*.

But with United tiring and Benfica regaining the initiative, Torres rose to meet Augusto's cross to beat Foulkes in the air, knocking it down, and as Eusebio took defenders' attention, a gap opened up for Graca, who from six yards beat Stepney. We were shattered, but got straight back in and I had another run at the defence. My shot rebounded off the keeper, and Sadler got to it, but his shot hit the keeper's boot and bounced over the bar.

Then Eusebio escaped Stiles, broke through Foulkes and Dunne, and seemed certain to score with only Stepney to beat, but the keeper pulled off the save of the match from the striker's fierce shot, and that was probably the turning point.

For only the second time, the European Cup final went into extra time with the score at 1–1. Busby urged us on, told us to keep possession, and felt we would finish the stronger. Players like Stiles and Crerand were fired up in practice matches so you can imagine their demeanour with just thirty minutes left to win the European Cup: they were fizzing to get at them.

Whatever anyone thought of my performance in the first half, I felt I improved in the second half and then three minutes into extra time Brian Kidd flicked on Stepney's long punt up field and, steering the ball away from a couple of tackles, I just went for goal with some defenders in hot pursuit. "George was off," recalled Charlton later, "giving a fair impersonation of Wembley's electric hare, supremely confident, doing ultimately what he always expected of himself in such situations. When George got away like that goalkeepers were inclined to feel they had chosen the wrong career, and I'm sure Henrique was no exception." They couldn't catch me; I sent the keeper the wrong way with a dummy and the ball rolled slowly towards the line. For a split second it seemed as though Humberto might catch it, but then the ball seemed to gather pace. Stiles did a cartwheel, and I turned away with one arm raised to celebrate my goal and the European Cup as good as in the bag.

"It was like something from *Roy of the Rovers*," I was quoted as saying afterwards. I was pretty ecstatic. I didn't mind being interviewed and was often widely quoted prior to a game and after it. I am sure on this occasion you couldn't have stopped me talking about it.

Benfica were on their knees. A minute later, Kidd, enjoying his nineteenth birthday, headed Charlton's cross over the keeper and in, off the underside of the bar. What a birthday present. Charlton lobbed a shot over the keeper for the fourth goal. "He wasn't a very big goalkeeper," the Geordie said modestly afterwards, but at the time he celebrated with a little jump in the air. We still had the second half of extra time to play but we might as well have come off – it was well and truly all over.

Busby's dream was fulfilled. So was mine, and everyone connected with Manchester United. A fitting and long-awaited tribute to all those who perished in Munich. Bobby became a national hero all over again after winning the World Cup with England. But Bobby was also a survivor of the Munich air crash, which made it even more poignant for him. He captained United and scored two goals. What more could any footballer achieve? The emotions afterwards were impossible to describe adequately. Matt Busby had one of those faces that could illuminate a room, like the pictures you see of saints. Charlton smoothed down his flyaway hair as he went up to the royal box to receive the trophy. Although he'd looked as though he could keep on going while on the pitch, he couldn't lift it above chest height. The fans went wild anyway.

There was no mistaking Busby's feelings when he said: "I am the proudest man in England tonight. The boys have done us proud. They showed in Madrid that they have the heart to fight back and tonight they showed us the stuff that Manchester United are made of. I am proud of them all."

We all left Wembley and headed in to central London where the club had arranged a big dinner-dance. Bobby Charlton was so ill that, once again, he couldn't attend the celebrations, leaving his wife Norma alone. Joe Loss and his band played "Congratulations". Matt Busby was persuaded to sing, and there was only one appropriate song: Louis Armstrong's "Wonderful World".

I had quite a few drinks that night and don't recall too much about the celebrations. The party apparently moved on to a nightclub but I had moved on to meet another girlfriend, Jackie Glass. But the skinny boy who seven years earlier had come off the ferry from Belfast had done his job. And I remember that. This match had just about everything for me.

That day, 29 May, was most definitely my finest hour; not just beating Benfica, but winning in some style. It was Manchester United's finest achievement for many reasons. The mere fact that the club was attempting to win the European Cup so soon after the Munich disaster was just incredible. Matt had built a brand new team, and a brilliant team at that. Yes, it was the pinnacle of my career and the best moment for the club.

Whenever I get together with some of the players from that night, there remains an inner glow that will live with us for as long as we live. As Bill Foulkes said: "For those of us who had survived Munich, the memory of the players who had died was never out of our mind. They were the reason we wanted to win. It was one of our best European performances. At the end I remember embracing Matt Busby. He was holding back the tears and so was I. We didn't need to say anything."

Personally, I never wanted to play for anybody except Manchester United. But I don't think there's anything wrong with moving. Manchester City tapped me once. It wasn't what you'd call subtle, they just told the press they'd like me in their team. No big deal. They weren't the only ones. I had both the Milan clubs, Real Madrid, one or two others. But they were all wasting their time. We were winning things, weren't we? I mean, we won the big one, the European Cup. You couldn't leave a team like that.

I thought nothing other than everything was in front of me, and our achievements would be limitless. We had such a formidable side, and everything was set up at the club for true greatness. You could sense something special. I had never known disappointment from day one in football. Life could not have been sweeter. The warm glow of expectancy could not have been greater. At twenty-two, I had already won everything, every major honour, every major trophy, every top individual honour. For the next ten years I thought I would be at the top of my game with the best club in the world winning trophy after trophy, season after season. It is hard to believe that, within four years, it would all go horribly wrong; that I had won my last trophy, the European Cup.

## 1967–68 ROLL OF HONOUR

*Champions:* Manchester City

*FA Cup:* West Bromwich Albion

*League Cup:* Leeds

*European Cup:* Manchester United

*European Cup-Winners' Cup:* AC Milan

*Footballer of the Year:* George Best

*European Footballer of the Year:* George Best

# 6

# 1968–69

The Don Revie era at Leeds United was up and running, and although both the manager and his team were much vilified by fans and opponents alike, I had nothing but the utmost respect and admiration for the club and the team.

In my opinion, Don Revie's remarkable transformation of Leeds was, if anything, even more dramatic than Shankly's at Liverpool. The Yorkshire club were flirting with relegation to the Third Division in 1962, yet by the middle of the decade they were a formidable football machine challenging for all the major honours. Now that is some achievement and I for one can recognise how much hard work and talent it would have taken to achieve it, even though, as we were all to discover at a much later date, there were some unsavoury shenanigans going on, instigated by Revie himself.

For a multitude of reasons Revie is a fascinating and successful character, a man driven to achieve success and obsessional in his determination to prove himself. His background gives an indication of how much he was immersed in the game. He had been a deep-lying centre forward in the Manchester City side of the mid-1950s, and Footballer of the Year in 1955. As a manager he had a gift for spotting influential players. Players of the stature of Billy Bremner, Bobby Collins, Jack Charlton and Norman Hunter were the names synonymous with this era, as Revie assembled an enormously powerful side, strong in every department and with a garrison spirit that bordered at times on the fanatical.

Remarkably, only three players cost a transfer fee: Johnny Giles, £33,000 from Manchester United, England outside left Mike O'Grady, £30,000 from Huddersfield Town, and striker Mick Jones, £100,000 from Sheffield United. That was a tribute to Revie's scouting system and youth policy, which unearthed and brought on the Scottish wingers Peter Lorimer and Eddie Gray.

I am always intrigued by how star players first emerged and how much the manager went out of his way to ensure their signing. Certainly Revie knew the importance of capturing Gray, a player who would become a cornerstone of his playing empire. When, in 1963, Gray left Our Lady of St Margaret's school in Glasgow, waiting at the school gates for the fifteen-year-old that day was Don Revie. Every club in Britain, Arsenal among them, wanted a young footballer who would later be described as "Nureyev on grass". But, determined and dynamic, Revie had got in first even though Leeds were then in the Second Division and had never won anything. "I'd come down on the Christmas before. I was just fourteen," said Gray, recalling how Revie had snapped him up. "I trained with the first team because Don wanted to impress upon me that Leeds was the place to come even though they were only a Second Division club. I had a lot of clubs chasing me and to be honest I had never heard of Leeds, because they weren't a fashionable club. They were a yo-yo team. Don put a lot of effort into attracting young schoolboys; him and the chairman Harry Reynolds used to come up to Scotland. They did it the year before with Peter Lorimer and Jim McCalliog. I came down and enjoyed it and the day I left school Don picked me up in Glasgow; he'd been to my school to see my headmaster. I left school then. I suppose that's my first real Leeds memory." Other products of the youth scheme included Welsh international keeper Gary Sprake and the versatile Paul Madeley.

One of the most important cogs in the Revie machinery was Johnny Giles, who, of course, had been part of Manchester United's 1963 victory over Leicester City in the FA Cup Final, but he ended up moving on to Leeds. He moved in from the wing when Bobby Collins broke a thigh and remained a key figure as a midfield schemer, striking up a formidable partnership with the dynamic Billy Bremner.

Revie was a great innovator on the field and it was he who decreed that Leeds United wear all white instead of blue and old-gold halves. Revie wanted Leeds to have the appearance of Real Madrid in the hope that one day they would play like them. No point in aiming low, he would always say. His team quickly gained a reputation for a high grade of possession football, an aspect of their play that caught my attention right from the start. All season long Leeds were tormenting opposing teams, making them expend their energy in pursuit of the ball. It was a demoralising experience, cruelly inflicted, but it provided for a captivating spectacle. The technique of creating and exploiting space, coupled with the unstinting support of colleagues for the man in possession, had long been the hallmark of Leeds' training ground sessions; it was soon proliferating throughout the First Division.

Leeds lost not one of their first nine league games until 28 September, when they went down 3–1 to Manchester City. They bounced back, winning the next three before a surprise 5–1 defeat at Burnley. But that would be Leeds' last league defeat of the season. Crucially, Revie's team were not distracted by going for too many honours. They were out of the League Cup, beaten 2–1 at Crystal Palace in the fourth round in October, and in January, courtesy of a Sheffield Wednesday 3–1 win, had departed the FA Cup. But Leeds were still immersed in the Fairs Cup, and had to face a tough and nasty match with Napoli in Italy in November, losing 2–0. But they drew the tie 2–2 and went through on the toss of a coin. Their European hopes were ended in March when Leeds were knocked out of the competition by Hungary's Ujpest Dozsa.

B ut there was a less likely English team left in the competition who eventually went all the way. Joe Harvey managed Newcastle United to its first European success when the team beat the Hungarians 6–2 on aggregate. They had to beat Sporting Lisbon along the way in the second round; the difference between the clubs on that night was Bryan "Pop" Robson – all 5ft

8in of goal-poaching excellence. The winner he struck in the second leg on Tyneside is regarded as the finest ever scored by a Newcastle player in the club's one hundred matches in European competition. Tommy Gibb floated a free kick to the edge of the box, Wyn Davies got his head to the ball, and "Pop" got on the end of it with a volley. Robson sprung a good three feet off the ground to get his right foot to the ball, and he connected with some force. It secured a 1–0 win on a chill November night and a 2–1 success on aggregate. Robson plundered six goals in total as the leading marksman in that triumphant campaign. "The continental sides hadn't come across a player like big Wyn before," reflected Robson. The Gallowgate crowd used to chant "You'll not see nothing like the mighty Wyn" in tribute to Robson's 6ft 1in striking partner. The plan was to aim balls into the box for Wyn and Robson to pick up the pieces in the archetypal "little and large" strike partnership. Willie McFaul in goal, and Bob Moncur and Ollie Burton at the centre of defence made them strong at the back too. Robson played in England's top division as a thirty-eight-year-old. In his last game in the old First Division, in May 1984, he scored a goal that saved Sunderland from relegation. "The best striker England never capped," Jimmy Greaves called him. "Pop", whose nickname came not from his ability to score swiftly, but from being one third of a group of schoolfriends known as "Snap, Crackle and Pop", reckoned he owed much of his sharpness and poise to the extracurricular training he undertook with Len Heppell, a former professional ballroom dancer. They started working together after Robson's prowess as a county standard table-tennis player brought him into contact with Heppell's daughter, Maureen, an England international player. "Lennie could spot things in your movement and he knew how to improve them," Robson said of the man who became his long-time father-in-law. "I spent the summer of 1968 working with him – playing table tennis and running and doing little exercises to improve my sharpness. It was just simple stuff, working on reactions and balance and poise, but it made a massive difference to me. I had been a canny little player before that, getting nine or ten goals a season, but that next season I scored thirty – twenty-four in the league and FA Cup and six in the Fairs Cup. The season after that I scored twenty-five." Robson continued to prosper as a top-flight scorer after moving from Newcastle to West Ham, earning the Football League's Golden Boot for his twenty-eight First Division goals in the 1972–73 season.

Normally, exit from Europe would have been too much to bear for Revie, but it did now mean that Leeds could concentrate solely on the league. There was an inner will to make sure there were no slip-ups this time. Seven straight victories from 24 January to 8 March, with just three goals conceded, set the tone for the title run. It was pretty obvious to me that the title was destined for Leeds, but there were a couple of big hurdles first. A 2–1 victory at Arsenal put the title within their reach. The match was typically Leeds – moments of solid, good defence and tactical skill interspersed with outbursts of violence, and all seasoned with more than a fair sprinkling of luck, which helped them grab two valuable points. It was lucky

– and surprising – that Gary Sprake was allowed to play on after punching Arsenal centre forward Bobby Gould. Even luckier, for the northern team, were the errors from the unfortunate Arsenal centre half Ian Ure, whose mistakes in defence gave Leeds both goals, first letting Mick Jones past to score, then hitting a back pass well wide of the keeper, so that Leeds player Giles could almost walk the ball into the net.

Leeds didn't care if their football wasn't stylish; they were simply determined to win at any cost. Whatever tactics, games-manship or trick at their disposal, they employed them in the last minutes of the match, passing among themselves and blatantly wasting time, intent on keeping the ball away from Arsenal. But Revie's squad were thick-skinned enough to brush aside all the adverse criticism their methods attracted. Tricky Revie, though keen on good public relations, was not going to sway from his methods with the title so close. Winning was far more important to him.

A win at home to Leicester City, followed by a draw at Goodison Park on a night when their nearest challengers Liverpool were held at Coventry, left Leeds five points clear with two games to play. Only Shankly's team, with three games left, could mathematically catch them. Fate and/or the fixture compilers decreed that Leeds' penultimate match, on the Monday night after the FA Cup Final, took them to Anfield. Leeds travelled to Liverpool with the league title in their hands. Only Bill Shankly's side could stop them. A point and the title would be theirs. The Anfield crowd displayed incredible sports-manship towards Bremner and his team.

Even so, the match was played in a furious atmosphere. In front of the inevitable Liverpool onslaught, Leeds did not falter, and hung on to win the point that guaranteed them the championship. It was appropriate, in so many ways, that their defensive ability, the basis of all they had achieved, clinched the title for Revie.

Beforehand, Revie always thinking ahead, had instructed Bremner, if they should get that decisive point, to lead the players after the game towards the Kop. Bremner took some persuading but, after they had celebrated before their own travelling support, Bremner obeyed his manager's rather bizarre intructions and marched his men forward. The stadium fell silent but, instead of an adverse reaction, the Leeds team were stunned when loudly hailed as "champions" by the 27,000 Koppites. The ecstactic Leeds players stayed put for twenty minutes, jumping on one another and paying their tributes to both sets of fans. They had been despised for so long that one could not blame them for enjoying their newly found adulation.

"Being cheered by a rival crowd – any rival crowd – was a new experience for us," Eddie Gray recalls. "This in itself was as much of a turning point for Leeds as the championship achievement." In the dressing room, where Shankly provided a crate of champagne, Revie was intoxicated by the extraordinary events because he was also stunned by the Kop's reactions. "The reception given us by the sporting Liverpool crowd was truly magnificent," he said, "and so, for that matter, was our defence tonight. It was superb in everything."

Eight years after he had been appointed, at an undistin-guished club heading for insolvency, Revie had taken Leeds to the top of the domestic game. And, after all the animosity directed at Leeds, it was made worthwhile by the enlightened Kop, a group of fans who appreciated and applauded excellence when they witnessed it, even if it was from the opponents. Bill Shankly gave Leeds his stamp of approval. "Leeds United are worthy champions," he proclaimed. "They are a great side." And Shanks didn't hand out such praise often – or lightly.

"That wonderful night at Anfield saw our burning faith in ourselves justified," Bremner reflected. "At last we were well and truly vindicated."

A goal by Johnny Giles five minutes from the end of their last league match on 30 April against Nottingham Forest gave Leeds a 1–0 win and the two points they needed to set a new First Division record of sixty-seven points, pipping Arsenal's 1931 tally by one. After three more seasons of finishing in the top four, and defeat in the 1966 Fairs Cup Final, Leeds United had finally won the title and they had done it in style, with a formidable record of losing just twice. Revie also transformed Jack Charlton from a solid club centre half into an inspirational defensive lynchpin and the fierce-tackling Norman Hunter into another England international. With Paul Reaney and Terry Cooper behind them, Leeds were masters of defence and possession football, conceding twenty-six goals, fewer than any previous champions in a forty-two-match season. Mick Jones was top scorer with only fourteen league goals and that gave critics plenty of ammunition about the team's style of play, a destructive, defensive force rather than the sweet, flowing football of a Manchester United. Yet that's deceptive, as only two clubs in the First Division scored more than Leeds. Leeds had figures of sixty-six scored, twenty-six conceded compared to Spurs fabulously talented and attack-minded double-winning team which had scored 115 and let in fifty-five in 1961; in the same year, even relegated Newcastle United had scored eighty-six.

English teams were by now regularly coming up against continental opposition and in particular the miserly *catenaccio*, which literally means padlock, a system operated by Italian sides. Tight defence was seen as the key to success, and that policy was perfected by Revie, whose contribution was comprehensively recognised when he was awarded Manager of the Year in both 1969 and 1970, the preceding winners being Matt Busby and Jock Stein.

Revie had fulfilled the target he had personally decreed in the summer of 1967: Leeds had won two competitions, the League Cup and UEFA Cup. In 1968 he narrowed his ambition to just one, the title he knew Leeds needed in order to establish a justifiable place into English football's elite. Billy Bremner recalled his deep-rooted philosophy: "When you haven't won anything, you're delighted to win something, but as soon as a new challenge is offered you have to climb higher. And so we climbed that little bit higher in going for the league." After five years of close calls, mainly finishing second best, Leeds finally peaked. Leeds' rise was timed to perfection as the chief rivals Manchester United and Liverpool were on the wane,

Manchester City hadn't the resilience to establish a dynasty, Arsenal and Everton were fine-tuning rebuilding programmes, and the challenge from the capital, in the form of Chelsea and Tottenham, was confined to the cups rather than the consistency required to win the championship.

Leeds had that elusive consistency at long last and the secret was in the reliability of their star performers. Bremner, Hunter, Reaney and Sprake played in every league game for Leeds; Jack Charlton missed only one, Mick Jones two.

I was surprised to learn that Torino, so impressed by the Revie method, offered Leeds £70,000 to buy him out of his contract. Revie was offered a cash inducement of £24,000, plus a generous salary and bonuses. But Revie announced that he wanted to stay and aim higher: the European Cup and World Club Championship.

As for myself and our stars at Old Trafford, the magic of Wembley had proved hard to come down from. "What else is there left to do?" seemed to be the regrettable attitude after winning the European Cup. Matt Busby had reached the summit, and there was a strange acceptance of the rapid decline. What we should have been doing was building a new team to do it all over again. There were a couple of young players such as myself and Brian Kidd who had emerged through the youth system, but the home-produced talent dried up. There was also a feeling that certain veteran players had reached their peak. Denis Law was carrying lingering injuries and Bobby Charlton was approaching the end of his illustrious career. And, of course, my well-chronicled problems off the pitch didn't help, though I increasingly had the feeling that I was carrying the team at times on the pitch.

Complacency ran right through the club to the very top, where the board had failed to reinvest in big-name signings. There was a lot of speculation about the dominant centre half Mike England coming to Old Trafford but he went to Spurs instead. There was a big loss. We were similarly linked with David Nish but he went to Derby County. The players we ended up recruiting were not up to the necessary high standards. A Manchester United without Best, Law and Charlton seemed improbable, though that's how it was soon to end up, and there needed to be special players arriving to fill those enormous boots.

It was a season that failed to find any consistency. Our statistics read: won fifteen, drew twelve and lost fifteen; goals for fifty-seven, goals against fifty-three. We finished a bitterly disappointing eleventh. I managed, however, a respectable tally of nineteen goals. Memorable games were few and far between – an 8–1 mauling of QPR in the league and a 6–0 win over Birmingham in the FA Cup – and there was a painful realisation that the magic had disappeared.

Sir Matt Busby – his new title having been bestowed in the Queen's Birthday Honours – would retire as the league's longest-serving manager at the season's close, perhaps sensing that our time as the great entertainers, and a team with that precious winning mentality and an overruling team spirit, had deserted the dressing room.

Manchester City built on their league success the previous season by winning the FA Cup. It had been a mixed season for Joe Mercer's team. It started well enough, beating West Brom 6–1 in the Charity Shield, but they went out in the first round of the European Cup against Turkey's Fenerbahce and managed only thirteenth place in the league (two below us) as defending champions. Both FA Cup semi-finals were settled with a single goal against the previous year's finalists, Leicester overcoming West Brom at Villa Park and City beating Everton at Hillsborough. The FA Cup Final was given the biggest-ever build-up, starting at 11.25am on *Grandstand* with coverage until 5.15pm. The final also made history by being broadcast simultaneously on BBC2 in colour for the first time. A Neil Young shot beat a young Peter Shilton to win the trophy. It was the fourth time Manchester City had scooped the prize, but it was their first success since 1956. For Leicester it was the third Cup Final defeat in nine seasons and three weeks later the Foxes were relegated.

As with QPR the previous year, Third Division Swindon Town won both promotion and the League Cup, defeating Arsenal 3–1 in the final to cause the biggest shock of the season on a pitch that was more mud than grass. Two goals in extra time from Don Rogers sealed an unlikely victory against an Arsenal side that had finished fourth in the championship. The League Cup was finally beginning to emerge as a competition worth winning.

It had had a chequered history since the Football League secretary Alan Hardaker had championed it at the beginning of the decade. With three European trophies to aim for, a second domestic cup was hardly an attraction. In its inaugural year Aston Villa had won it in extra time. But when Second Division Norwich City beat Fourth Division Rochdale over two legs in the 1962 final, the competition was in danger of losing all interest. The turning point came in 1967 when the final became a one-legged affair at Wembley and the status was further enhanced with the award of a Fairs Cup place to the winners, provided they were in the First Division. That stipulation meant that Queens Park Rangers and Swindon, winners in 1967 and 1969 respectively, weren't able to embark on a European adventure. By the end of the decade the League Cup was firmly established, although it always remained a poor relation to the premier knock-out competition.

England went into the 1968 European Championships as favourites, but after beating Spain in the quarter-final, it all went wrong for the World Cup holders against Yugoslavia. Alan Mullery was sent off for retaliation, the first England player to receive his marching orders, and the team went down 1–0. This was a time when being sent off while playing for your country carried a heavy stigma. (I should know, as I was sent off during a game against Scotland two years later – for throwing mud at the ref!) It was rare, and the player was inevitably thrust into the media spotlight, whereas today, with red cards pulled out of refs' pockets for hardly anything, it hardly carries the same kind of shame. Goals from Bobby Charlton and Geoff Hurst gave England third place, with the hosts Italy beating

Yugoslavia 2–0 in the final replay, having drawn the original match 1–1.

There was one major title left for us at Old Trafford – and one of the biggest. United played Estudiantes in the World Club Championship, having qualified as European Cup winners. We were all looking forward to the contest, particularly as the Argentineans had apologised profusely for their team's previous behaviour when they last played in this tournament and kicked the shit out of Celtic. It was so bad they dubbed it the Battle of River Plate. We were assured that Estudiantes were a university team of medical students, and their manners would be vastly different to those at the River Plate. We should have known. No one tackled harder or dirtier than this Argentinean team. Matt Busby always said I was the best tackler in the club. You wouldn't have credited it, but that's what he said, and I wasn't afraid to go into a crunching tackle, nor was I afraid to be tackled. But this lot were something else.

In the first leg in Buenos Aires, which we lost 1–0, Bobby Charlton needed three stitches after being hacked down, while Stiles, a marked man from the start, was back-headed in the face, and was later sent off for dissent. Back at Old Trafford for the second leg, Estudiantes went ahead after only five minutes. Denis Law had to be substituted after getting the stud treatment from the keeper. Then this guy, Medina, just came up to me and kicked me, no intention of playing the ball, no intention of playing football of any description, just whacked me as hard as he could and spat at me for good measure. He was booked for it, but I wasn't finished with him, and I smacked him in the mouth, turned round and walked off – didn't even wait for the ref's decision – and he went off too, as you would have expected. Willie Morgan equalised but United failed to score again, which is perhaps a blessing in disguise.

I was too often in trouble with referees by now, mainly for foul and abusive language. Well, I was hardly likely to be kicking anyone. So I began to become acquainted with some intimate knowledge on disciplinary cases. I'm sorry but I don't have an awful lot of time for referees. The trouble with refs is that they have never played the game so they are clueless as to what really goes on inside players' minds.

Despite our indifferent form at home, it was business as usual in Europe and I might well have won the European Cup in successive seasons. After seeing off the likes of Anderlecht and Rapid Vienna, we found ourselves paired in the semi-finals against the might of AC Milan. In front of 83,000 fans in the first leg in the San Siro, Milan had established a lead with Angelo Sormani opening the scoring and, despite young John Fitzpatrick's close attentions, the second was scored by Hamrin. But it got a lot worse for Fitzpatrick. John had a pretty hot temper and when Hamrin spat at him, he saw red and chinned him. He knew he shouldn't have retaliated but spitting, well, it doesn't really get any lower and, put it this way, if he had spat at me I'd have chinned him too. The army had to escort John back to the dressing room, and on the way back to the airport our coach was stoned. Of course, John was suspended for the second leg.

Yet we still felt we remained capable of overturning the 2–0 deficit from the first leg. And after a great display in the return leg, we were heading back to the final but for one incident, the same sort of thing that cropped up recently when Manchester United played Tottenham at Old Trafford and the ball had crossed the line by a yard. When I saw that Tottenham incident, it brought back memories: the ball was probably the same distance over the line.

Two goals down from the first leg, United gained hope when Bobby Charlton, taking a pass from myself, pulled back a goal with a characteristic blast after seventy minutes. Then a late goalmouth scramble resulted in Law poking the ball over the line for the "equaliser", which would have taken the game into extra time. A Milan defender lying on the floor managed to hook the ball back, however, and the French referee waved play on. The incident was probably the first example in Britain of a television replay showing the ball having crossed the line. It had crossed it by some distance but the holders were on their way out of the competition 2–1 on aggregate.

We can't, in fairness, lay all the blame with the referee. We were also eliminated after a defiant goalkeeping performance by the man known as "The Black Spider". After Bobby's strike, The Black Spider resisted the subsequent siege. The 6ft 3in Milan goalkeeper, Fabio Cudicini, playing in an all-dark strip, managed to get in the way of everything that came his way, including a piece of brick thrown from the Stretford End. He was struck on the head and knocked unconscious as coins and other missiles were thrown from fans in the terraces. Play was held up for five minutes as Cudicini received treatment; the pitch was cleared and order restored. The goalkeeper was able to play out the match and United's players recovered some dignity by applauding the Italian side at the end. Milan, coached by Nereo Rocco and captained by Gianni Rivera, went on to beat Ajax 4–1 in the final.

All these years on, Cudicini recalls in graphic detail the events of that tumultuous May evening at Old Trafford and still takes a keen interest in the affairs of the English game. His son, Carlo, is second-choice goalkeeper at Chelsea. "I remember that match at Manchester very well," seventy-year-old Cudicini said at his home in Milan. "I was given the name 'Il Ragno Nero' – The Black Spider. I think it was the English press who thought of that. Well, it was very complimentary, but all of our team had to work hard to keep the ball out of our goal a second time that night. There was a lot of tension in the match and it became a little dangerous. The spectators threw stones, metal and various other objects on to the pitch. I was hit and knocked to the ground. I was unconscious for a few minutes."

Cudicini was also grounded, with his back to the ball, when United almost levelled the tie and sent the teams to a replay in Brussels. "I cannot say whether or not it was really a goal because I could not see," Cudicini says. "It must have been very close but some of our players said that not all the ball was over the line. I think it was like the famous goal in the 1966 World Cup final at Wembley."

Goal or no goal, it was to be the last European stand for Busby and his legendary players.

# 1968–69 ROLL OF HONOUR

*Champions:* Leeds

*FA Cup:* Manchester City

*League Cup:* Swindon

*European Cup:* AC Milan

*Cup-Winners' Cup:* Slovan Bratislava

*Footballer of the Year:* Tony Book of Manchester City

and Dave Mackay of Derby

*European Footballer of the Year:* Gianni Rivera (AC Milan)

# 7

# 1969–70

It was fascinating watching the bitter conflict develop between Leeds United and Chelsea, the north-south divide, the ultra hard-grafting professionals against the glitzy late-night clubbers and drinkers. Whatever the reasons, the rivalry was there for all to see, a fierce competitive edge whenever the pair got together on the football field.

The King's Road set of the 70s included Peter Osgood, Charlie Cooke and Alan Hudson.

Osgood was always said to be Chelsea's answer to George Best. Like me, he had come through the ranks. In fact, Chelsea had a solid reputation for developing young talent: Brabrook, Greaves, Tambling, Bridges, Shellito, Bonetti, and then Osgood.

But really there was no comparison between me and Ossie. I was relatively short, he was tall and thin – 6ft 2ins – and he was an ugly sod! A strip of a lad and outrageously skilful, while he was still only eighteen, he equalised in the third round of the FA Cup at Anfield in 1966 against the cup holders and Chelsea came away with a 2–1 victory. But Ossie then broke his leg in a tackle with a young "Crazy Horse" Emlyn Hughes in a League Cup tie at Blackpool. Tony Hateley was bought for £100,000 to fill in the gap, and Osgood eventually returned a heavier character but still with sufficient brilliance as a goalscorer. Nine months later and two stone heavier he scored on his comeback the following season with two goals in the 6–2 home defeat by Southampton, one a run past half of the opposition. Only four England caps was a poor return for someone of his outstanding talent. He famously performed a lap of honour when he scored his hundredth goal for Chelsea, blowing kisses to the crowd.

There was a diverse amount of characters at Stamford Bridge, from goalkeeper Peter Bonetti to strikers like Osgood. Peter Bonetti was voted "Chelsea's Greatest Ever Player" halfway through his Stamford Bridge career. He was affectionately known as "The Cat" for his amazing agility. Despite his slight frame and mere 5ft 10in, he dominated his area with his ability to catch crosses. He also had a sense of style, with green shorts and socks to coordinate with his jersey. He was an all-round distinctive star, the first to wave to the fans when they chanted his name before games. Bonetti played on past his thirty-fifth birthday before he retired in 1979 after 729 games. From 1960 to 1979 thirteen other keepers started a game but Bonetti was always first choice because of his ability to stay the distance, and as a consequence of such consistency Chelsea sold a young promising keeper to Manchester United, Alex Stepney. Stepney proved to be an outstanding acquisition for us, one of the best keepers I have had the good fortune to play alongside.

Unfortunately for Bonetti, he was two years younger than Gordon Banks, which restricted him to just seven England caps. Alan Hudson said of him: "Bonetti was somebody who shouldn't have been a goalkeeper; there was nothing of him. I called him a Biafran runner; he'd run for miles. I was stood right behind Bobby Charlton one day and he whacked it and the whole ground stood up and shouted goal, and 'Catty' didn't just save it, he caught it. I played against Gordon Banks and with Peter Shilton and Pat Jennings, but he was the best."

Though perhaps not as much of a showman as some of his team-mates, another player I admired for his sheer energy, work-rate and commitment was the versatile John Hollins. He played 592 times for the club. He was voted the club's Player of the Year in both crucial seasons of 1970 and 1971. He played right back and midfield, and even scored the BBC's Goal of the Season against Bob Wilson at Highbury in January, 1970.

As a winger, I appreciated the skills of Charlie Cooke, who was twice Chelsea's Player of the Year (1968 and 1975). The fans would sing "Cooke's better than Eusebio", and only the brilliance of Franco Zola eclipsed Cooke as perhaps the greatest, most naturally gifted, winger in the club's history. Charlie destroyed England at Hampden Park in 1968 with his dribbling prowess although the game finished 1–1. "When Charlie Cooke sold you a dummy, you had to pay at the turnstiles to get back into the stadium," was the tribute paid to Cooke by the legendary Jim Baxter.

For Manchester United the realisation began to bite that we were not going to achieve anything special this season, the way things were going. We were simply not good enough, and that was hard to take. We lost our first two home games to Everton and Southampton and it took us seven games before we actually won in the league – a 3–1 win over Sunderland, which also featured my first goal of the season.

Once I'd broken my duck, my goals began to flow and I notched eight league strikes in September alone. This tally included three braces, one in a 5–2 win over West Ham, the others against Leeds and Sheffield Wednesday. We also recorded an impressive 4–1 at Anfield in December. But equally we could get stuffed ourselves in any given game. City had thumped us 4–0 at Maine Road the month before in front of 63,000 fans. Consistency was non-existent. There was no change by the end of the season: during the last few games we were humiliated 5–1 by Newcastle at St James's Park, then beat West Brom 7–0 four days later. I spoke out at the time that I felt matters would get worse before they got better. There were a lot of players we could have signed but failed to do so for one reason or another. We finally finished eighth in the league, a minor though largely insignificant improvement on the previous year.

I suppose a mild consolation was that I equalled the FA Cup-scoring record on 7 February with six goals in Manchester United's 8–2 fifth-round victory at Northampton. I had returned from a month's suspension as punishment for a silly piece of petulance, and thoroughly enjoyed myself in the mud at the

County Ground in front of a 22,000 crowd. I scored with my head, with shots, dribbling around the keeper, against a Northampton side that had been in the First Division four years earlier. Brian Kidd scored the other goals for us that day while McNcil and Large were on target for the Cobblers. It was not the first time a player had scored six in the cup, though. Denis Law, of course, did it at Luton in 1961 in his first spell at Man City, but the match was abandoned and the records expunged – and City lost in the replay.

The nearest we came to glory was yet another FA Cup semi-final. It took Leeds United and ourselves three games just to score a single goal. Billy Bremner, who was voted Footballer of the Year, broke the deadlock with the winner at Burnden Park in the second replay.

The final itself, between Leeds and Chelsea, also went to a replay: Wembley's first drawn final. The teams met again eighteen days later at Old Trafford before Ron Harris became the first Chelsea skipper ever to lift the FA Cup.

This FA Cup Final was no ordinary contest. It was a classical contrast in philosophies and styles, the cultured against the methodical, and the two games were bitterly fought. As Charlie Cooke recalls: "They were our arch rivals for quite a few years. It was cut-throat. This constant whining at referees they did, the referee baiting. That gamesmanship used to ruffle our feathers." After ninety minutes of kicking each other all over the hallowed turf, the teams were happy to hear the final whistle, particularly Chelsea's David Webb. Webb had been turned inside out throughout the game by Eddie Gray as Dave Sexton's side grabbed a 2–2 draw to earn the replay at Old Trafford. Many believed Chelsea had got away lightly after taking a real battering. Peter Bonetti was crocked early on by Mick Jones but this was a time when there was no replacement sitting on the bench to take his place. The Cat struggled on, without taking goal-kicks, yet still managed to pull off a string of fine saves. Leeds took the lead through Jack Charlton after twenty-one minutes, but the Blues levelled matters four minutes before the break courtesy of Gary Sprake's howler. Peter Houseman, never a favourite with the Chelsea faithful, drove in a long-range effort, which Sprake allowed to creep under his body. Chances came and went at both ends in the second half as the usually immaculate Wembley pitch took its toll on the players.

The Horse of the Year Show had been held at the stadium shortly before the final and the heavily sanded turf did neither side any favours. But with six minutes remaining, Leeds thought they had finally killed the game off when Jones beat Bonetti. Chelsea, however, had other ideas. They threw players forward and Hutchinson struck just two minutes later to earn the Londoners another crack at the cup.

Come the replay Sexton moved Ron Harris to right back in place of Webb, who filled in at centre half. Chopper Harris wasted little time in putting Gray in the stand time and time again – and the winger unsurprisingly struggled to have the impact he did at Wembley. It may be hard to picture in today's age of bookings and red cards galore, but Chelsea and Leeds literally kicked – and punched – lumps out of each other. It was a battle, pure and simple. Osgood and Charlton squared up to each other, while Bremner and Harris pretty much hacked down anything that moved. Jones was on target again to hand Leeds a first-half lead after thirty-five minutes. But Chelsea refused to lie down and although it was a long time coming, they equalised in the seventy-eighth minute. Osgood had scored in every round of the cup and he kept the record going with a fine diving header.

Apart from the odd bruise, nothing separated the sides come full-time. And it appeared extra time would fail to settle the occasion, until Hutchinson wound up one of his trade-mark long throws. Webb arrived at the far post and bundled his way towards the ball, forcing it in off his cheek to stun Leeds after 104 minutes of pulsating action. The Blues dug in to hold on.

Sexton had his Cup Final problems. With Hudson injured for the final, Peter Houseman filled in, but in extra time and for the replay Cooke switched to midfield. It was from Cooke's superb chip that Osgood headed the equaliser in the replay. "I remember feeling that the game was kind of drifting, we were going nowhere," recalls Charlie. "We need to crack something open, that was on my mind, and when I picked up the ball, it was pretty far out, and I was just trying to force something to happen." Cookie ran with the ball, created a crossing opportunity and steered a superb diagonal ball for Ossie to convert. "It was a beautiful cross. Ossie always makes the most of those things."

Osgood recalled: "There is no doubt that of the great memories I still cherish of my days playing for Chelsea, the best would have to be winning the FA Cup in '70. That was a great year for me: third in the league, called up for England to go to Mexico in the World Cup squad with great players such as Alan Ball, Bobby Charlton and Nobby Stiles, who had won the World Cup in 1966, and to win the FA Cup. The only pity was that we had to win it at Old Trafford in a replay instead of Wembley. But yes, that was the icing on the cake: simply fantastic and the memories will live with me for ever. It's every kid's dream to win at Wembley, to run out for an FA Cup Final. As a kid I would watch the Wembley finals and then I'd go out to kick a ball around, pretending to be one of the players. I always seemed to be Jimmy Greaves. Funnily enough we share the same birthday, 25 February.

"Scoring in every round of the FA Cup was something special. We played the final on a Wednesday; it went to extra time and then on to a replay two days later. Dave Sexton told the players that there was no point training; just have a swim and a sauna. It was traditional after a match to have a night out followed by a day off and so we carried on that tradition. Charlie Cooke, Tommy Baldwin and myself, the usual pack, went down to the Hilton Hotel, had a right old session and spent the next day lying around the pool sobering up. I had missed the semi-final against Manchester City with an injury, but I played in the final with the aid of cortisone injections. But when they wore off I was in absolute agony, so I sat around the pool dangling my foot in the water. Alan Hudson strolled past and took a look at us

ABOVE: George Graham at his wedding with wife Maria, mum, and best man Terry Venables. All smiles here, but they faced each other later the same day in the North London derby!

RIGHT: Ever the gentleman, Bobby Moore helps wife Tina into the car before an evening out.

ABOVE: Looks like I was taking the Manchester derby at Old Trafford very seriously in March, 1969. Despite the determined look on our faces, City pipped us 1–0 on the day.

LEFT: Journalist Max Urbini presents me with the 1968 European Footballer of the Year award. By then I was winning so many awards I needed a bigger mantelpiece to put them on.

ABOVE: Tony Book lifts the FA Cup and Mike Doyle lifts Tony Book, as they celebrate winning the 1969 final against Leicester City with team-mates Glyn Pardoe, Franny Lee, Harry Dowd and Colin Bell.

RIGHT: An emotional moment after the same final for Mike Summerbee and City manager Joe Mercer, who always had a good relationship on and off the field.

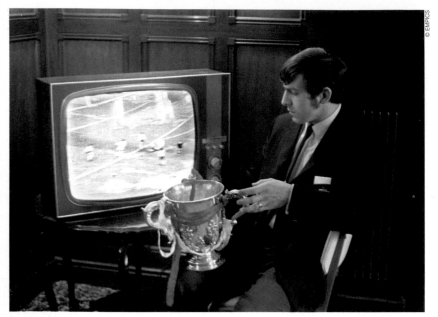

Don Rogers, two-goal hero of Swindon's 3–1 League Cup
Final win over Arsenal in 1969, takes a serious view of the
match highlights with the trophy for company.

Champagne and cigars (and a cigarette for Billy Bremner)
as Leeds celebrate winning the 1968–69 Championship
after a goalless draw with Liverpool.

So close to a second European Cup Final – Ugly scenes at Old Trafford during our semi-final second leg against AC Milan in 1969, where a missile from the crowd knocked out Milan 'keeper Cudicini.
At 1–0 to United, Law poked in a shot which was well over the goal line, but disallowed. Instead of a 2–2 scoreline and extra-time, we were instead controversially out of the competition 2–1 on aggregate.

Young Ipswich manager Bobby Robson pinpoints another player to have caught his eye in 1969. Robson's shrewd signings and willingness to put faith in continental technique transformed Town from minnows into genuine title contenders in the 70s.

ABOVE: Another photo
opportunity for PM Harold
Wilson, another award for me!
Picking up the *Daily Express*
Sportsman of the Year gong at the
Savoy Hotel in 1969.

RIGHT: Not the proudest day of my
international career – Trudging off
for an early bath after being
dismissed for throwing mud and
spitting at the referee in Northern
Ireland's match against Scotland
in April, 1970.

Like me, Colin Harvey knew how to grab a goal or two and was lovingly known to Everton fans as "the white Pele". Here he does his bit at the back as the Toffees defend a corner in 1968.

Howard Kendall eyes up another opportunity in the box, watched by Everton team-mate Alan Ball and Chelsea's Alan Hudson in the 1970 Charity Shield. Kendall scored the second goal in their 2–1 win over the Londoners.

Manager Harry Catterick gets his hands on a well-deserved bottle of bubbly as Everton celebrate winning the Championship in 1970.

1970 saw the first series of the BBC's long-running quiz *A Question of Sport*, on which I was a guest for the very first edition in January. On this later edition, a seemingly confident Bobby Moore sits with Geoff Hurst and Alan Mullery. Standing behind are legends Tom Finney, Johnny Haynes and Stan Mortensen.

Having apparently visited the airport's hat stall with Emlyn Hughes, Jeff Astle sticks a record on a forerunner of the iPod, as they wait with Geoff Hurst at Heathrow, before flying out to Mexico in 1970. At the time, the squad had the number one hit record with "Back Home".

ABOVE: A famous trio
and a famous double –
Frank McLintock,
George Graham and
Charlie George celebrate
the FA Cup win over
Liverpool in 1971.

RIGHT: Arsenal captain
Frank McLintock and
manager Bertie Mee
show off the other piece
of silverware from the
Gunners' double-
winning 1970–71
season, the League
Championship trophy.

Not for the first time, a priceless trophy being given the dirty
bath treatment at Old Trafford! This time it's Chelsea
celebrating their win over Leeds in the Cup Final replay in
Manchester in 1970, with Tommy Baldwin, John Hollins, Peter
Bonetti, David Webb and Peter Osgood making the most of it.

Chelsea followed up their 1970 FA Cup win with the Cup-
Winners' Cup in 1971. Peter Osgood laughs at his passport photo
with my old adversary Ron "Chopper" Harris (second left) as
Eddie McCreadie (left) contemplates the flight to Athens.

The biggest giant-killing of them all – Excited Hereford City fans in February, 1972, celebrating their team's 3rd round defeat of Newcastle that became FA Cup folklore.

Ronnie Radford (left) scored the non-leaguers' goal that shocked Newcastle, the quality of the strike as stunning as its significance. Ricky George (right) then scored the winner after Newcastle had equalised. No wonder they look so delighted.

The one that got away, but it made no difference to Derby's season in the end. County boss Brian Clough failed to bring the much sought-after Ian Storey-Moore from Nottingham Forest to the Baseball Ground in March, 1972, the player signing instead for Frank O'Farrell's struggling Manchester United after a lengthy transfer battle.

Derby's finest hour – Brian Clough and assistant Peter Taylor hold the 1971-72 League trophy aloft at the Baseball Ground in August, 1972. Clough and his players had already set off on holiday by the final day of the season when Leeds and Liverpool both failed to win with their last match, meaning the Rams took the title.

When a linesman limped off injured in the Arsenal v Liverpool clash in September, 1972, commentator Jimmy Hill was the only qualified substitute available, much to the amusement of Arsenal's Charlie George and Reds' manager, Bill Shankly!

The Doc reads speculative reports of his move to United on the plane to Manchester, seated next to the exit. My own exit from Old Trafford was to follow shortly after he arrived.

Sunderland manager Bob Stokoe hugs his players after
their shock 1–0 win over Leeds in the 1973 FA Cup Final.

Off! Billy Bremner of Leeds and Liverpool's Kevin Keegan
are sent off for fighting in 1974 in the so-called Charity
Shield match. They both threw their shirts on the ground
in disgust at the dismissals and earned themselves lengthy
bans for their trouble.

A terrible day for Manchester United as Denis Law's instinctive backheel for the old enemy Man City condemns us to relegation in 1974. Denis later told me this was the worst moment of his career. How sad that it was also the last goal in this, his final appearance of a fabulous career.

A photocall for the greatest England side ever, reunited in 1974. By then, a new era had begun – Don Revie was at the helm, and things were very different as England failed to qualify for the '74 tournament in West Germany.

During my fallout with Manchester United, I played a few matches for my old friend Barry Fry at non-league Dunstable Town. Ironic then that I scored against United's own reserves in Town's 3–2 win in August, 1974, when still technically a United player…

lot and wondered what was going on. He was a fresh-faced lad at that time and was concerned about our state for the replay. We told him not to worry: "Make sure you do your job and we'll do ours." In the replay Charlie was the man of the match. Of course it didn't take Huddie long to see our way of thinking!

"I noticed that Jose Mourinho likes his players in for training at 9am sharp. Well, that would have suited Huddy and the rest of us. We were always getting into trouble for being late, and that was in the days when training was much later than Mourinho likes it. But 9am would have been fine as we would just be coming back from a night out – we would all be early for a change!"

The name of Peter Osgood will always be inextricably associated with the FA Cup, not merely because he secured a winner's medal with both Chelsea and Southampton in 1976, but also because he took the trophy home with him when he won it with the Saints. "I did – but not that night," he says. "It was about three months later. We were all at a casino, attending a big function. I was a bit bored, so I said to Peter Rodrigues [the Southampton captain], 'I bet you a bottle of champagne I can take the cup home and sleep with it.' He said: 'You're on.' Me and Steeley [the defender Jim Steele] went outside, and I said to a security guard: 'We're going to have our photo taken with the FA Cup.' He said: 'No problem.' So, off we went with it, put it in the car and I drove home with it. I slept with it that night. I've slept with worse, I tell you ... The next day, I woke up and thought, 'Bloody hell, what have I done here?' Anyway, I left it outside Lawrie's office door. I got a right good ticking off, but he laughed in the end."

Leeds were left with a bruised ego as Chelsea paraded the cup. Revie, an exultant Manager of the Year, had every right to celebrate during the summer of 1969 but he recognised the dangers of complacency and took the reckless route of publicly announcing his targets for the forthcoming season. Attacking the idea that his team had already reached its pinnacle, he revealed that he had set his players the goal of retaining their league title and winning both the FA and European Cups. It is a reflection of the esteem in which his players held him that they probably believed it too. A double was difficult enough; only one team had managed it all century. But a treble, that was improbable.

Yet, remarkably, as late as early March, with only six weeks left of a season brought forward to accommodate Sir Alf Ramsey's preparations for the World Cup in Mexico, Leeds were top of the league with seven games to play and in the semi-finals of both cup competitions. Progress, however, had come at a price and their programme had become so congested at that critical stage of the year that the club's doctor had warned Revie that six of his shattered team were on the verge of exhaustion. This left Revie facing a dilemma and he solved it by downgrading his league campaign and selecting reserves for their remaining games.

Revie's second string picked up only three points from a possible twelve, earning the club a £5,000 fine from the Football League for fielding an uncompetitive team; the league refused to believe Revie's claims of an injury epidemic. The nine points squandered in this spell were the difference between themselves in second place and the eventual champions Everton. This sacrifice required the winning of at least one of the other two competitions to prove that such a compromise was justified.

The European Cup, given its status, was in theory the least gruelling of all the leading tournaments to win in the 1960s and 1970s, with only four rounds in total before the final. That season, Leeds had cruised past SK Lyn Oslo of Norway, 16–0 on aggregate, twice thumped Ferencváros, their old Hungarian adversaries 3–0, and beaten Standard Liège 1–0 home and away. Celtic, in contrast, had required a huge slice of luck to get past Benfica in the second round, winning 3–0 at home but losing by the same score in the Stadium of Light.

It all led to a mouth-watering prospect of Don Revie's Leeds United meeting Jock Stein's Celtic, a team firmly on course for their fifth of nine successive league championships with their sights on their second European Cup.

Celtic set off by train to Yorkshire to face the overwhelming favourites, with comedian Lex McLean in their private carriage to help take their minds off their task The game at Elland Road, on April Fool's Day, was Leeds' sixth match in twelve days, a pile-up caused by their failure to see off Manchester United until the second replay of the FA Cup semi-final. Missing Norman Hunter through injury, Leeds were taken apart in the first half by Jimmy Johnstone's ability to beat Terry Cooper at will, and by Bobby Murdoch and Bertie Auld's supremacy over Billy Bremner and Johnny Giles in midfield. Conceding their first goal in the competition to George Connelly in the first minute, Leeds never recovered. They managed to keep the deficit to one goal, despite Celtic's brilliance in attack. Late in the second half, Bremner was concussed when his head hit the ground and spent the last twenty minutes wandering dazed up and down the tunnel. He was eventually found by the club doctor in the Celtic dressing room. Bremner's headache hardly improved when he eventually came round to discover Everton confirmed as the league champions that night, beating West Bromwich Albion at Goodison for their third win of the Easter period. Leeds had only themselves to blame for abandoning that prize for Europe.

L eeds followed the first-leg defeat by losing at home to struggling Southampton on the Saturday, their first home defeat in the league, and were then thrashed 4–1 at Derby on the Monday. The second leg took place a fortnight later at Hampden Park in front of an official attendance of 136,505, the biggest in the competition's history and still the largest crowd before which an English club has played. Both sides had played in cup finals four days before the decider, Celtic losing 3–1 to Aberdeen, Leeds, playing at the top of their game for the first time in weeks, throwing away a 2–1 lead to allow Chelsea to equalise and force a replay with their late goal, a draining experience for Revie's team.

Revie's pre-match briefing concentrated on how to stop Johnstone. With the left-footed Hunter now back to support Cooper on the vulnerable side of United's defence, Revie's plan revolved around the two players dropping off to cover the winger, forcing him to lay the ball off. Initially the plan worked, with Johnstone far less influential than he had been at Elland Road, as Leeds gained the upper hand when Bremner whacked in a thirty-yard shot after fifteen minutes to level the tie and silence all but the 3,000 travelling supporters. Not for long, as Celtic peppered the Leeds goal. Gary Sprake, keen to amend for his Wembley disaster, was in fine form but he couldn't stop Celtic going back in front with a goal by John Hughes just after half-time. Unfortunately, shortly afterwards, Sprake was carried off on a stretcher after a collision with the goalscorer. David Harvey, Sprake's replacement, had little chance with Celtic's second – the only time Johnstone was left one-on-one at the back, crossing for Murdoch to slot home from close range. Exhausted Leeds couldn't respond as it turned out to be a comfortable victory for the Scots. The tie had been lost in Leeds.

Regrettably Celtic lost to outsiders Feyenoord in the final in Milan, where Wim van Hanegem and Wim Jansen, the latter a future manager at Celtic Park, were outstanding to upset Celtic's normal rhythm.

After sixty-one games, Leeds' whole season hinged on the FA Cup Final replay – and they lost it in extra time. Leeds failed on every target set by Revie. "Leeds, like Sisyphus, have pushed three boulders almost to the top of three mountains," Geoffrey Green wrote, "and are now left to see them all back in the dark of the valley." Revie would never be so unrealistic again.

Five years later, with Revie by then at Lancaster Gate, his ageing team finally made the European Cup final. They were met there by Michel Kitabdjian, who had refereed the Elland Road tie with Celtic. It was not a happy omen.

For my money, Everton fielded one of the finest sides seen in English football at this time. They were a joy to watch and, indeed, play against. Most teams wanted to play attacking football, and it made it a pleasure for me to take part, because that is how I see the game being played. That's not to say any team made it easy for me – they didn't, because by this time I was well and truly a marked man, in every sense. The Toffees launched their challenge for the championship in style, with the Holy Trinity of Kendall, Harvey and Ball providing silk and steel to the Everton midfield. They had finished the previous season top scorers with a total of seventy-seven goals. It set up their confidence for a realistic assault on the title.

Because of the Mexico World Cup, the new season was squeezed into eight months. The rearranged schedule involved seven games in the first three weeks of the new season. I was to get a first-hand view of just how good Everton were as we were due to play them twice in August in the league.

Everton won their opening match against Arsenal 1–0 despite missing Ball through injury. Four days later they were in Old Trafford, and won 2–0. Now, I really admired that performance. We had our own usual Holy Trinity, but their big-name players put us to the sword. The player I most admired that day was the little fellow, Alan Ball. He was all over the place. Hurst collected the opener after thirty-eight minutes, thanks to one of Alan's passes, and Ball finished us off with a second-half header from Royle into our box.

The following Saturday Everton saw off Crystal Palace 2–1 and the following Tuesday we were off to Merseyside seeking revenge over Everton for the Old Trafford defeat. We didn't know what hit us. Everton stormed into a 3–0 lead after just twenty-six minutes, yes, twenty-six minutes. Goals from Ball, Morrissey and Royle delighted the Everton fans, who chanted "Easy, easy, easy". Everton were on the march and United were most definitely out of sorts.

Our Manchester rivals City at least gave Everton a tougher game at Maine Road the next week. Despite an Everton lead after just two minutes, City fought back, eventually managing a draw. A 2–1 midweek win over Sheffield Wednesday cemented their top spot in the table and set up nicely their confrontation with Leeds on 30 August.

Although it was so early in the season, I was sure this was virtually the title decider, with Leeds unbeaten since the previous October – a remarkable run. Everton raced into an incredible three-goal lead with Husband's first goal coming after just four minutes. Royle was unstoppable, crashing a header against the bar after twenty minutes but recovering quickly enough to head it into an empty net. Straight after half-time, he was at it again, with a shot into the top corner. Leeds, as you would expect, responded and got it back to 3–2 with goals from Giles and Bremner, but it was too late.

The injured Kendall was back for the midweek League Cup 1–0 win over Darlington, and now at full strength, Everton maintained their lead. By the end of October they had played seventeen league games, winning fourteen, drawing twice, and losing just once, taking thirty points. They took a 3–0 thumping from Liverpool in December, and more crucially, lost 2–1 at Leeds two days after Christmas.

Tellingly, during much of November and December, Colin Harvey had been missing when he almost lost the sight in one eye after an infection. He returned in mid-January, by which time Ball was missing. A bundle of energy, Ball was also tempestuous and was always getting into trouble with referees. Sent off again, he was suspended for five weeks. In total the team's three midfield stars had been separated for three months. In the eleven games they were apart, Everton won six, drew two and lost three – emphasising their importance to the team as a unit. In that time Everton had fallen from top spot in the First Division and Sheffield United had knocked them out of the FA Cup.

Injury had plagued their early season, but now came a huge blow: their powerful and influential centre half captain Brian Labone was ruled out for the rest of the season with a back injury. Catterick reacted quickly, and surprisingly appointed Ball captain in Labone's absence. "It is a psychological move to give Alan more responsibility and make him more aware of referees' and players' problems," Catterick explained at the time. It worked. Ball revelled in the captaincy, redirecting his aggression. In his famous white boots, he played his first game as the new skipper against Tottenham on 11 March. Whittle grabbed the winner on nineteen minutes, blasting a shot past Pat Jennings to restore Everton to top place in the table. Three days afterwards the two sides met again and Everton won 3–2 at Goodison. Royle scored the winner, his twentieth goal of the season – and that put Everton three points clear. Revenge followed in the Merseyside derby at Anfield, when goals from Royle and Whittle gave them a 2–0 win. In my view this was the defining moment for Everton, with Ball majestic in midfield and Royle so dangerous in attack.

Wins over Chelsea and Stoke put the championship within sight. On 1 April, at Goodison, a win against West Brom would deliver the title. In relaxed mood, after a two-day break, Whittle collected his eleventh goal in fourteen games. Harvey completed his comeback with the goal that secured the title – a strike that I personally feel was one of the best ever to win a championship. The fans chanted "We are the champions" and, with reference to the number of players in the England squad, "Send our team to Mexico". The players received the trophy in front of a crowd approaching 60,000.

"They have won it by applying their individual skills to the team as a whole," was Catterick's conclusion, "and I would like to believe they have also managed to entertain spectators all over the country in the process ... Our success has been a team effort and the credit must be shared all round."

Royle finished with twenty-three goals and Whittle eleven from fifteen games, not bad for a stand-in striker. The team had an average age of twenty-four so the future looked bright. Ball predicted: "I can see five great seasons ahead. This team is certain to go better." It was the same kind of thought I had after we won the European Cup.

I could see the signs of the emergence of Arsenal, adopting a philosophy more akin to Revie's Leeds than to Everton or Manchester United. There was a gradual shift of power towards Highbury and a turning point in Arsenal's history holds a special place in fans' memories, a glory night in Europe against Anderlecht on 28 April. That night the Gunners ended a seventeen-year wait to finally cast off self-doubt and begin to look confidently forward rather than nervously back. And, perhaps more importantly, for a whole generation of fans too young to remember Bastin, Drake and James, it was the night that they were at last part of a triumph that belonged unquestionably to them rather than to their fathers and grandfathers.

The match was the second leg of the final of the Fairs Cup, later the UEFA Cup, then played on a home and away basis. In the first leg in the Parc Astrid in Brussels, the brilliant Anderlecht duo of Jan Mulder and Paul Van Himst gave Arsenal a chastening evening. When Mulder climaxed another thrilling passing move by crashing in Anderlecht's third goal after seventy-five minutes, it looked as if Arsenal's years in the wilderness were to continue. But five minutes from time, eighteen-year-old Ray Kennedy, a substitute for Charlie George, headed home George Armstrong's cross and suddenly they had a toe-hold on the tie.

Manager Bertie Mee summed up the significance of the away goal so late in the tie with Anderlecht. "By getting one goal the game has been opened up and it will be a tremendous second leg."

In the all-seater era, when Gunners fans are conditioned to Arsène Wenger's educated style of football, Highbury has been likened to a library – due to the lack of real passion from the crowd. But when the teams emerged on that chill, damp April night for the second leg, the entire atmosphere was remarkably transformed.

"The noise, it was really frightening even though you were the home side," Bob Wilson recalled. "I thought, 'God! This is unreal.'" I couldn't help but admire the way an hysterical crowd of 51,612 roared their team on from the start. I always thought the real passion could only be found among the northern fans, and there was nothing more intimidating for opponents, particularly on European nights, than Old Trafford in full voice. But this occasion proved to me that such emotions could also be generated by southern supporters.

After a nervous opening Arsenal were rewarded when Eddie Kelly's thumping shot put the Londoners ahead on the night after twenty-five minutes. All the artistry came from Anderlecht and the match turned on an incident on the hour when Thomas Nordahl met Wilfried Puis's near-post cross and saw his effort come back off the post. A goal then would have made the aggregate score 4–2. Reprieved, Arsenal went on the offensive and George Graham and Bob McNab combined down the left to create the space for John Radford to head past Jean Trappeniers. A minute later, Jon Sammels chested down a long, high ball and moved smoothly forward before shooting emphatically into the corner. For a player who had endured some torrid times at the hands of the boo-boys in this Highbury crowd, the goal was a satisfying moment for the stylish midfield player, who had taken until this point in his Arsenal career to win over the home fans.

In *The End*, actor-turned-author Tom Watt's colourful book about the history of the North Bank, he recalled: "I remember thinking after that game, 'If I'm at Arsenal for another ten years, there could never be anything better than this feeling.' That was a fantastic night for everybody. You saw some of the old boys who had been watching Arsenal for years, they were crying. The whole thing was lovely."

When the final whistle sounded, thousands of fans swarmed on to the pitch, lifting captain Frank McLintock and Charlie George on to their shoulders. The trophy was presented by Sir Stanley Rous, the president of FIFA, and Mee emerged in the directors' box to acknowledge the adulation of the supporters. Eventually, they left the pitch but even then thousands congregated on Avenell Road to continue the celebration. Secretary Bob Wall, who had worked for the club for more than forty years, said: "I've witnessed many wonderful occasions here in the past, particularly in the pre-war days, but I must say I've never seen anything quite like these scenes at Highbury before."

Mee confronted the press with an extraordinary air of calm while the frenzied celebrations continued. Mee told them, "We badly wanted to win the Fairs Cup but the players realise that this is only an interim step," he said. "The First Division is the toughest competition in the world and no club, whatever they achieve outside it, can call themselves great until it has been won."

I took careful note of Arsenal's emergence, but their achievement against Anderlecht did not create a lasting stir beyond north London. The next evening, millions of Britons tuned in to the BBC's coverage of the Chelsea-Leeds United FA Cup Final replay at Old Trafford, while in Vienna, Manchester City ensured that two of the three European trophies would be lifted by English clubs when they defeated Gornik Zabrze in the Cup-Winners' Cup final.

At the end of a turbulent decade, English clubs had made their mark in Europe, winning five trophies in all, and the national side were World Cup holders, ready to defend their crown in Mexico with an even better team than the one that triumphed at Wembley in '66. Of course, it is one of my big regrets that I never made it on to the biggest football stage of all. I never played in a World Cup final, and never expected to because I was playing for an unfancied nation, although there were a couple of times we came close.

I loved playing for my country, enjoyed everything about it, and I still go back to Belfast to appear on talk shows and the like. In training with the Irish I would often swap places with Pat Jennings. He thought of himself as a centre forward and I always fancied going in goal. We used to love it, but while Pat was hopeless in attack, they couldn't get a goal past me! Pat Jennings was my room-mate with the Northern Ireland team, while David Sadler and I shared a room when we were away with Manchester United. They were the only two I ever shared with. You would always want to share a room with somebody you got on with, which I suppose is stating the obvious. Pat is a lovely man, and we are very good friends. He's the perfect room-mate: very quiet, and as soon as he gets into bed he is off to sleep.

Dave Sadler was very similar and you need really good friends if, like me, you're always getting yourself into a right pickle. There was one night that I didn't come back to my room and dear old David packed all my gear up for me and put it on the coach ready for our morning departure. I arrived back at the team hotel just before departure time for the airport. Jack Crompton, the trainer with the responsibility of seeing that we were all tucked up in bed at night, jumped on the team bus and asked me where I had been that night. I told him I had just been for a stroll because I couldn't sleep. He said, "That's fine, but I was just wondering whether you always make your bed before you go off for a stroll?" Of course he knew what I had been up to and that David had covered for me, but he never said a word!

When Wilf McGuinness took over the team he tried out a new idea to integrate the players more, to create a better team spirit. He suggested that we changed room-mates on trips and that we put all the names in a hat and pick out the one we would share with. We would all stay calm, pick out the names, then go off into a corner and switch the names until we were back to the ones we wanted. Funnily enough, I had picked out David Sadler as my room-mate. Wilf quickly realised it was a total waste of time and never asked us to pick the names out of the hat again.

Pat Jennings is one of the game's all-time legends. Pat joined Spurs from Watford in 1964, the year that he made his international debut. He won the FA Cup, two League Cups and the UEFA Cup before Keith Burkinshaw, then the Tottenham manager, sold him to Arsenal for a knockdown £40,000 in 1977, erroneously imagining that Jennings was past it. Jennings continued to play immaculately for Tottenham's arch-rivals, racking up 326 appearances and another FA Cup triumph, in 1979. Having studied him so closely I can safely say that his best attributes were peerless positional sense, glacial cool and a huge pair of hands that Bingham called "Lurgan shovels". Jennings won 119 caps, a Northern Ireland record, and the nation's achievement in reaching back-to-back World Cup finals looks to me increasingly impressive with the passing of time. Jennings first played for the Irish team in 1964 and must have thought his chance of a World Cup had gone until we made it in 1982. To get there again in 1986 was a tremendous feat for such a small country.

Back in 1970 Northern Ireland were never in the running, so I sat back to enjoy England's defence of the World Cup in Mexico. Expectations were high in this country, but England had never really performed that well in World Cups on the other side of the globe, and no European nation had ever won in South America.

I was just transfixed, like everybody else, by all the controversy that surrounded the England camp. There were misfortunes, it seemed, at every step, from Bobby Moore and the accusations of the stolen bracelet to Sir Alf's errors in his substitutions against Franz Beckenbauer's West Germany in the quarter-finals.

When Bobby Moore was detained for questioning by the Colombian authorities over the theft of a £625 diamond and emerald bracelet, it was not just the world of football that was stunned by the scandal. Some of the British press claimed it was a Latin American plot against the captain of the World Cup champions and England's greatest footballing hero. But I was fascinated to read of newly released Foreign Office documents uncovered at the public record office, which appear to bring the truth about who really stole that bracelet one step closer. The files provide tantalising further evidence to support the suggestion that the real thief was an unidentified third man, possibly an England footballer, who was also in the hotel jewellery shop with Bobby Moore and Bobby Charlton when the bracelet went missing.

Moore had hinted to Jeff Powell, his autobiographer, before his death from cancer in 1993 that "perhaps one of the younger lads with the squad did something foolish, a prank with unfortunate circumstances". Powell claimed in a television documentary that Moore had told him the full story but only on the promise that he would take it with him to his grave. He said it reflected Londoner Moore's East End upbringing in which it was a matter of honour "not to grass". At the time of the World Cup, all Moore told the press about the allegation was: "I'm not too sure what it's all about. As far as I can make out, there's nothing in it. I can assure you of that."

I was also greatly amused to read that during the investigation, Colombian security police measured the size of Bobby Moore's fist to see if it could have fitted through the hole in the glass cabinet from which the bracelet was stolen. It was too big.

Moore was held for four days before he was released to fly on to Mexico to play in the crucial game against Brazil, after the personal intervention of prime minister Harold Wilson.

England and Brazil were the joint favourites, and they were drawn in the same group. Each side recorded an opening game victory then met in Guadalajara. Pele set up Jairzinho for the only goal of the match fourteen minutes into the second half, but England had good reason to feel optimistic still; Peters and Lee had missed chances, and Astle missed a golden opportunity when he came on as substitute. There was every indication that the two teams would meet again in the final. Although England lost that game, they still made it through to the quarter-finals, where Banks's late withdrawal through illness was widely seen as the key factor in the team's defeat against West Germany.

England went two up through goals from Mullery and Peters, and looked to be heading for the semi-finals. In the second half Beckenbauer beat Peter Bonetti to pull one back for the Germans, and suddenly the momentum switched. Ramsey took off Charlton and Peters, replacing them with Colin Bell and Norman Hunter. A back-header from Uwe Seeler looped agonisingly Bonetti's head, forcing extra time. England's misery was complete when Gerd Muller, who would go on to be the tournament's top scorer, volleyed the winner from close range. With England going out to West Germany there would be a new winner, and the clear favourites were Brazil.

The final was probably the greatest of them all, with goals from Pele, Gerson, Jairzinho and Carlos Alberto securing a 4–1 win for Brazil over Italy. Carlos Alberto Torres, who played alongside Pele in the great Santos side of the 60s, captained the Brazilian team which, in my opinion, took part in the finest World Cup victory of all.

Carlos Alberto's strike at the Azteca Stadium, Mexico, on 21 June, 1970 is probably, for me, the best goal of all time. Brazil were already 3–1 up against Italy in the final when Clodoaldo jinxed magically in midfield and Rivelino glided down the left wing before passing to Jairzinho. Then Pele, playing in his last World Cup, majestically rolled the ball perfectly and nonchantly to his captain running on his outside, and Carlos Alberto duly obliged with a cracking shot past goalkeeper Enrico Alberosi. Legendary 1966 commentator Kenneth "They Think It's All Over" Wolstenholme summed it up with another of his classics: "That was sheer, delightful football". Carlos Alberto stepped forward, fittingly, to accept the Jules Rimet trophy and take it back to Brazil for good.

If Carlos Alberto arguably scored the best goal, then it is universally accepted that Gordon Banks pulled off the best World Cup save with that mystical stop from Pele's header. I am in full agreement with that one. Gordon Banks was a brilliant keeper in my view. He earned his first cap in 1963 and after his debut became a fixture in the England side for nearly a decade.

Pele is quite a small guy, around the same size as myself, yet he could score some wonderful goals with his head, and he could beat the tallest of defenders in the air, creating the space and producing power with his headers. On this occasion, after a bright start by England, Jairzinho beat Cooper on the right wing, and picked out Pele with his perfect cross. Pele leapt with such purpose and menace you could only see one outcome – a certain goal. His header was powered downward just inside the far post. In fact Pele himself says that he shouted "Go-o-o-o-al" from the second he made contact with the ball. But Banks defied all logic when he somehow scooped the ball off the ground and over the bar. Banks pulled off that mind-boggling save just ten minutes into the World Cup tie.

Banks began his career at Chesterfield and established his reputation after moving to Leicester City in 1959. In the 1961 FA Cup Final he was on the losing side when his team went 2–0 down to Spurs, and he picked up another losers' medal two years later. Banks moved to another unfashionable club, Stoke City, in 1967. Five years later, as soon as he signed a long-term contract with the Potteries club, his career was cut short by a car accident in which he lost an eye. But Banks will be fondly remembered for his exploits for club and particularly country, and nothing will erase that Banks save from Pele.

The 1970 World Cup is as good a time as any to assess the brilliance of Bobby Charlton. It was during the tournament in Mexico that Bobby played his final game for England, in the quarter-finals against West Germany. In that searing heat many believe, and I share that view, that England manager Sir Alf Ramsey made the error of judgement in substituting Bobby in the second half when England were leading 2–1. You can understand the thinking behind the change, to save Bobby for the semi-finals, and managers live and die by their tactical switches when it comes to substitutions. Bobby's record of 106 caps was subsequently overtaken but his forty-nine goals has yet to be beaten. No doubt Michael Owen now fancies his chances, having surpassed the thirty-goal mark with his hat-trick in the friendly with Colombia in England's summer tour of the United States. Given Michael's age, and the club he is playing for, and the fact that he is an England regular, he has every chance of finally cracking Bobby's proud goalscoring record. But no matter what Bobby might say, he will deeply regret losing that record, if he ever does.

Bobby quite rightly became Sir Bobby in 1994 when he was honoured for his services to football. Sir Bobby captained our side which lifted the European Cup, scoring twice in that unforgettable 4–1 win over Benfica at Wembley. It was an emotional night for all of us, but Bobby was perhaps more prone to showing his emotions than the rest of us. Bobby would play his 606th, and last, game for United at Stamford Bridge in 1973. He won just about every honour in the game, at both club and international level. The Charlton brothers were the footballing family of its generation, with brother Jack such a dominate force too for club and country. They were related to Jackie Milburn, a legend on Tyneside in the 1950s.

Bobby signed for Manchester United in 1955 as part of Busby's grand scheme to recruit the best youngsters. It tickles me that Charlton scored against Charlton on his debut. Well, that is, Bobby scored against Charlton Athletic in his first game for United in 1956; actually, he scored twice that day. Bobby and the rest of the Busby Babes had everything going for them to dominate the game domestically and in Europe for a decade but the team was all but wiped out in the 1958 Munich air crash. Among the survivors was Bobby himself, and he recovered sufficiently to receive the first of his 106 England caps just a few weeks after the tragedy.

I suppose you would term Bobby a deep-lying centre forward. He was originally a winger or inside forward but he developed into his role during the 60s and became a key player in Busby's new team and equally influential for his country. He distributed passes with pinpoint accuracy but he was renowned for shooting from distance, and believe me that wasn't so easy with those heavy leather balls. But he had power in those boots, and unlike modern players he was two-footed. During England's 1966 World Cup triumph, both Portugal and Mexico discovered just how venomous Bobby could be with his long-distance shooting. His performances that season rightly earned him the European Footballer of the Year award.

While I was branded the rebel, Bobby was the true gentleman of football, famed for playing the game in the spirit of genuine sportsmanship. I have often heard it said that Bobby was the boring one, and I made up for it. But boring isn't a term I would use to describe English football's number one gentleman legend. Remarkably, in a sparkling career that spanned twenty years he was booked just once, for time-wasting when his side were losing.

# 1969–70 ROLL OF HONOUR

*Champions:* Everton

*FA Cup:* Chelsea

*League Cup:* Manchester City

*European Cup:* Feyenoord

*European Cup-Winners' Cup:* Manchester City

*Footballer of the Year:* Billy Bremner

*European Footballer of the Year:* Gerd Muller (Bayern Munich)

# 8

# 1970–71

Purely as a fascinated observer, I could see an affinity developing over the years between the Everton and Arsenal clubs and even now Arsenal vice-chairman David Dein is a close friend of Everton owner, Bill Kenwright.

I could always feel at the start of every season whether it was going to be a good one for me and for the team. Every team can sense whether it's going to have a good season, depending on the outcome of the opening game, not necessarily in terms of the result, but how the team is going to gel, how new players will mould into the team, whether there is a chance that this will be "our" year.

The Arsenal team arrived at Goodison full of the usual aspirations and expectations, determined to set the tone for the entire season. This match would be a sound indicator for Arsenal as Merseyside was not always an easy place for footballing visitors, whether they were performing on the Anfield or Goodison stages, as the pair had amassed a total of three league championships and a couple of FA Cups between them in recent years.

But there was an even greater air of anticipation at the outset of a new decade, with the football industry booming. This was reflected in a whole new generation of fans being turned on to the sport via television.

The opening *Match of the Day* of the season was watched by an incredible twenty million, with the programme unveiling its new theme tune, which is still being used today. David Coleman introduced the programme's new format and Leeds United's Mick Jones won the first Goal of the Month with his winner against us on the opening day of the season. The following week Arsenal put four past us including a John Radford hat-trick.

While there were grounds for optimism, the whole industry had to be vigilant, particularly as gates were dipping and there was a major concern about whether the saturation levels of television coverage were responsible (and this was before today's wall-to-wall satellite coverage!). There were concerns, too, that hooliganism off the field was a major deterrent to attendances, while on the field, coaches and managers were becoming more interested in playing a defensive game, which was not so entertaining.

The new decade kicked off with everyone wondering how it would pan out. Would managers want to entertain, or simply to win at all costs? The opening day of the season seemed to indicate that football was not being fatally damaged, whatever the managers had in mind. The public's fascination for the game continued and was, in fact, reflected in a forty thousand increase in overall attendances on the same period the previous season.

Nowhere was there more of an upbeat feeling than the home of the league champions, Everton. A week earlier Everton won the FA Charity Shield, beating Chelsea 2–1, with goals from Alan Whittle and Howard Kendall. On the same day, Derby County had beaten us 4–1 in the final of the Watney Cup, which had been introduced as an event for the two top-scoring teams in each division who had failed to qualify for Europe or gain promotion. That United was playing in it was a sign of the times in my eyes. Commercialism was taking a grip and this was an aspect that concerned me as much as tight-marking defenders. Commercialism had its positive side: the influx of new money meant players' wages were rising, but so too were transfer fees. The downside was that commercialism sucked out the remaining sportsmanship. The game became less fun, and more a business.

While Football League secretary Alan Hardaker could condone the pre-season tournaments such as the Watney and Texaco Cups, he was against extending other forms of advertising: "I do not think anyone in the game wants to see in this country the kind of advertising prevalent on the Continent, where one team's shirts endorse a certain brand of alcohol, while another team carries plugs urging male supporters to use a particular brand of eau de cologne.

"This is not sponsorship, it is merely advertising, which does nothing whatsoever for the game." Well said, Alan. Shame that his crystal ball was a touch cloudy.

At Goodison, Everton dominated Arsenal from the start of the match, and they could not prevent Joe Royle's header from Tommy Wright's cross. With just twenty minutes to go, Bob McNab cleared off the line from Whittle. The Gunners staged a fight back after Charlie George beat keeper Gordon West to equalise, but George's goal cost him dearly: as he scored, Gordon West fell on his ankle, giving him a double fracture.

The goal stalemate didn't last long. Keeper Bob Wilson turned the ball against the post and Alan Ball set it up for winger Johnny Morrissey to score a close-range goal. Arsenal demonstrated their determination by grabbing another equaliser for a 2–2 draw. The Gunners had shown they were a fighting force with a fair degree of skill – a potent combination that could certainly make them championship contenders – but no one anticipated just how skilful and combative this side would become.

The debt owed to Bertie Mee in the development of the Arsenal machine has long been the subject of frenzied debate and speculation. In the mid-60s Mee took over a team with a great tradition but an uncertain future. Just how this prim little physiotherapist managed to succeed where far bigger names had failed remains a mystery to many even now. His playing credentials with Derby County were modest. He was no coach, and in fact knew little about tactics. He was dwarfed by his contemporaries – Busby, Nicholson, Shankly and Revie. Yet within five years of becoming Arsenal manager he had led the club to a Fairs Cup win. On the surface that doesn't sound very much like instant success, but it has to be assessed in context.

When Mee was put in charge, Arsenal had not won a major honour for thirteen years. The club's championship successes of 1948 and 1953 had been followed by seasons of mediocrity. Billy Wright, after a triumphant career as captain of Wolves and England, took over at Arsenal, an appointment greeted with enthusiasm by fans and media alike, but Highbury soon realised that the immensely likeable Wright did not possess management qualities, or certainly not the sort needed to turn around Arsenal's fortunes. On a May evening in 1966 when Arsenal were at home to Leeds while television was screening the Cup-Winners' Cup final between Liverpool and Borussia Dortmund from Hampden Park, the meagre crowd of 4,554 for that Arsenal fixture remains the smallest attendance for a league match at a major ground since the Second World War. It hastened the departure of Wright, a one-time national hero, and led to the appointment of a virtual unknown in Mee. On the surface it seemed a complete U-turn, from the high-profile, affable Wright to a man with no profile at all! Yet Tom Whittaker, a club physio under Herbert Chapman and George Allison in the 30s, had revived Arsenal in the post-war seasons. So Arsenal looked to the treatment room in search of another saviour.

Bertie Mee could be engaging, but beneath the surface there was a hard streak. The then chairman, Dennis Hill-Wood, father of the current chairman Peter, had appointed Mee in desperation at Arsenal's lack of trophies. The old Etonian chairman was a sound judge of character and he made the bold decision to appoint Mee, clearly having some inside knowledge about his credentials. He knew something the rest of us didn't. Mee believed in winning as a priority even, if need be, at the expense of entertaining. Yet his teams could do both, but they were essentially functional first; fancy was a bonus.

Mee's strength was that he knew what Arsenal FC was about, just as George Graham did when he returned as manager, having blossomed as a midfielder during the Mee era. Captain Frank McLintock had a keen insight into Mee's management skills: "Bertie Mee was a stickler for discipline and other great Arsenal managers, like George Graham, have copied his methods with success ... I thought he was a bit like Captain Mainwaring from *Dad's Army* in some respects and I had several run-ins with him, but he did a fantastic job for Arsenal."

Rather than McLintock benefiting from Mee's management, Mee was fortunate to have McLintock, a player of huge intelligence, experience and skill. McLintock was as inspirational off the field as he was on it. He had started out at Leicester before moving to Highbury and becoming one of the few defenders to win the Footballer of the Year award.

Mee's greatest asset was his ability to delegate and he left the playing side to the well-organised, defensive expert coach Don Howe, the former Arsenal and England full back who proved to be the ideal partner. In the late 50s and early 60s Arsenal fielded various individual talents – Vic Groves, Danny Clapton, George Eastham – without establishing a dominant team to disturb the elite of that generation.

Ironically, Arsenal began to disturb the established order

just when they never possessed the glittering stars of previous recent years. Of course they had the potential of the young Charlie George, so he naturally attracted the headlines. Ray Kennedy and John Radford made more modest news but, in reality, were just as effective as the maverick George. Arsenal's re-emergence was built on commanding defence and organisation masterminded by Howe. Pat Rice, who won forty-nine caps for Northern Ireland, had a distinguished career at Arsenal after joining in 1967. He spent fourteen seasons there, making 397 league appearances at right back. Bob McNab, who won four caps for England, filled the berth at left back and missed only two of the sixty-four games this season. He first played for Huddersfield, the town of his birth, joining Arsenal in 1966. An old friend of mine, James Lawton, who then worked for the *Daily Express*, wrote how the Highbury backroom staff made a video of a defensive performance that Bob McNab put in against me. It was described in Lawton's piece as "a tactical masterpiece". McNab reflected: "Peter Simpson and I made an alliance against Best over the years. I stuck so close to George it would have been impossible if Peter hadn't been filling the space behind me. He was the ultimate challenge for a defender. You couldn't lunge at him because that's what he wanted ... if you did it, he bit."

Like Ashley Cole more recently, McNab had been tapped up by a big club after a contract dispute. He was playing for his home team Huddersfield Town, and each week saw his name linked with Manchester United and Liverpool. After playing a full season, he thought, as Cole did, that he was worth a rise on his modest wages – in McNab's case up to £25 a week with £10 appearance money. Huddersfield said that they could not afford it. Eventually, he realised that as their most saleable asset, the grand plan was for him to move. A modest rise would have placated him but Huddersfield declined, and then came the tap. It was from the mighty Liverpool: Bill Shankly. High-powered agents were not involved because they did not exist in this era, but even without them, there were a variety of intermediaries who were capable of perfecting the top-up. In this case, the word from Shankly came from a local schoolmaster, a neighbour of the Scot when he was manager of Huddersfield. McNab was made aware, through this "third party", that his progress was being closely monitored.

McNab got the bus to Huddersfield station and was met off the train by Shankly in Liverpool. He was told that he could earn as much as £125 a week with win bonuses in Europe. However, Arsenal had also made a bid and when McNab saw the marble halls his head was turned. He recalls how Huddersfield handled his transfer request: "I took a couple of days composing it, not having an agent, and it consisted of two sentences – one said I was disappointed not to get a rise and the other was I wanted a move." That night, the Huddersfield evening paper reported the club would have to bow to McNab's demands. The manager Tom Johnson told him: "You've got what you wanted. Liverpool and Arsenal have agreed a fee. Go and talk to them – and don't come back here expecting any money." Huddersfield received £50,000 in 1966, £15,000 more than the previous record for a full back. Arsenal gave McNab a signing-on fee of £5,000, paid over four years, and a tailored blazer. After two years in the first team he was able to put down a deposit on a modest house in north London.

McNab played in 277 league games in nine years for his beloved Arsenal, then had one season at Wolves before playing for San Antonio in Texas.

Another outstanding full back was Sammy Nelson, signed originally as a seventeen-year-old winger in 1966, before he eventually moved to full back. Nelson landed in hot water when he bared his bottom to the North Bank after scoring a rare goal. Sammy considered his act of "mooning" as a moment of fun, part of his affinity with the fans. But his act was taken far more seriously by his club and by the football authorities.

Alongside McLintock at centre back was the reliable Peter Simpson. Born in Great Yarmouth, Simpson was a commanding central defender in his own right, but always overshadowed by his captain. He played in 370 league games for the Gunners.

Behind the defence was the highly capable, brave and reliable Bob Wilson. Originally from Chesterfield, Wilson joined Arsenal from Wolves in 1963. During the next ten years he made 234 league appearances between the posts and though initially an England schoolboy international, he won two senior caps for Scotland.

Peter Storey was the hatchet man as a player whose "hard man" character led him later into a life of crime. He won nineteen England caps between 1971 and 1973, and played 391 league games for the Gunners after joining as an apprentice in 1962. He then moved to Fulham. In 1979 he was fined for running a brothel in east London. A year later he was jailed for three years for financing a plot to counterfeit gold coins, and subsequently spent further time in jail for attempting to import pornographic videos.

In midfield there were a couple of no-nonsense Scots. Eddie Kelly made his debut for Arsenal in 1968 and added his name to the history books three years later when he became the first substitute to score in an FA Cup Final. In eight years at the club he made 211 appearances. George Graham was a robust midfielder who had played for Aston Villa and Chelsea. Graham was Mee's first signing in 1966. He spent six seasons at Highbury, scoring fifty-nine goals in 227 league games. He had less success at Docherty's United but eventually moved into management at Millwall before returning to fill the trophy cabinet at Highbury during one of Arsenal's most successful eras.

Up front, the team was built around John Radford, an ideal target man, and the utility striker Ray Kennedy. Radford joined the Gunners as an apprentice in 1964 and scored 111 league goals in 379 games, spending twelve years at the club, being capped twice for England. Kennedy joined Arsenal as an apprentice in 1968, scoring fifty-three goals in 158 league games as a bustling forward. After six seasons he was signed by Liverpool for £180,000. Bob Paisley moved him to left midfield, where he thrived, winning seventeen caps for England.

George Armstrong was an unusual, multi-purpose left winger. Armstrong was totally astute, the indispensable link between defence and attack. Armstrong signed as a seventeen-year-old in 1961 and was seldom out of the team. An energetic runner who could play on either wing, he had signed on as a seventeen-year-old in 1961, and later played for Leicester and Stockport before turning to coaching. He was enticed back to Highbury in 1990 by his old team-mate George Graham to join the backroom staff, collapsing and dying at Arsenal's training ground in October 2000 of a brain haemorrhage.

Such a collection of players hardly smacked of the kind of success that was generated under the Bertie Mee regime. But the Mee-Howe combination worked, as Arsenal set about replacing the wing play of Tottenham and Manchester United by the 4–3–3 system that prevailed with Ramsey's England. Howe's knack of putting players in the right positions for the overall good of the team was simplicity itself. Storey, a full back, became the midfield rock on which many an opponent foundered. The strength of Graham in the air, previously seen only as a source of goals, became equally important in cutting out high balls between the penalty areas. Frank McLintock, once an attacking wing half for Leicester City, fully developed into a cultured centre back. We all have our flaws, though, and Howe's was buying the radiantly tricky Peter Marinello from Hibernian for £100,000 in 1970, who starred in milk adverts and, sadly for him, the reserves at Highbury. Howe preferred George Armstrong, a human supply line to the prolific foreheads of John Radford and Ray Kennedy to the erratic Marinello. Marinello was hailed as London's answer to me. He had the looks and the outlandish fashion sense, but he failed to fulfil his enormous potential and ended up a peripheral member of the squad because Howe would not contemplate any form of favouritism, even towards players bought for a large transfer fee like Marinello.

And then there was Charlie George. It's doubtful that Mee, or any other manager, could have handled the effervescent nature of George, who had signed schoolboy terms with the Gunners at thirteen. He made his debut aged eighteen, but earned only one cap for England after a run-in with the national coach, Don Revie.

Regrettably, the magic moments at Manchester United were few and far between.

It was a traumatic time at Old Trafford for me as I was suspended by the club for breaches of discipline. On 4 January I appeared before an FA disciplinary commission after acquiring three cautions for misconduct in a period of twelve months. I arrived three hours late for the hearing, not a good move to get the commission on my side, and was fined £250 and given a six-week suspended sentence. Then on 8 January I missed the train taking the team to play Chelsea in London. I got a later train and spent the weekend with actress Sinead Cusack, an episode that made both front and back pages of the national press for three days solid. Three days later the club suspended me for two weeks. On 17 January I played and scored for a joint Rangers-Celtic select side in a benefit game for the sixty-six victims of the Ibrox disaster, and on 27 January scored my only ever international hat-trick in a 5–0 win against Cyprus in Belfast.

I did make it to Derby's Baseball Ground, though, on Boxing Day, and scored as the teams shared eight goals that day.

Dave Mackay and Frank Wignall put the home team two ahead; we then scored three in four minutes, two from Denis and one by myself before Kevin Hector equalised. Archie Gemmill restored Derby's lead but Brian Kidd headed the final goal of the game from a Bobby Charlton corner. Two days later Wilf McGuinness was temporarily replaced as manager by the man he succeeded, Sir Matt Busby.

In the FA Cup, the cameras seemed to be on hand at every major upset. In the third round, Blackpool beat West Ham 4–0 and in the fifth it was the turn of Leeds United to suffer humiliation. On 13 February they had to travel to Colchester United of Division Four and were left with egg all over their faces when the home team went 3–0 up with two goals from Ray Crawford and one from David Simons. Norman Hunter and Johnny Giles replied for Leeds but that was not enough to avoid one of the most famous of all FA Cup upsets. In the next round, Everton put three past Colchester at Goodison Park to end their dream.

Recovered from his broken leg, Charlie George made his comeback in the FA Cup fourth round replay against Portsmouth, returning to the side at the expense of George Graham, and of course scored with a low twenty-yard drive as Arsenal continued its march in a tournament that became particuarly interesting at the semi-final stage. Liverpool beat Everton at Old Trafford in one semi, while Arsenal were two down to Stoke in the other but recovered to draw and won the replay 2–0.

The turning point in the season's tussle between Leeds and Arsenal came when the northern team's reputation for aggression unwittingly aided the Gunners' cause. With a comfortable seven-point lead over Arsenal, Leeds met West Brom in a crucial league game at Elland Road. They went a goal down in the last quarter of the game when the linesman waved for offside against Colin Suggett. The referee Ray Tinkler, however, waved play on and with a two-to-one advantage, Jeff Astle scored easily. Revie's players angrily surrounded the referee, dozens of fans ran on to protest and it took the police several minutes to regain order. Totally ruffled by this bizarre moment, Leeds went on to lose the game and their lead over Arsenal in the title race. As punishment for the pitch invasion, they were forced to play the first four games of the following season at neutral grounds. Leeds finished second for the fourth time in seven seasons but had the consolation of winning the Inter-Cities Fairs Cup for the second time in four years.

Arsenal secured the league title on the Monday night at White Hart Lane, of all places. It was tense enough playing against the bitter local rivals, but the tension was unbearable the longer the game went on, with just so much at stake. It took Arsenal until the eighty-eighth minute to pip Leeds to the title by a point with a 1–0 victory, with more than 51,000 inside and more than 30,000 people locked outside White Hart Lane.

For me the symmetry was fascinating, as it had been ten years earlier when Spurs first landed the double. Now their north London rivals had won in their own back yard to give them the opportunity to emulate that astonishing feat.

The tension at that final match on the home territory of their fiercest local rivals was incredible. This was a good Spurs side: Pat Jennings, later to join Arsenal, was at his athletic best, those plate-size hands stopping everything thrown at him. Martin Chivers, Alan Gilzean and Martin Peters all caused problems but Armstrong was at his best and, with three minutes to go, George pinched the ball off Joe Kinnear, Jennings saved from Radford and I remember Armstrong keeping the ball in play before crossing for Kennedy to thump a header in off the crossbar. Mayhem followed. Arsenal defended for the remaining seconds, retiring referee Kevin Howley blew his whistle and north London exploded. The pitch invasion lasted an hour and Arsenal's players were drinking champagne out of tea-cups.

There was little recovery time. The Cup Final was the team's sixty-fourth competitive game of the season, and only seventeen players had been used in the fifty-one league and cup matches.

Howe and Mee, as ever the astute double act, gave the team Tuesday off and ordered the preparation of a perfectly mown practice pitch at London Colney to replicate the Wembley surface. All the players did during Cup Final week was play light practice games.

Bob Wilson recalls: "Bertie had told us to be prepared for 'a cacophony of sound' on the day. He was right. The noise was deafening, the atmosphere incredible. There is something special about FA Cup Final days."

Despite Arsenal's domination, it was goalless as this fascinating final went into extra time. To put the match into context, they were facing a Liverpool team undergoing a massive revamp. Players such as Ian St John and Ron Yeats, as well as Tommy Lawrence and Peter Thompson had left as Shankly, looking to the future, began to revitalise the club. Emlyn Hughes, then still in his teens, arrived in 1967 from Blackpool, and had been joined by John Toshack. Brian Hall, Larry Lloyd and Steve Heighway were new faces too, as well as two other youngsters. One had cost the club £100,000 – striker Alun Evans from Wolves. He was, however, never considered to have been good value, as his occasional flashes of brilliance were not consistent enough for Anfield. The same could not be said of Shankly's £35,000 purchase from Scunthorpe, a player who was watching his new team-mates take on Arsenal: Kevin Keegan. And Keegan could see for himself the task he faced to ensure Liverpool's status among the game's elite.

Arsenal left it very late before Charlie George beat Ray Clemence from distance for a memorable historic goal that remains one of Arsenal's most significant strikes of all time. Wilson remembered: "My orders had been to help out the two central defenders, Peter Simpson and Frank, against the threat of John Toshack, and to go for everything. I was edging forward all the time when Steve Heighway caught me out. I still worry today that my reputation would have been ruined for ever if we had not equalised and gone on to win the match. FA Cup headlines are littered with goalkeeping blunders. We got the craziest of goals to equalise, through Eddie, though I still think George Graham got a touch."

Few goals live in the memory as long and as vividly as the one scored by Charles Frederick George on 8 May, 1971. Yes, it was an exceptional goal, but Wembley finals are littered with spectacular strikes which, from time to time, will merit inclusion among the "greatest of all time" category. It was the context in which George scored that made it so special. Well, firstly it was the defining moment of a terrific match, goalless after ninety minutes, only to finish 2–1 after extra time. "It was an almost intolerably dramatic, pulsating Cup Final," wrote Brian Glanville in *The Sunday Times*. And that the winning goal "should be scored by a youngster born virtually on the club's doorstep" added to the occasion. Local boy made good is the hallmark Charlie George has enjoyed living with ever since.

Coincidently, Bob Wilson was formerly a teacher at Holloway School when Charlie was still a pupil there. They ended up in a double-winning side together. Quite remarkably, Wilson summed up the emotion of that success: "After the final whistle, I dragged Frank back around the pitch, telling him to take it all in, to savour it. It is hard to explain the elation. After the match, we attended the banquet in the evening, interviews on *Match of the Day* with David Coleman, and front-row seats at Danny La Rue's nightclub in London, where he put on a special show for us. The next morning we toured Islington, where Frank famously fell asleep on the steps of the Town Hall. On the following Wednesday, we had to sing 'Good Old Arsenal' live on *Top of the Pops*, lyrics courtesy of Jimmy Hill. The gold disc still hangs on the wall of my downstairs toilet at home. Years later, I spoke to Bill Shankly about the '71 Cup Final, and in his mind, having pipped Leeds, he believed we were very much in our prime, while his team were in transition with a young Emlyn Hughes, Ray Clemence and Steve Heighway in their first seasons. Shanks later admitted that he believed if we'd met ten times, Arsenal would have won eight of those matches. His psychology was his great tactic and he certainly managed to wind me up before the game, saying it was a nightmare pitch for goalkeepers. The pitch had been soaking wet on the Friday, but on the day it was about ninety degrees, with almost every player suffering with cramp in extra time."

Charlie's goal did not just win the FA Cup for Arsenal; it clinched the league and cup double for only the second time in the twentieth century, matching Tottenham Hotspur's achievement a decade earlier. Cup doubles have become commonplace since the start of the Premier League; Arsenal and Manchester United have won it five times between them and even league and FA Cup doubles don't quite have the same charisma as they did then. In 1971 it still represented English football's Holy Grail, enabling George to be worshipped for years.

Now, what about George's peculiar goal celebration – lying prostrate on his back? Could it have been as mundane as time-wasting? So how did Charlie earn his place as an Arsenal legend?

"I used to think ahead of other people, and I knew it would take quite a while to pick me up off the floor," Charlie recalls. "But I'm amazed people don't remember that I scored two goals in the fifth round at Man City and done exactly the same thing. I laid on the ground just their side of the halfway line. It wasn't just something I did in the final."

Radford was shouting at him: "Get up, you lazy f*****! There are nine minutes left!" But Charlie was oblivious to the reaction of his team-mates, even if he could have heard them above the din of the crowd. Whatever the reasons for it, Charlie's posturing as well as his goal remains one of the most potent of FA Cup Final images. Also his long, lank, untidy hair matches the place to a time: unmistakably the early 70s. These days the hair is much shorter but he is still the same skinny frame and the identical look. There's also a finger missing on his right hand, a giveaway that this is a man of mystery. "Caught it in a lawn mower, years ago," he explains.

Just as sharp are the memories of the '71 Cup Final: "I remember going to look round Wembley on the Friday. The younger players, like Ray [Kennedy], Eddie [Kelly], Peter Marinello and myself hadn't played there before, and for us it was an absolutely awesome place. Then we stayed that night in the Grosvenor House, Park Lane. Very nice. The match itself we should probably have won four- or five-one. Liverpool were a very good side, with good youngsters like Steve Heighway and lots of experience in the likes of Tommy Smith and Chris Lawler, but we played much better than them. I wish I had a penny for every time the goal's been on telly or spoken about. As soon as I hit it I knew it was in. If Clemence had got to it, it would have broke his hand."

While Charlie George became synonymous with the clinching of the double, the same cannot be said of Mee, irrespective of his impressive managerial career. George, as he made clear in his recently published autobiography, had scant respect for

Mee. "I thought he was a pompous little man. I was Billy Wright's last signing. Just after he signed me, we only had 3,900 people here for the last game of the season against Leeds, and we got beat 3–0. So the board decided on a change. To be fair, we won three trophies in three years. But a lot of that was down to the coaches, Don Howe and Dave Sexton before him."

Mee's star faded in the mid-70s and he resigned in 1976 under pressure from Hill-Wood. Former England manager Graham Taylor, who appointed Mee as his assistant at Watford in 1977, described him as "probably the best signing I ever made". Mee stayed at Watford even after Taylor's first departure and served as general manager, and then on the board, until he left the club in 1991 at the age of seventy-three "He was a physiotherapist who became the manager – can you imagine that happening now?" Taylor said. "He was a great organiser so I could leave a great deal with him."

While much admired by Taylor and the managerial fraternity, Charlie George's dislike for Mee was one of the reasons he left for Derby in 1975 after a season wasted on the bench at Arsenal. George's only honours came at the beginning of his career, the Fairs Cup and the double. His England career consisted of sixty minutes in a friendly against the Republic of Ireland in September 1976, when Don Revie played him out of position on the left wing, then substituted him. "I played well, too, as good if not better than the majority of players, who included Keegan, Wilkins, Brooking, Stuart Pearson. But at half-time Revie come in the dressing room and wanted me to go down the left-hand side. I'm not a left winger, and I told him so.

But I knew when I saw Gordon Hill warming up that I was coming off, and I told Revie what I thought of him in no uncertain terms. So I had an hour for England and that was it." When Revie tried to shake his hand as he left the field, George advised him loudly to "go fuck yourself!" "And that was the end of me," he said. He concedes that "it wasn't the brightest thing I've done or said in my life", but that "I am not sad or apologetic about it".

Two years later, playing for Derby under Tommy Docherty – and with the disgraced Revie out of the England job – an offer came from Ron Greenwood, the new national manager. "Tom was as good as gold with me," George said. "He let me play and enjoy my football. One day he told me Ron Greenwood had picked me for the B team. I went in the office and told him: 'C is for Charlie, and C is for class – he can stick his B team up his arse.' Unfortunately, the Doc relayed the response word for word."

The injustice of a wasted opportunity to represent his country still rankles. "How could I play one game for England? I don't even say 'one cap'. I had an hour. Absolutely farcical. But it happened. It's finished. It's gone." Yet, despite all the downs, there were sufficient ups for Charlie to have. He loved his career and he had a great time overall.

In the 70s, Charlie epitomised the problems of being flamboyantly skilful. Original was somehow deemed to be suspect. He was frequently misunderstood. After the Cup Final, for example, Brian Moore, the television commentator, asked him to explain how he had scored the winning goal. George deadpanned: "Well, Brian, I hit it – and there it was in the back of the net." It was interpreted as evidence that George, who had famously spent most of his school days playing truant, was thick. But George explained: "He'd asked a silly question and I was just trying to be flippant."

It was certainly a season for London Pride. The double for Arsenal, and a wonderful European adventure for FA Cup holders Chelsea. The west London club were full of confidence with the return to fitness of Alan Hudson and the £100,000 signing of Keith Weller from Millwall, who played in all the games but one of the European campaign. First-round opponents were Greek side Aris Salonika and after a 1–1 draw in the away leg, Chelsea triumphed 5–1 at home with Hutchinson scoring twice. Marvin Hinton was on target, while John Hollins collected a double including a long-range left footer. CSKA Sofia of Bulgaria were beaten 1–0 home and away in the next round to set up a meeting with Bruges of Belgium. Trailing 2–0 from the first leg, the stadium, often accused of lacking atmosphere, vibrated to the passions of the fans, and when Houseman cut the deficit, and Osgood levelled, the supporters erupted. Osgood then put Chelsea ahead in extra time but classy Bruges were also a threat until Baldwin finally put the tie beyond doubt.

The semi-final against holders Manchester City lacked the previous rounds' flair as City had several of their star names injured. In the event, Chelsea won both legs 1–0. Derek Smethurst scored the winner at Stamford Bridge and at Maine Road it was left to Keith Weller to steer Chelsea towards a final against Real Madrid. At the final in Athens on 19 May, Real Madrid were led out by Di Stefano and Puskas. This was the club that had collected a formidable five successive European Cups just a decade earlier and had become champions again in 1966. Osgood was injured and only managed to play with the help of a cortisone injection. Followed by 5,000 fans, Ossie put Chelsea into a fifty-seventh-minute lead, but when the cortisone wore off he had to leave the field. With seconds to go, Real equalised through Ignacio Zoco.

The replay was scheduled two nights later, with most Chelsea fans forced to head home and watch on television, though hundreds made up all sorts of excuses to their bosses and wives to stay on, those who had run out of money sleeping rough on the beaches. The players, meanwhile, headed for the bar – typical way to kill time for the boozers from the King's Road. Osgood went out with Cooke and Baldwin the night before the replay to sample the delights of the local beer and nightclubs. What a way to prepare for a final! But it was hardly the first time – or the last. Some of the Chelsea stars of this era became stereotypes, and justifiably so.

But it was Real who had the hangover, in front of a 35,000 crowd. Webb's burst from the back forced a corner, taken by Cooke, and when half cleared, Dempsey scored with a spectacular volley – one of only seven goals he scored in more than a hundred appearances for the club. They were two up in the thirty-eighth minute when Harris and Baldwin combined to set up Osgood for a clever low shot into the corner from twenty yards. Ossie was again forced to retire early. Fifteen minutes from time Real rallied with a goal and in the final seconds Bonetti pulled off a flying save from Zoco's header.

Charlie Cooke was the star of the replay, again in the centre of midfield with John Hollins injured and Keith Weller on the flank. Spanish international and Real Madrid striker Amancio said before the final: "If we stop Cooke, we will win." They didn't. Cooke said: "We deserved to win. I think we wore them out." The fans who stayed on in Athens had a wonderful night of celebrations, and the players ... well, they headed back to the bar.

Osgood had scored in every round of the 1970 FA Cup, and now he had scored in both the European Cup-Winners' Cup final and the replay. There is no doubt in my mind that he was the most naturally gifted and spectacular centre forward of his generation, yet he made only four appearances for England, including two as a substitute. He recalled: "Sir Alf didn't really like flair players. He preferred grafters and workers, which is why Frank Worthington, Rodney Marsh, Stan Bowles, Tony Currie and myself won so few caps. But if you want my opinion he made a big mistake when he brought on Jeff Astle instead of me against Brazil in the 1970 World Cup finals in Mexico. I was flying then. Chelsea had just won the FA Cup, I was top scorer in England with thirty-one goals, I was only twenty-three and playing the very best football of my life. It was another three and a half years before Alf picked me again, against Italy at Wembley. We lost 1–0 in what was Bobby Moore's last game for England. It was also my last. At twenty-six, I was never picked again. I'll never understand it. I broke into the World Cup-winning team in '69 when I was twenty-two. We beat Belgium. I was picked for Mexico and thought, 'This is it.' Only recently big Jack Charlton said one of the worst crimes in English football was me not playing."

I have met up with Peter Osgood many times and we have compared notes on our livers – not that I am saying that Ossic's a big drinker. He told me: "I had to come off the booze on the orders of my doctors, just the way you did. I was really worried and never took a drink for months because the bad news was that my blood count in the liver should be around the seventy mark and it was as high as 520." He was really alarmed until I told him my count was 1,200. He said: "You were always that little bit better than me, and still have to be!"

But not all the Chelsea crew were heavy drinkers, late-night socialisers or womanisers, and ironically the hardest man in their team was perhaps the tamest off the field.

Captain Ron Harris wasn't too concerned about picking up glittering individual awards, or England caps, as he was the first Chelsea captain to lift the FA Cup and the first to receive a European trophy. "Chopper" Harris arrived as a crop-headed, uncompromising defender and that's how he finished nearly 800 games later. The players at the Bridge called him Buller, but the fans nicknamed him Chopper. Chopper stuck, as did Ron when he marked a player, particularly me. He seemed to enjoy marking me. There was one occasion when a photo shoot was organised, with the plan to show me in flowing action at Old Trafford. But the pictures were useless because the photographer discovered that in virtually every shot Chopper, who had been shadowing me mercilessly, was snarling over my shoulder. Ron remembered it well: "I was marking him, that was my job. I didn't know there was some fancy photo shoot going on, but George tells me it was ruined because I was in fifty of the fifty-two frames."

Chopper wasn't a rare breed at that time, he was the norm. There were hard men in every team. Jimmy Armfield captained England and played no fewer than 568 games for Blackpool between 1952 and 1971. He recalled: "There were hard men in those days, real hard men. It was much harder refereeing. I got booked once and it made headlines, it was so rare, but a modern referee refereeing one of those games would have booked everyone."

Johnny Haynes is an authority on football in this era, having made 594 appearances for Fulham between 1952 and 1970. Was it fairer in the 60s and 70s or did players not cheat, play-act and try to win penalties in his day? "That's always happened. People just don't remember. Everyone wants a penalty when they need one, don't they?" Fans were thought of as providing "good-natured banter and friendly rivalry" as part of the fun, but Johnny remembers getting plenty of abuse from the terraces: "Whenever I played north of Watford I got loads of stick, but I dealt with it."

And Jimmy Armfield said that the crowd weren't alone in using bad language: "I remember Stan Cullis on the touchline at Wolves when I was overlapping – he was shouting, 'Who the f***ing hell's going to stop this devil?' Running down the touch-line screaming at us. Today people would have lip-read that. And I can remember Blackpool beating Wolves in a cup replay on a Wednesday afternoon. Blackpool had a player sent off and they had to protect a referee at the end of the match. All the crowd were swarming on to the field."

All of which prompts questions about the accuracy of our impressions of the game then, and our perception of declining standards now. "The simple truth is that the bad stuff is high-lighted more now," said Jimmy. John Haynes agreed: "Yes, the media today just make more of it. I feel quite sorry for the play-ers – not that you can ever feel really sorry for them because they make so much money they should put up with whatever they need to put up with – but it's hard for them because every-thing they do is picked up."

Ron Harris may have been one of the best markers, but no matter who you played in those days – Billy Bonds at West Ham, Arsenal's Peter Storey, Paul Reaney at Leeds, Liverpool's Tommy Smith – you often got a kick now and then when you were marked. Although little Nobby Stiles was our man marker at United, I had to face him as well whenever Northern Ireland played England. The first time he played against me was at Wembley, and he apologised to me before the game because Sir Alf had told him to kick shit out of me and to follow me wher-ever I went. I actually scored in that match with a header past Gordon Banks but we lost 2–1. It was an injustice because I scored an "original" goal. Too original for the referee, as it was ruled out. As Banks released the ball from his hands to punt it upfield, as goalkeepers would do time and time again during a game, I just stretched out my foot, without making any contact with Banks, and clipped the ball away at the very second he had released contact, and was therefore no longer in possession of the ball. We outplayed England in the first half, but their late winner from Allan Clarke was an injustice again. Derek Dougan and our defence were outstanding that day.

The domestic season was to be a watershed for Manchester United, and for me. While the Best, Law, Charlton triumvirate was on the wane in Manchester, the King's Road set must have thought, like we had done, that they were off and running. As we discovered, sometimes the glory doesn't last.

Well, London ruled all right for the time being, Arsenal winning the fabulous double and their north London rivals Spurs bringing the League Cup silverware back to White Hart Lane. Leeds landed the Inter-Cities Fairs Cup to make up for all of their previous disappointments in Europe, but the season's final blast of glory belonged to the Pensioners.

## 1970–71 ROLL OF HONOUR

*Champions:* Arsenal

*FA Cup:* Arsenal

*League Cup:* Spurs

*European Cup:* Ajax

*European Cup-Winners' Cup:* Chelsea

*Footballer of the Year:* Frank McLintock

*European Footballer of the Year:* Johan Cruyff (Ajax)

# 9

# 1971–72

I simply adored Brian Clough's management style, and perhaps it is one of my regrets that I was never a player under his leadership; I feel sure I would have enjoyed it immensely. I can imagine many people thinking that I was such a rebel that there would be no chance of Cloughie and myself hitting it off. How wrong they would be. I had no time for liars and cheats, but Brian Clough was the genuine article and I wish he had been my manager because I know, under the right guidance, I could have stayed on and played at the highest level for longer than I did.

This was the season that cemented the Brian Clough legend. And, yes, in my eyes, this man could walk on water. I could never tire of listening to the exploits of Clough, who was managing Hartlepool United at thirty when he knew that, but for a knee injury, he had a stack of goals left in him, having averaged close to one a match for Middlesbrough and Sunderland. Jose Mourinho, who has been likened to a modern-day Cloughie, has no playing pedigree and first appeared in the football world as Bobby Robson's interpreter. He has something to prove, just as Clough did.

Clough's Derby County had finished fourth in the previous season and having signed Dave Mackay to add a vastly experienced component to his young team, the next major step in my view was the acquisition of Archie Gemmill, a little Scot with a big heart, signed from Preston. Cloughie had the direct approach, and in those days he wasn't afraid to nip around to the player's house and make sure that the new recruit signed before Clough left. That's what he tried to do with Gemmill.

Clough usually got his way, but he didn't with Archie, whom he later called "an awkward little shit", but one that he swore by as a key player in the transformation of his Derby team. Gemmill said he wanted to sleep on it. So Clough said, "No problem, so will I," and suggested he slept in the spare room. Cloughie did the washing up and next morning Archie's wife Betty cooked him bacon and eggs. She was at the time heavily pregnant with Scot (who later ended up playing for Cloughie at Nottingham Forest).

As the Mackay era was drawing to a close, another key Clough signing in addition to Gemmill was Colin Todd, a young defender he had worked with during his short spell in charge of the youth side at Roker Park. Cloughie splashed out £175,000, a substantial fee in those days. Clough's exploits in the field quite rightly turned him into a legend, but off the field he was one of the most colourful characters ever in the game.

I admired the qualities that made Clough so outspoken and abrasive, but, naturally, those same traits had not always endeared him to the directors at the Baseball Ground, who feared that his controversial outbursts might land the club in difficulties. In the autumn of 1973 relations worsened and Clough and his managing partner Peter Taylor dramatically parted company with Derby County.

Cloughie adored Derby, as he stressed: "I loved what we had created at that old-fashioned club. I realised I could be as a manager what I had been as a player – the best in the business. It was a feeling that I simply could do no wrong. The players we had signed – Dave Mackay, Roy McFarland, John O'Hare, Alan Hinton, Archie Gemmill, Colin Todd and the last of the arrivals, Henry Newton – were all of the highest class."

He spoke of his relationship with his managerial sidekick, Peter Taylor. "Taylor had an unrivalled eye for talent, and no one could match my recruiting skills. Our ability to blend them into a balanced, exciting and successful team was proven for all to see. Nothing could halt the march. That's the way it seemed and that's the way it should have been – but for a combination of my ego, Taylor's pride, and the stubbornness of an old man who wanted to be seen to be running his club and regaining control of his outspoken, outrageous manager."

Cloughie felt that Derby chairman Sam Longson had become jealous of his television profile and his unrivalled power within the club. However, there were plenty of reasons for Longson to argue his case against his manager, as Clough himself pointed out: "There had been many a controversy since our arrival, not least the fiasco over the proposed signing of winger Ian Storey-Moore in 1972. He was on his way to

Manchester United for £200,000 when we stepped in. We almost kidnapped him. Taylor and I were masters of the cloak-and-dagger transfer – we tapped more people in our time than the Severn-Trent Water Authority. United thought they had him nailed but we shipped him to Derby, and hid him away like Salman Rushdie before unveiling him as 'our new signing' to a packed house at the Baseball Ground. Even I hadn't bargained for the kind of shit that hit the fan over that. You couldn't mess with Manchester United, the great Matt Busby's club, in those days. We were left waving goodbye to Storey-Moore as he departed for Old Trafford and our tails were very definitely between our legs."

But Clough blamed Taylor for indirectly poisoning his relationship with the Derby chairman. Clough explained: "He began telling the chairman, 'It's time you realised how well Brian runs this club.' He was right. I did. But instead of heightening Longson's appreciation, Taylor's words had the reverse effect. Longson began to believe that we had too much power and, to a certain extent, he was right. I had let it go to my head."

Before he died, Clough noted the similarities with the coach everyone has described as a "breath of fresh air", and yet, just like Cloughie, courted controversy at every turn, whether willingly or not. "That new Portuguese bloke at Chelsea," Cloughie said in typically flamboyant mood. "He's got a lot to say. He reminds me of what I was like at his age – but I was better looking."

Differences are equally significant and it is hard to imagine Mourinho taking the League Cup home, as Clough did later, after one of Forest's successes, and putting it on top of the television set while the family sat round eating fish and chips. When Jose won the Champions League with Porto he hardly seemed to want to hold the trophy at all; he knew he was off to Stamford Bridge and had done his job and left the club with the most precious piece of silverware.

But Clough did more than run successful football teams. He led and captivated whole communities, something more easily achieved in the provinces than in west London. Cloughie was a complex character and at times he caused mayhem wherever he went, but there was another side to him: there are many stories of Clough's generosity.

One statistic would have earned the wholehearted approval of Clough and Peter Taylor, and that has been Mourinho's Chelsea specialising in clean sheets. In the 70s and 80s, no one talked more obsessively about clean sheets than Clough and Taylor.

It mirrors the clarity of vision that Clough showed at Derby when his first three signings, John O'Hare, Roy McFarland and Alan Hinton, went on to play 1,150 games between them, having cost £70,000 in transfer fees. Circumstances are vastly different at affluent Stamford Bridge these days in that Mourinho has access to Roman Abramovich's colossal fortune, whereas Clough and Taylor had to generate money for transfers.

The modern trend is to disrespect officials. Not so Clough. Quite the opposite. He advocated that his players obeyed officials. Referees enjoyed officiating in Clough's matches. Clough demanded respect for them and forbade his players to dispute decisions, instructing that they take up positions to face the free kick rather than waste time with any form of dissent. Clough was a stickler for players to conform on their appearance. Perhaps my hairdresser might have objected had I actually signed for Cloughie! He also would have had no time for designer stubble. At Derby, he went for a haircut before every home match and liked his players to be properly presented. He respected talent and addressed the Liverpool managerial legend as Mr Shankly.

Clough had taken Derby up to the top flight as Second Division champions in 1968–69, reaching fourth in their first year back, an excellent achievement by anyone's standards. But not Brian's. He was a perfectionist and when they finished a respectable ninth the following year, it was far from good enough for him.

On the opening day of the league programme the defending champions Arsenal defeated Chelsea 3–0 at Highbury, having strengthened the side with Alan Ball from Everton for a then record £220,000, while Liverpool beat Nottingham Forest 3–1 in a game that saw a twenty-year-old Kevin Keegan turn and score in the box on his debut.

Manchester United were still the country's favourite second team and the one everyone wanted to watch. That's why the television cameras always followed us. We made thirteen TV appearances this season and one of them featured one of my best-ever goals: a cracker against Sheffield United in October at Old Trafford. With the end of the game rapidly approaching and the score still 0–0, I collected the ball, ran to the right, beat four Sheffield United defenders, then calmly slotted the ball inside Sheffield United keeper John Hope's far post. On 18 September I bagged a hat-trick in the 4–2 win over West Ham at Old Trafford and managed a second the following month at The Dell as we beat Southampton 5–2. Leeds outdid us in March, putting seven past the Saints including a Peter Lorimer hat-trick and then toyed with their opponents, famously stringing twenty-seven passes together on *Match of the Day*. A fortnight earlier Leeds had even put a humiliating five past us at Elland Road.

Despite the occasional up-beat snapshot, it was not a good season for Manchester United by any means, and one of bitter disappointment for me personally in so many ways. I was sent off against Chelsea, I was prevented by my club from playing for Northern Ireland against USSR in Belfast on 13 October because of death threats, and just ten days later I received further death threats that I would be shot whilst playing for Manchester United at Newcastle. I played that day and scored the only goal of the game, and although I hardly gave it a second thought once I was on the pitch, security was tight and I had police protection after the match at St James's Park.

On 17 November I was the subject of Eamon Andrews' *This Is Your Life*, but the New Year did not start happily, as on 4 January I missed training for a week and was inevitably dropped by Frank O'Farrell for the home game with Wolves. I flew off to London and spent a much-publicised weekend with the then Miss Great Britain, Carolyn Moore, returning a couple of days later. I was fined two weeks' wages, around £400. I was ordered to do extra training and instructed to move out of my house and back to live in my previous digs with Mrs Mary Fullaway and concentrate on getting fit.

Next month I was on the point of a break-up with football, and I confided to *Daily Express* journalist John Roberts that I was so fed up playing in such a poor Manchester United side that I would even consider playing elsewhere.

The FA Cup was full of even bigger surprises than the previous year – and that's saying something. In November, Ted MacDougall of Bournemouth put himself in the record books by scoring nine in the 11–0 win over Margate, and only one was a penalty. MacDougall scored five in the first half, at which point the Margate boss jokingly asked manager John Bond to substitute their tormentor. Bondie would have loved such cheek. Of course he kept on Super Ted, who went on to score another four after the interval.

The following day, MacDougall, one of the game's relatively poor relations, received a telephone call from none other than World Cup hero Geoff Hurst, inviting him to turn out for a Rest of the World XI against West Ham in his testimonial game at Upton Park.

"We assembled at the Hilton in Park Lane," MacDougall recalled, "me in my beat-up, second-hand car where I looked around the lobby and thought, 'What the hell am I doing here?' Bournemouth's Ted MacDougall standing beside Eusebio, Simoes, Uwe Seeler, Jimmy Greaves, Dave Mackay and Jimmy Johnstone, stars I'd only ever seen on TV. Anyway,

I managed to score in front of 40,000 spectators, which was something special."

It certainly was a year of FA Cup shocks, and for me the biggest of all time came on 5 February, when Colin Addison's Southern League Hereford United knocked out the mighty Newcastle United in a third-round replay. Having already drawn at St James's Park, the replay conjured the most replayed goal in the history of the cup. Malcolm Macdonald put the Geordies ahead before Ronnie Radford unleashed a forty-yarder out of the Hereford mud that flew into the net, sent the 15,000 crowd delirious, and guaranteed the scorer FA Cup immortality.

I can remember how a very young John Motson was beside himself. The police restored order after the fans stormed on to the pitch, and in extra time substitute Ricky George turned and shot low into the goal. Cue the second pitch invasion.

Yes, I would agree that Radford scored the goal of the season. But while I must say that Radford's goal was spectacular, Ricky George netted the winner and yet he hasn't quite been given the same status in the FA Cup history. For a man who had been handed four free transfers before his twenty-first birthday and spent the rest of his career basking in the anonymity of non-league football, Ricky George is one of the unlikeliest of football legends in my view.

George recalls the two ties with Newcastle that turned him from a total nonentity into an overnight legend: "There were 39,000 inside St James's Park and I will never, ever forget the noise. We'd never seen or heard anything like it. When you looked at the Newcastle team running out your heart sank: Malcolm

Macdonald, Bobby Moncur, Tony Green. We kicked off to a deafening roar and were a goal up in seventeen seconds. For the next twenty minutes it was like trying to stem the Charge of the Light Brigade. John Tudor equalised, Supermac put Newcastle in front and the Geordie crowd sat back awaiting an avalanche." Instead of which, Addison made it 2–2 to earn a replay.

The night before the replay, John Motson, who's an old pal of mine, and myself were enjoying a few drinks. We weren't drunk but it was well after midnight when we bumped into a group of journalists in the lounge bar. Motty introduced me around and I was suitably impressed to meet Jackie Milburn. "You know," said Milburn sadly, "it's lads like you who make me glad I gave up management. You should be in bed."

"But I'm only a sub," I replied defensively. "Only a sub?" he snapped back. "You might come on and score the winning goal." For one of the few times in my life, I took heed of someone's advice and fled to bed.

For eighty minutes the replay raged end to end until Macdonald climbed above the Hereford defence to send a bullet header into the net.

"That's it!" cried Motson in the BBC commentary box. "Newcastle have scored the winner." Famous last words; George was summoned from the bench and actually won a tackle in midfield, "a rare occurrence, indeed", and slipped a pass to Radford who unleashed the shot which still features on *Match of the Day* whenever FA Cup day comes round.

"Into extra time and my moment of glory in the 103rd minute," recalled George. "I found myself in possession on the edge of the box and, unsure what to do, I decided to have a pot at goal. I was more surprised than anyone when the ball flew across Newcastle goalie Willie McFaul and into the far corner of the net. To be truthful it could have gone anywhere. At that moment you want to do everything: a lap of honour, laugh, cry, hug someone ... The crowd ran on, I was embraced by thousands of small boys and ten team-mates in mud-splattered shirts. It's a moment that will live with me for ever; the memory still brings tears to my eyes."

After a home draw in the fourth round against a West Ham side containing Bobby Moore and Geoff Hurst, Hereford's cup run came to an abrupt end when they lost 3–1 at Upton Park. George himself left the club soon after to return to Barnet, for whom he would play more than 300 games.

Leeds easily brushed aside Second Division Birmingham 3–0 at Hillsborough. Two goals from Mick Jones and one from Peter Lorimer took Don Revie's side to Wembley for the third time in eight years. The other semi was a repeat of the previous season's, and once again Arsenal beat Stoke, this time after a replay. Perhaps Leeds' finest display en route to the final was the sixth-round victory over Tottenham. Although the margin of the win was a modest 2–1, it was the manner of the triumph that so gladdened Revie. Pat Jennings was in superlative form to prevent a hammering, and afterwards the keeper described Leeds as the best team he had ever seen. But with their league form not quite as consistent as Revie had wanted, there was also a bust-up between the Leeds manager and FA secretary Alan

Hardaker over their fixture pile-up. Revie was acutely aware of the need to strengthen in the centre and sought to buy Asa Hartford from West Brom, an attacking midfield player. But the deal, subject to the normal thorough Elland Road medical, fell through when it was disclosed that Hartford suffered from a heart defect. It halted Hartford's big move to Leeds but it did not prevent him from pursuing a full and fulfilling career.

As Leeds approached the Centenary Final, the double was still in sight and Revie observed: "If we do the double, I think we should not be classed as on par with Real Madrid but just as Leeds United." Revie sensed that Leeds were gaining the aura of being a big club.

Leeds deservedly won the 100th FA Cup Final with Allan Clarke's diving header from a Mick Jones cross taking the trophy to Leeds for the first time. However, the grand occasion, attended by the Queen, was not the best advert for football. The two sides knew each other far too well, and it was beginning to look as though Arsenal had taken over from Chelsea as Leeds' number one enemy. Both Leeds and Arsenal had developed a method of football based on stopping the opposition playing creative football. Hunter and Charlton completely subdued the threat of Radford and George, although George did provide one moment of his magic when he hooked the ball fiercely on to the bar. In the first half Alan Ball hit a perfect volley that Reaney instinctively cleared off the line. Apart from those two efforts it was mostly Leeds in a final ruined by a succession of fouls. Four players were booked: McNab and George for Arsenal, Bremner and Hunter for Leeds. The only injury, though, was when Leeds striker Mick Jones dislocated an elbow in a last-minute collision with Arsenal keeper Geoff Barnett. It still had serious repercussions as it meant that Jones was missing for Leeds' vital assault on the title two days later.

Entry to the League Cup was now compulsory and competition was fierce. Stoke City and West Ham fought out a seven-hour semi-final marathon; a Terry Conroy goal settling the tie for Stoke after two legs and two replays.

"Blue Is The Colour" was released before Chelsea played the League Cup final against Stoke, but there was a surprise in store. Tactically ambitious, Stoke were consequently vulnerable, but against Chelsea they memorably confounded the odds, and indeed the run of the play on the day. Conroy was far too often injury-prone, but the Irish winger had the talent to go past defenders with ease when he was in the mood. He was part of the five-pronged strike force – with Peter Dobing, Jimmy Greenhoff, John Ritchie and veteran George Eastham on the left flank – that left only Mike Bernard holding the midfield. "We filtered back if we lost the ball," Conroy reflected. "If you wanted to go, you went. Tony [Waddington] had faith in us."

After going one down to an early scrambled goal headed by Conroy, Chelsea's fluid play earned them a dominance. The turning points were three saves characteristic of World Cup-winning Gordon Banks, two regrettable fouls on the flying Garland by Stoke's strong-arm defence – Alan Bloor and Mike Pejic were booked – and an injury to Paddy Mulligan, Chelsea's right back, which necessitated two further positional changes in the second half with the introduction of substitute Tommy Baldwin. "We had a lot of the ball, but overall Stoke deserved it," recalled Hudson. "I was disappointed with the way we played – it was one of those days."

Another scrambled goal, by Peter Osgood, had made it level at half-time, but the switching of Ron Harris to right back and Peter Houseman from midfield to left back with Tommy Baldwin playing up front saw Chelsea's grip loosened. Stoke regained the lead through Eastham, but still required the world-class Banks to keep Chelsea out with two electric saves from Chris Garland and Osgood shots, then another, desperate save at Garland's feet in the final minute.

"I only remember the last one clearly," Banks, who succeeded the late Sir Stanley as club president, says. "Bernard gave a long back pass, not realising how near Garland was. I wasn't expecting it and, as I sprinted off my line, it was fifty-fifty. But Garland got there first, I spread myself towards his feet and fortunately his shot spun off me for a corner." Another of those few hundred "fortunate" Banks saves.

"To save Ossie's header, seven minutes from time, he came from nowhere." Hudson is still impressed with the memory. Stoke played twelve games to get their hands on their first piece of silverware in their 109-year history. The thirty-five-year-old George Eastham hit the winner, his first goal for nearly two years. It was also a first medal at club level for thirty-four-year-old Gordon Banks, who was also named Footballer of the Year. Those were good times for clubs like Stoke City, the little clubs that have next to no chance of winning major trophies these days. Millwall reaching the FA Cup Final in 2004 was as near as anyone outside of the Establishment has got in modern times, although they were well beaten, outclassed and really out of their depth in the final against Manchester United. Millwall went into that game with trepidation, but when Stoke City played Chelsea in this final, it was in an era when workrate had not yet suffocated improvisation. The League Cup final was contested between two sides whose philosophy was to attack.

Stoke City is England's second oldest senior league club after Notts County, and to this day have still only won just one major trophy in 143 years. For seventeen years, 1960–77, Stoke City manager Tony Waddington revived the finest Potteries years of the 30s, by using the cunning ruse emulated by Lawrie McMenemy: signing older, intelligent players nearing the end of their careers and letting them run the team. First it had been Stanley Matthews – at forty-six – and Jimmy McIlroy master-minding their return to the old First Division, then Dennis Viollet, Roy Vernon and David Herd. The side of the early 70s brought the peak: successive FA Cup semi-finals in 1971 and '72, and finally the Wembley victory over Sexton's distinguished European Cup-Winners' Cup holders.

It was a vastly different tale for the losers. The break-up of the King's Road set was imminent. Charlie Cooke was one of the few to show top form in the final, but the guts of the Chelsea side was about to be ripped out. Hudson was about to leave: "I was still only twenty-two when I went to Stoke, and Waddington gave me the tactical responsibility that brought out my best football. No doubt."

Hudson had become part of the fashionable Chelsea scene that Sexton could not control and both he and Peter Osgood were sold off. Hudson played 189 times for Chelsea, scoring fourteen before ironically joining Stoke for £240,000 in January 1974. Hudson took unfashionable Stoke to the top of the table while Chelsea were relegated, won a couple of England caps, and moved on to Arsenal where he reached a Cup Final only to lose, surprisingly, to Ipswich. Typically, he had an argument with Terry Neill, and walked out to play in America with Seattle Sounders, returning to the Bridge nine years later, but left after another argument to return to Stoke. He retired through injury when he was thirty-four. Alan Hudson was the Gascoigne of his day, equally talented and ultimately unfulfilled. Sir Alf Ramsey once said: "There is no limit to what this boy can achieve." He won a European Cup-Winners' Cup medal in 1971, still only nineteen, to make up for the heartache of missing the FA Cup Final the year before. But he went AWOL when he was supposed to join the England Under–23s tour and was suspended from international football for two years.

On the international front, Sir Alf himself was beginning to show signs of cracking. This was the year that Northern Ireland last beat England and, of course, it was a game that I managed to miss. Losing to Northern Ireland, minus myself, must rank as one of Ramsey's worst defeats. Terry Neill was Northern Ireland's player-manager at this historic time and also the scorer of the only goal in an epic 1–0 victory at Wembley.

A few weeks earlier England had been knocked out of the European Championship by West Germany so it was a bitter blow to Sir Alf to lose to Northern Ireland. Neill, the former Tottenham and Arsenal manager, recalled: "As soon as the referee blew the final whistle, Alf left the bench and walked across the pitch to me. He shook my hand and said, 'Well done!' I've never forgotten the dignity he showed in defeat that night. He was a great role model in that sense and his behaviour would put some of today's coaches to shame. What goes on now between some managers shows a lack of dignity, intelligence, courtesy and perspective."

England haven't lost to Northern Ireland since that defeat in the Home Championship match. In fact, Northern Ireland have won only two matches against England, stretching back to 1928. "I think we surprised a lot of people that night," said Neill, who was also player-manager of Hull City at the time. "Not many gave us a chance but we had a good team." He was right. Surprising as it might seem, there was some talent in that Northern Ireland team. Just look at the back four that night – Pat Rice and Sammy Nelson from Arsenal, Allan Hunter from Ipswich, and Terry Neill wasn't bad as an out-and-out stopper centre half. The truth is, of course, that Northern Ireland had one of the world's great goalkeepers in Pat Jennings. He kept us in it for the first thirty minutes. We owed him a lot. We usually did.

Although England dominated possession they created few chances, and that was to become a worrying trend for Sir Alf. They paid the price after thirty-three minutes when Wolves' Danny Hegan took a corner and Brighton's Willie Irvine headed the ball down to the feet of Neill, playing his fiftieth international. "The way I remember it, I picked up the ball in my own half, dribbled past five defenders and sent a screamer past Peter Shilton from thirty yards," a typically mischievous Neill said. "Time plays tricks, doesn't it? Actually I scored from two yards – but it was a volley with my left foot. I thought, 'Oh no! It's going to be on my left.' I only used my left to stand on. It was a memorable night for us. Significant wins of that sort were few and far between. In the dressing room afterwards the only regret among the lads was the absence of George Best. He'd gone on one of his periodic walkabouts and missed the match."

A youthful Martin O'Neill turned out that night as well, and he recalled Terry Neill's winner: "We dined out on that for five years!" But Martin can also recall waiting to see if I ever turned up or not for the Northern Ireland team. Martin usually has a go at me about the time that the Northern Ireland team were playing a Home International match in Scotland when they stayed at the Marine Hotel in Troon. Martin said: "We were looking wistfully at the aircraft on the horizon and wondering whether George Best might be on one of them, but he never was."

The Home Internationals were an annual event, and Martin remembered the relaxed attitude when he was first selected in the early 70s: "We looked on the games against the other home countries as convivial get-togethers. There was very little pressure on Northern Ireland to get a result and we just looked forward to the comradeship over the three games, which we played in a relatively short space of time at the end of each season. Because of the troubles at home we played in some quite diverse places. I recall playing at Goodison Park in 1973 and we played other games at places like Coventry and Craven Cottage, though they were against European opposition. Being all over the place over a number of years made us feel more together and we used to joke that we had all shown up in the vain hope that George might arrive. But, as I say, he rarely did."

Thanks, Martin. Of course, I did miss many games when I shouldn't have done. I know that I was considered at the time as one of the world's outstanding players but it is one of my great regrets that my international career from 1964–78 brought a haul of just thirty-seven Irish caps and nine goals. I know I should have played a hundred times for my country and if I could turn the clock back and do it all again I would have done. Of course, it is vastly different for goalkeepers, but Pat Jennings went on to win 119 caps.

Despite being considered a "small" nation we still produced some outstanding individual talents, many of them icons of the game in English game, like Danny Blanchflower, Billy Bingham, Peter McParland, Jimmy McIlroy, Pat Jennings, Harry Gregg, Norman Whiteside, Gerry Armstrong and Martin O'Neill.

From the age of seventeen I was playing for one of the best club teams in the world and even if I was never in a Northern Ireland side that beat England, I did score against them at Wembley. It was that most audacious "goal", when I kicked the ball out of Gordon Banks' heroic gloves and nicked a "goal" against England. They disallowed it. But really I still claim it. That makes ten goals in thirty-seven international games.

I got more pleasure playing for Manchester United. It was the total opposite to appearing for my country. When I ran on to the pitch with United, we never believed we'd be beaten. When I played for Northern Ireland, we never thought we would win. But the pleasure was beginning to drain away at Old Trafford as the team slowly disintegrated.

While Old Trafford was in a complete state of turmoil, and my own enthusiasm for the game had waned to breaking point, the championship was in Cloughie's sights. At the turn of the year, Derby were in outstanding form. Clough was always sensitive to criticisms that his Derby side had no right to be classed with the giants of the game.

The season had developed into one of the closest championship contests for many years, and at the start of the final week, four clubs still had a chance. Manchester City were the first to fall away, finishing on fifty-seven points, and Derby ended their campaign with a 1–0 win against Liverpool that left them one point clear at the top on fifty-eight.

Peter Taylor took most of the Derby players, those who hadn't to report for international duty, to Cala Millor, the resort in Majorca, a venue which was to become quite distinctive to the Clough-Taylor era. Cloughie headed for the Scilly Isles with his wife Barbara, and their three children and his mum and dad, leaving Liverpool and Leeds – who both had one remaining fixture – to take the title for themselves.

This is part of the Clough style that made me laugh: he would often take holiday breaks during the school half-term, going missing while the players were at training. He couldn't give two hoots. His family came first, and he didn't care who objected. Tough. He was in charge.

It could not have been a more dramatic and tense finale. Leeds needed just one point at mid-table Wolves. If they failed, Liverpool could go top with a win at Arsenal. As it turned out, neither club could meet its target. Leeds went down 2–1, while Liverpool were held to a goalless draw. Liverpool thought they'd won it with a last-minute goal from Toshack, but it was disallowed. Derby were champions for the first time in their history, with Cloughic's boys sitting in the sunshine, with a glass of Sangria no doubt in hand, lapping up the exciting news from back home.

That definitive game with Wolves came back to haunt Don Revie in more ways than merely the lost opportunity to land the double. Months later Revie was accused of attempting to "fix" that match, allegations first made by the *People* that three players claimed they had been approached and bribed with offers of £1,000 to "take it easy". Both the police and the FA investigated without reaching a conclusion, though the suspicion of scandal around Revie never fully dissipated.

I went off at the beginning of May to play for the Rest of Europe against Hamburg SV in a testimonial match for Uwe Seeler in Hamburg and by the end of the month I was sunning myself in Marbella when I announced I had decided to retire from football. I had been drinking a bottle of spirits a day.

But it was an on-off, on-off decision, and it wasn't long

before I thought about playing next season. I flew back from Marbella and was immediately suspended for two weeks for breach of contract and ordered into lodgings with Pat Crerand, although that was just a temporary measure while I sold my house. I was soon back in my old digs with Mrs Mary Fullaway and reported for pre-season training on 10 July.

## 1971–72 ROLL OF HONOUR

*Champions:* Derby County

*FA Cup:* Leeds United

*League Cup:* Stoke City

*European Cup:* Ajax

*Cup-Winners' Cup:* Glasgow Rangers

*Footballer of the Year:* Gordon Banks

*European Footballer of the Year:* Franz Beckenbauer

(Bayern Munich)

# 10

## 1972-73

Despite all the problems, both on and off the field, I was there for the opening game of the season against Ipswich at Old Trafford. Somehow I wish I hadn't been. Kevin Beattie's spectacular debut in an unforgettable 2–1 victory heralded a new dawn for Ipswich Town as "The Robson Years" really kick-started and Manchester United's downward spiral was well and truly underway. That's how much a good start can be valued.

We were catapulted into a relegation fight for our lives from the very first game. The first three games were lost and then after a string of four draws came two more defeats. It wasn't until the tenth league game that we collected our first win when we beat champions Derby County 3–0 at Old Trafford on 23 September after signing Wyn Davies for £60,000 from Manchester City. Davies scored on his debut against Derby and a week later O'Farrell went out and bought another striker, Ted MacDougall from Bournemouth for £200,000.

The Third Division goalscorer got off the mark with goals against Birmingham, Liverpool, Southampton and Norwich, but these victories were surrounded by too many defeats. Having scored 126 goals in 165 appearances for Bournemouth, manager John Bond had turned down bids from Wolves, West Ham, Coventry and Terry Venables' Crystal Palace. But Bond was finally forced to relinquish his prize asset in October when Manchester United tabled the then-fabulous offer of £200,000. He might have written his name in the record books for his FA Cup-scoring feat against the "mighty" Margate, but he was not the kind of player who would step into the goal-scoring shoes of, say, a Denis Law.

But it is interesting to listen to MacDougall's assessment of the state of Manchester United when he arrived, because he was spot on in that respect. "Old Trafford was not the happiest dressing room back then," he recalled. "The manager, Frank O'Farrell, was a lovely man, but United were an ageing side in decline, lying about fourth from the bottom. Bobby Charlton, George Best and Denis Law were still there from the glory days, as was Sir Matt Busby, though he never spoke a word to me in the five months I was there. Clique is too strong a word, but there was a definite 'them and us' mentality between the older players and the new guys like me, Wyn Davies, Ian Storey-Moore and Alex Forsyth. I never thought to ask why, but at training, we always got changed in the reserves' dressing room. I scored on my debut at Old Trafford, which was memorable, the rest of my time is best forgotten. Let's just say there was itching and a lot of blaming everyone else."

The First Division table had an odd look about it, Manchester United struggling down at the wrong end, and a club like Ipswich at the top end. Perhaps it had a lot to do with managers, and a growing realisation that the men in charge of the team might just be as important, if not more important, than the players. Sir Bobby Robson was a case to underline this theory. I knew him when he was still plain Bobby, as enthusiastic and exuberant as he is today. You just knew he was a manager the players loved to play for. He was an infectious character. He was also someone who had a sense of humour – and he needed it with so many players taking the mickey out of his legendary inability to get people's names right! There's the typical story of how he greeted Bryan Robson when Bobby was manager of England and Bryan was the country's captain. Bobby said, "Hello, Bobby," to which Bryan responded, "No, I'm Bryan, you're Bobby!"

But Robson was never afraid to make tough decisions with his players, as he did right from the start of the glory years with little Ipswich Town. Robson risked the wrath of the Town supporters by opting to exchange the highly rated Rod Belfitt for Everton's David Johnson. But Ipswich Town became a fixture in the top flight's top six all season, eventually finishing a solid fourth. Johnson and Whymark quickly built a strong partnership with powerful support from Bryan Hamilton and Colin Viljoen in midfield, helping to secure the club's first-ever UEFA Cup qualification. Ipswich also beat Norwich 3–2 over two legs in the Texaco Cup.

Yet, just a couple of seasons earlier, Ipswich had been the

scene of tumult and controversy over the infamous "goal that never was", a furious mid-season bust-up between manager Robson and club captain Bill Baxter. It had happened at Stamford Bridge, when a Chelsea shot clearly bounced back into play off the outside of a goal stanchion holding Town's net in place. Both sets of players were astonished to see the referee award a goal, which perhaps explains why 60s Ipswich hero Baxter got angry enough to physically attack Robson shortly afterwards. The Scottish hard man disappeared to Hull City early in the next season, which saw the Town finish nineteenth in the division.

Next season, transfer success Allan "Big Al" Hunter shored up the defence but results away from home were patchy. An important corner was turned when construction of the then-enormous Portman Stand (now known as the Cobbold Stand) signalled an exciting new era, with Robson's solid management proving his doubters wrong. New captain Mick Mills attracted the attentions of Manchester United, but Robson refused to release him unless a replacement for Mills was secured. Almost unnoticed behind the scenes, Robson's insistence at the end of the 60s that the club overhaul its under-performing youth policy was beginning to bear fruit as they climbed up the ranks to finish thirteenth.

While Ipswich were beating us on the opening day of the season, Liverpool beat Manchester City 2–0, and in December took a significant stride to establishing their title credentials, having recovered from 3–1 down to beat Birmingham City 4–3.

Bill Shankly brought in the excellent Peter Cormack from Nottingham Forest for a £110,000 fee in the summer to supplement his impressive squad. Shankly and his backroom staff had developed a distinctive style of play which was designed, initially, to avoid injury. Shankly recalled: "The team played in sections of the field, like a relay. We didn't want players running the length of the field, stretching themselves, so our back men played in one area, and then passed on to the midfield in their area, and so on to the front men. So, whilst there was always room for individuals within our system, the work was shared out."

Four wins in their first five games gave Liverpool a great start to the new season and already the rest of us knew this was a club to fear. They crashed to two successive defeats at the hands of Leicester and Derby, but recovered superbly as they went on a run that took everyone's breath away, losing only once more until the end of January.

Shankly always ensured opponents were demoralised when they stepped from the coach outside Anfield, let alone trod on that celebrated pitch. He orchestrated ambushes in reception or around the dressing-room area, seemingly chance encounters designed to sow seeds of doubt in visiting minds. When Don Revie's Leeds arrived at Anfield, having been delayed in traffic, with less than thirty minutes to kick-off, Shankly lay in wait. Shankly put Leeds on the back foot, when he told them: "I thought you were frightened to turn up." Revie and his team were already down in the psychological battle before a ball was kicked. As experienced internationals in the camp went past,

Shankly had a greeting for each. "Oh, Big Jack," Shankly told Charlton. "The pitch is terrible, it won't do for a big player like you." Then came Billy Bremner. "Oh, wee Billy, the pitch won't suit a small player like you." Liverpool inevitably won.

In my view the game is all about players, but the very best managers, as well as implementing tactics, create a winning mood in their players. The most successful sides have the most rousing managers. Liverpool had Shankly and by this time we had the dreaded Doc, who couldn't cure anything. Ian Callaghan, who scored fifty goals for the club, described Shankly as the "best motivator in the world".

As Liverpool prepared for confrontation with the might of Matt Busby's Manchester United, Shankly was leaning over a Subbuteo-type pitch as Ray Clemence, Tommy Smith, Emlyn Hughes et al paid attention. "I took the models of Bobby Charlton, Denis Law and George Best off the model pitch and put them in my left-hand pocket," Shankly says. "Then I told our players: 'Don't worry about them, they can't play at all.' It was psychology, of course. Charlton, Best and Law were three of the best players in the world." Liverpool were appropriately motivated.

Acutely aware of the quality of the individuals at West Ham in 1965, Shankly informed his players: "That Bobby Moore can hardly walk. As for Geoff Hurst, he looks ill to me. Don't be cruel to them. Stop when you've got five." Liverpool romped to a 5–1 win, Roger Hunt collecting a hat-trick.

Preparing to face Paul van Himst and the outstanding Anderlecht side of the mid-60s, Shankly was at his inspirational peak. "You're OK, boys," he growled. "You're playing a load of rubbish tonight." On Liverpool's victorious return, Shankly proclaimed: "Congratulations, lads, you've just beaten one of the best teams in Europe!" That Anderlecht tie illustrated another of Shankly's wiles. That night, Liverpool appeared for the first time in an all-red kit. "It had a huge psychological effect," recalled Shankly. "The players looked like giants and played like giants." Anderlecht were suitably stripped of any sense of invincibility.

Shankly's instruction that the "This Is Anfield" sign be placed in a prominent position en route from dressing room to pitch was a psychological weapon of immeasurable power and influence, put there to emphasise to the Liverpool players the extent of the club's expectations but also to frighten the opposition. Shankly relentlessly built up the reputation of his own players to such an extent Revie described it as a "torrent of adulation" from the manager on his players.

Emlyn Hughes was a key figure at the start of this incredible run in the 70s. Hughes was signed by Shankly as a teenager in February 1967 for £65,000, a record fee for a full back. He had then played fewer than thirty professional matches for his club, Blackpool, but Shankly had seen in him much of his own childlike enthusiasm for the game, as well as Hughes's innate stamina and drive. In later years Hughes liked to tell the story of how Shankly had pranged his car in his haste to drive Hughes over from Blackpool to Lytham St Anne's to register him with the Football League. As a constable began to take down Shankly's details, the increasingly irate Scotsman asked the officer if he knew who was in the vehicle. "No – not me!" he went on, point-ing at Hughes. "The future captain of England!"

Although Shankly's prediction was to be fulfilled, in his first few outings for his new team Hughes demonstrated that, as yet, his energy far outweighed his skill, with his wild charges upfield, and even wilder tackles. It attracted the nickname "Crazy Horse". Yet he quickly settled down, and once more proved that Shankly had a genius for spotting unknown players – among them Kevin Keegan and Ray Clemence – whom he could groom to replace the likes of Ian St John, Ron Yeats and Roger Hunt, who had helped to make the club's modern repu-tation in the mid-1960s.

Hughes started as a left-sided defender but soon moved to the centre, where he would forge successive partnerships with Larry Lloyd, Tommy Smith and then Phil Thompson. For all his dynamism – never better exemplified than by his post-goal cele-brations, in which he would frequently run the length of the pitch, frenetically windmilling his arms – Hughes was also a level-headed reader of the game, with a sound touch and good passing range. This brought him into his own in the early 70s, when Shankly decided that if Liverpool were to prosper in Europe they must dispense with the traditional type of English centre half, a one-dimensional stopper uncomfortable in posses-sion, and build their attacks from the back. It was the team's ability to blend British aggression and work-rate with a conti-nental style of movement that made them so irresistible for the next fifteen years.

Having missed the 1971 FA Cup Final defeat by Arsenal,

Hughes was more eager than most to land his first trophies. And after that blistering start there was no stopping Liverpool, both home and abroad. Having just failed to win the league the previous season, Shankly was on a mission not to fail this time and the manager was also determined to conquer Europe. Liverpool faced Spurs in the UEFA Cup semi-final in one of the first all-English contests, which Liverpool won on away goals. After a goalless encounter at Anfield, the second leg was a lively contest. Alec Lindsay scored after a free kick to give Liverpool a slender lead. Martin Peters scored twice for Spurs, the holders, but Steve Heighway's away goal sent Liverpool through to the final after the aggregate score had finished 2–2.

In the two-leg final Liverpool faced a highly rated Borussia Mönchengladbach side that included Netzer, Bonhof, Heynckes and Vogts. The first leg at Anfield showed Shankly at his cunning best. He played Brian Hall instead of John Toshack, feeling that the smaller, quicker man might get more joy against the German defence. Anfield was packed, but torrential rain forced an abandonment after thirty minutes, during which time the Liverpool boss had seen that Mönchengladbach were susceptible to the high ball. Twenty-four hours later, Toshack was in the side, naturally all fired up after being left out of the original line-up. For the price of 10p admission, Liverpool fans saw their team gain a 3–0 lead, courtesy of Toshack as a target man whose flicks created two goals for Kevin Keegan. As Mönchengladbach would score twice in the second leg, an acrobatic penalty save by Ray Clemence at Anfield became startlingly crucial.

Although winning his first European trophy gave Shanks immense pleasure, it was landing his third league championship that pleased him the most. As he said at the time, "That was the greatest triumph of all of them. Winning the championship early on was a novelty. This one was won with a new team. This was definitely the greatest moment that I had in football."

Liverpool took the league title with a goalless draw with Leicester at Anfield. The team went on the obligatory lap of honour, and Shankly tore off his jacket to reveal a bright red shirt and red tie, and he marched towards the Kop to take a solo bow. As he punched the air, the Kop responded with an enormous cheer and then chanted his name. Defender Phil Thompson recalled an incident when the fans threw their scarves on to the pitch for their heroes to wear, and a policeman kicked one away. Shankly spotted it and came running over and pushed the policeman away. "Don't be doing that," he said. "That's somebody's life. People have paid good money for that. Give it here." And with that he picked up the scarf and wrapped it around his neck. That summed up Shanks's passion for the game, for his team, and for the fans.

Liverpool finished three points ahead of Arsenal, with Leeds third and Bobby Robson's rapidly emerging Ipswich Town in fourth place. Liverpool strode to their record eighth championship using just sixteen players all season. The league and European double brought huge satisfaction to the club – and I, and everybody else, recognised that the shift in power had moved to Anfield. Only Matt Busby could claim to have won more championships since the war.

The bootroom had become bunker, the HQ, the think tank, the focal point of Liverpool's success, the tiny room measuring twelve foot square, containing, as you might expect, the players' boots. Shankly had his own office but after training, or a game, he preferred to gather his personally approved backroom staff in the tiny confines of the bootroom. His coaching staff Paisley, Fagan, Bennett and later Moran formed the Anfield dynasty. They'd make a cup of tea and sit down for a chat, with Shankly in his woolly cardigan, Bob Paisley in his slippers, Fagan and Moran still sweating in their tracksuits from a good morning's workout.

But while the coaching team enjoyed the privacy of the bootroom to dwell on all matters concerning their team, the celebrations of their double feat involved their passionate fans. An estimated quarter of a million ecstatic Merseysiders lined the streets of Liverpool as the team triumphantly paraded the two trophies through the city with an immensely proud Shankly, again wearing his bright red shirt. When the motorcade reached Liverpool's Picton Library, the players left their bus, and Shankly spoke to the thousands amassed in front of the building: "This is the greatest day of my career. If there is any doubt that you are the greatest fans in the world, this is the night to prove it. We have won for you and that's all we are interested in, winning for you. The reason we have won is because we believe and you believe and it's faith and interest that have won us something. Thank God we are all here. You don't know how much we love you." With that, Shankly led the fans in a spontaneous rendition of "You'll Never Walk Alone", the Anfield anthem.

Leeds added to their impressive list of second placings by losing the European Cup-Winners' Cup final to AC Milan. Tottenham qualified for Europe by winning the League Cup for the second time in three years when Ralph Coates's goal was enough to see them defeat Norwich City in a dull final at Wembley.

There were few dull moments where Brian Clough was concerned. From beginning to end of the season I was kept busy trying to keep track of his antics. As defending champions, Derby County controversially did not appear in the traditional curtain-raiser at Wembley. Clough maintained that prior to winning the title he had booked a tour of Germany for pre-season, and as you got to know Clough you also got to know that he wasn't one for changing his mind. Though even then, Cloughie knew his chairman would never forgive him for missing out on a place in the royal box – as Cloughie put it so eloquently: "In the eyes of a football club director that is as big a crime as scarpering with the season ticket money!"

Derby eventually came a disappointing seventh in their defence of the title, probably, in my view, like so many other clubs, preoccupied with trying to win the glorious European Cup. At the start of the season Clough broke the British transfer record by signing David Nish from Leicester for £250,000. Clough was, of course, convinced he would land the European Cup at his first attempt, and knowing his ego, that hardly surprised me. They sailed through the early rounds and not even Portuguese giants Benfica, with Eusebio, could live with them. Clough went to spy on them, and didn't even rate them – or so he said. And just to make sure they couldn't play, Cloughie ordered the Baseball Ground to be waterlogged. "I arranged for half the River Derwent to be piped on to the pitch the night before the game." The old FIFA president, Sir Stanley Rous, who sat in the directors' box next to Clough for the evening match, pointed out that he hadn't been aware of a downpour that day. Sir Stanley was shocked when Clough started bellowing his instructions from the directors' box. Derby hammered Benfica 3–0 and although Benfica were vastly superior in the second leg in the Stadium of Light, Derby held out for a goalless draw.

The semi-final of the European Cup took Derby to Turin for a first-leg tie against the mighty Juventus. Derby lost 3–1 and even though that would dent the confidence of most men, it didn't surprise me again when Cloughie was cocksure he could reverse that scoreline a fortnight later. Cloughie might not have been steaming about the scoreline but he was incensed about something else. He talked about the "lousy stench" of what he described as "attempts at corruption". UEFA carried out an inquiry into Clough's allegations but nothing came of it. Clough spoke out because he had heard that the ref had received "some sort of bribe". Cloughie insisted that one of the Juve substitutes was seen going into the referee's dressing room before the match and again at half-time. Cloughie said: "I'll never know what was said, but one thing's for sure – he wasn't in there to brew a pot of tea."

Clough wrote in his autobiography: "I was livid. We had two key players booked well before half-time, Roy McFarland and Archie Gemmill. As far as I can remember their only crime was to stand somewhere adjacent to an opponent who flung himself on the floor. Now wasn't that a coincidence? McFarland and Gemmill – two players who just happened to have been booked in previous games. It stunk to high heaven. I'd heard lurid tales of bribery, corruption, the bending of match officials in Italy, call it what you will, but I'd never before seen what struck me as clear evidence. I went barmy.

Our anger afterwards saw Taylor arrested – for something minor like a murder threat to the referee, apparently. Meanwhile I was ranting to the press about 'cheating, fucking Italian bastards', and I meant every single word of it. "

But Clough still believed he was destined for the final, and it was a marvellous atmosphere at the Baseball Ground that night on 21 March, the first day of spring, and Clough's birthday. Alan Hinton missed a penalty when the Italians were under the cosh, then Roger Davies was sent off. With the game ending 0–0 and County having lost 3–1 on aggregate, Clough and Taylor left the ground with feelings of total frustration, still mixed with the anger from the first leg in Turin. But later that night Clough's brother Joe rang to tell him of the death of their mother from cancer – which put everything into perspective.

Clough and Shankly weren't the only managers making headlines. When Bob Stokoe arrived in late 1972, Sunderland, in the old Second Division, had lost their last ten matches. The next six months were to produce a spectacular transformation. "I didn't bring the magic," Stokoe reflected the following spring, on the eve of Sunderland's FA Cup Final. "It's always been here. I just came back [to the north-east] to find it."

I could hardly believe it at the time when Bob Stokoe's team produced one of the biggest Cup Final upsets in history, beating Don Revie's heavily fancied Leeds. It was supposed to be one of the easiest finals to forecast. All I can say is, good job I didn't put any money on Leeds.

Who can forget Jim Montgomery's fabulous double save? I know I have already said that I rate Gordon Banks' save from Pele's header as the best I've ever seen, but this one from Montgomery came pretty damn close.

Leeds choked with disappointment at a result which allowed the trophy go to the Second Division for the first time since West Bromwich Albion won in 1931. What impressed me the most was that Sunderland's achievement owed so much to their own wonderful resilience, their heart and spirit. Much of the football may not have been memorable, but there had probably not been such tension or excitement at Wembley since we won the European Cup.

The red-and-white Sunderland hordes were delirious from the very first deafening roar, when their team turned to wave before the presentation to the Duke of Kent. "Howay the lads," their fans cried, as stirring and emotional as 10,000 hunting horns. How their heroes responded.

Of course, there was that controversial moment ten minutes

after half-time when Dave Watson, Sunderland's superbly controlled and commanding centre half made his one serious error in bringing down Billy Bremner. The referee failed to give a penalty. Maybe Bremner was paying for years of influencing referees and Mr Burns subconsciously leaned the other way at the vital moment.

Bobby Kerr came back deep to cut off the inviting channels waiting for Eddie Gray, who slowly faded until he was substituted for Terry Yorath with a quarter of an hour to go. What encouragement the sight of Yorath coming on must have been to Sunderland. Without the expected penetration from Gray, it was up to Bremner and Johnny Giles to crack Sunderland. They could not. Dave Horswill and Ian Porterfield were superb, Horswill marking Giles, Bremner shadowed by Porterfield.

Even allowing for the fact that striker Allan Clarke should have won the match, with a glorious chance squandered, Sunderland's defence was still magnificent. Up front, the stocky Hughes and darting Dennis Tueart were always posing problems for a Leeds rearguard, which had lost some of its formidable quality.

Another flurry of fouls – Paul Madeley on Ray Guthrie as he came through, Clarke on Hughes. On the half-hour Gray had a half-chance at the back of the penalty area, but put the ball wide; half a minute later Sunderland were in front. Porterfield, whose elegance, particularly in his turning on his left foot, was an outstanding feature of the game, swept a thirty-yard cross-field ball to Kerr on the right. Seeing Harvey off his line, Kerr floated a high chip and Harvey had to back-pedal hard to turn the ball over the bar. Hughes sent over Sunderland's first corner, Vic Halom headed down and Porterfield caught the ball on his left thigh, swivelled and cracked it into the roof of the net with his right – reputedly weaker – foot.

Over the last half-hour they attacked with ten men. Repeatedly, Sunderland were on the ropes, hanging on. With twenty-six minutes to go, Montgomery made two unforgettable saves. Sunderland's resistance was draining away, but Montgomery's brilliance revived them. He had helped them beat Arsenal in the semi-finals, with remarkable reaction to a deflected shot when going the wrong way. At Wembley he improved upon it.

Lorimer's long centre from the right fell precisely on the stooping head of Clarke beyond the far post. Twisting in mid-air, Montgomery plunged to his right to turn the ball away. Lorimer moved in and only had to tap the ball inside the right-hand post. Instead, he drove it and Montgomery, lying on the ground, got his right arm to the ball to deflect it up on to the crossbar and away.

I have seen many elated winners at the finish, and plenty of dejected losers. But the scenes of celebration from the fans and the players alike took some beating. As for the Leeds stars, they were inconsolable. It was all some of the Leeds players could do to walk up the steps to collect their losers' medals.

Stokoe's death in 2004 at the age of seventy-three after a long illness tugged heartstrings on Wearside and Tyneside. This big, undemonstrative man unified the town, his impact in a way comparable to the return of Stanley Matthews to Stoke City in the 60s. League attendances at Roker jumped threefold from 10,000: more than 50,000 were there for the defeat of Manchester City in the fifth round. Like Matt Busby, Stokoe was a leader more than tactician. "Go out and *enjoy* yourselves," was his dressing-room message. As one of the players said: "It was the first time we'd heard the word." Dennis Tueart, who became an England winger, recalls that Stokoe's skill was in blending and understanding players. "He wanted us to play together – a wonderful motivator."

Outwardly unemotional, Stokoe eased his managerial tensions at Sunderland with long walks on the seashore with Jed, his Labrador, yet none will forget his uninhibited gallop, raincoat flapping, across the Wembley turf to hug the goal-keeper whose miraculous double-save had helped defy Leeds. Montgomery recalls that magical moment: "To this day I don't know what he said but I do remember Bobby Kerr pinching his hat. Then a fan ran on and started holding us as well. Bob singled me out because of a combination of saves I'd made in the cup run. Bobby and Billy Hughes didn't have their teeth in, which was the first thing they thought about though we had just won the cup. They headed straight to the bench for their dentures and then were happy and ready for the presentation and the photos. Afterwards, we had a banquet at the Grosvenor House Hotel and I remember sitting with Ian Porterfield and the realisation suddenly hit us. We'd won the cup."

Montgomery had made his league debut for Sunderland as a nineteen-year-old in February 1962, played in more than 600 league and cup games and picked up a European Cup-Winners' medal with Nottingham Forest in the twilight of his career.

I feel that Ian Porterfield's contribution is somewhat over-looked: after all, he scored the match winner. Porterfield recalled: "The special thing for me was the collective impact it had on the people of Sunderland. They have a great passion for football; it was a great day. The highlight was the camaraderie between the supporters and the atmosphere in the stadium."

Although Porterfield's lone goal sensationally lifted the cup – this was Sunderland's first Wembley appearance for thirty-seven years – it took another three years to regain First Division status, after which Stokoe returned to his cycle of lesser clubs.

No one, not even Bill Shankly, hated losing more than Stokoe. Prior to the final against Leeds, noted manipulators of referees, he held a press conference, as calculated as any by that arch-psychologist Jock Stein, for Friday's morning papers. "I want to be sure that the match is controlled by the referee and not by Bremner and Clarke," he pronounced. Ken Burns was on the ball, and Stokoe took his place in history.

Sunderland received a second trophy from Sir Stanley Rous this season, as Team of the Year at the BBC's *Sports Review of the Year*, when it was highly visible that the thick sideburns and fattest tie knots marked the fashion of the day for footballers.

Despite our poor start in the league at United, the crowds still flocked to Old Trafford, even for a testimonial game, with 60,538 turning out for an emotional night for Bobby

Charlton against Celtic. But as the club seemed to look back on past glories, the future looked grim.

The back pages were filled with stories of the manager's pending demise. O'Farrell had already spent £600,000, starting with defender Martin Buchan, and after a paltry return of three goals in eight league games he had bought Ian Storey-Moore. The start of the season, though, produced only four goals from the first nine league games, with Wyn Davies and Ted MacDougall leading the attack. In our game against Spurs at Old Trafford at the end of October, the scoring had been dominated by World Cup heroes. Unfortunately for us Bobby Charlton got just one, while Martin Peters hit us with four as we sunk to a 4–1 humiliation. Serious doubts about O'Farrell's future were being expressed publicly immediately after our embarrassing defeat by the north London club.

I for one had had enough by now. I was in a state of shock mixed with anger and disappointment and I made it clear that if Manchester United were relegated I would want out. I have no doubt that put extra pressure on the manager, but that is how I felt and I was not prepared to pretend otherwise.

A 3–0 defeat at Maine Road in November did not help the manager or improve my mood and I was fined four days later for missing training. My season was already over. I made my last appearance in the home game with Southampton. Four days later I was called in to see Frank after missing training yet again. He dropped me, and rumours started that I would be transfer listed. Early in December I left the club without permission and was later spotted in a London nightclub – where else?

The next day I was suspended for two weeks and transfer listed at a fee of £300,000. Derby County declared an interest. So, too, did Bournemouth and the New York Cosmos; even Malcolm Allison at Manchester City.

As the team suffered another home defeat 2–0 against Stoke, poor old Frank O'Farrell's days looked numbered. The club had not covered themselves in glory in the League Cup either; it took two games to beat Oxford United, winning 3–1 at Old Trafford after a 2–2 away draw. Then came humiliation with a 2–1 home defeat by lowly Bristol Rovers in a replay following a 1–1 draw.

The chairman, Louis Edwards, intervened and persuaded me to resume training with the team. Then came the 5–0 embarrassment at Crystal Palace on 16 December; that was the end for Frank, if indeed the decision had not already been taken, because in the stands that day was Tommy Docherty. After the game Sir Matt said to him: "If something happens over the weekend, are you interested in coming to Old Trafford?" Docherty indicated that he would. As if he wouldn't! It had long been his ambition to manage Manchester United; he was hardly going to turn it down. He had been a candidate eighteen months earlier when Wilf McGuinness had been demoted to reserve team coach, but the board opted for O'Farrell, no doubt taking the more cautious approach knowing the "baggage" that came with the Doc.

Frank was officially sacked on 19 December. The axe fell literally a few hours after he and the directors were wining, dining and dancing at what turned out to be a pretence at being one big happy Manchester United family at a testimonial dinner for Bobby Charlton. The banquet-ball at the Midlands Hotel lasted until the early hours and included the manager and his coach Malcolm Musgrove and chief scout John Aston. But early next morning the directors were together again in the Collyhurst offices of Louis Edwards, and the decision was taken. O'Farrell thought that long-serving Aston was being summoned to act as caretaker, but he too was sacked. Just eighteen months in the job and his time was already up. He complained bitterly initially that he had been given no explanation by the directors, although just looking at the results was explanation enough. If he had been in any doubt he had only to study the club's official statements. Manchester United were near the bottom and that, quite rightly, was not acceptable.

I had made life tough enough for Frank, which in retrospect I can only apologise for, but I had my problems at the time as well. I had come to the conclusion there was no point carrying on yet again so I dispatched a letter to the club directors informing them that I was finished with football. It was the second time I had announced my retirement. The letter read: "I had thought seriously of coming personally and asking for a chance to speak at the board meeting, but once again, I am afraid, when it came to saying things face to face I might not have been completely honest. I am afraid, through my somewhat unorthodox ways of trying to sort my own problems out, I have caused Manchester United even bigger problems. I wanted you to read this letter before the board meeting commenced, so as to let you know my feelings before any decisions or statements are issued following the meeting. When I said last summer I was going to quit football, contrary to what many people said or thought, I seriously meant it. Because I had lost interest in the game for various reasons. While in Spain I received a lot of letters from both friends and well-wishers, quite a few asking me to reconsider. I did so and after weeks of thinking it over I decided to give it another try. It was an even harder decision to make than the original one. I came back hoping my appetite for the game would return, and even though in every game I like to think I gave one hundred per cent there was something missing. Even now I am not quite sure what. Therefore I have decided not to play football again and this time no one will change my mind. In conclusion I would like to wish the club the best of luck for the remainder of the season and for the future. Because even though I personally have tarnished the club's name in recent times, to me and thousands of others, Manchester United still means something special."

The club issued a statement on 19 December which read: "In view of the poor position in the league, it was unanimously decided that Mr O'Farrell, Malcolm Musgrove and John Aston be relieved of their duties forthwith. Furthermore, George Best will remain on the transfer list and will not be again selected for Manchester United as it is felt it is in the best interests of the club and the player that he leaves Old Trafford. In the meantime, the board will assume responsibility for team selection and the position of manager will be advertised.

"The above statement was prepared after the meeting of directors this morning. In the afternoon a letter addressed to the board was received from George Best stating that he had decided he was unable to continue and would not play football again. This letter was opened at the board meeting at 4.25pm, when members of the staff were informed of these decisions."

Perhaps this time everyone took my retirement seriously because they removed my waxwork figure from Madame Tussauds and replaced it with Johan Cruyff's! I went off for a break in America and Mexico to leave them all to it. In fact, I came out of retirement again – just for a game of kickabout with a group of Mexican waiters. Again, New York Cosmos expressed their desire to sign me, but in the New Year I was once more in trouble, this time found guilty of assaulting waitress Stefanja Sloniecka and causing actual bodily harm during an incident the previous November in Rueben's nightclub. A few days later I flew off to Toronto to discuss the possibility of playing in the World Indoor Soccer League but it came to nothing. New York Cosmos approached Manchester United for permission to negotiate terms but the proposed deal failed to materialise. Terry Neill wanted me to join his Hull City players on a relaxing break in Jersey but nothing came of that, either. Harry Gregg wanted to take me on loan to Swansea, but it didn't work out.

Poor old Matt Busby had the club at heart but he took so much stick during this time, so many of the critics blaming him for interference and being the man who stabbed Frank in the back. There were even offensive notes slipped through his letterbox, something I found disgusting and totally unacceptable. I had been impressed, along with everyone else at Old

Trafford, when Frank first got to work, and for the first half of the previous season we had lost only two league games and had won most of the others. Perhaps it was just the first sweep of a new broom, just as we would see when Docherty arrived, but that doesn't last long if you haven't really got that Midas touch, which any manager at Manchester United needed, to follow Sir Matt. In the final twelve-month period, Frank's record read won ten, drawn eleven, lost twenty-one, and that was a recipe for the sack at any club, not just one with such great expectations. The board had backed him with £600,000 worth of new players, and that was a massive amount for the time. Yet there had not been any appreciable improvement, and my depression deepened about the future of the club under the current regime. I wasn't around but I heard that there was a "clear the air" meeting between the whole board of directors and the players.

Of course, after the usual couple of months, I started missing the game again. I wanted to carry on playing for my country but at the end of March Manchester United blocked it. Both Crystal Palace and QPR made bids for me. My on/off retirement was soon back off as I resumed training on 27 April, four months after announcing (for the second time) my retirement. I was beginning to make more comebacks than Frank Sinatra.

While all this was going on, United were wrestling with their relegation scare under new management. The ink was hardly dry on Docherty's United contract when he was off on his transfer shopping trips. He signed George Graham from Arsenal for £125,000 just five days after his appointment – the third time Docherty had linked up with Graham. As the young

Chelsea manager he snapped up Graham from Aston Villa for £80,000, and as Scottish manager he recruited Graham for the national team, even though he was losing his Arsenal place to Alan Ball. Typical of the flamboyant Doc, he said at the time: "From the moment I took the job I wanted George Graham. He's a midfield player of the highest class."

Within hours of completing the Graham signing, the Doc was on the move again, buying twenty-year-old Alex Forsyth for £100,000 from Partick Thistle. Forsyth became the fifth member of Scotland's international squad at Old Trafford. Capped four times under Docherty as Scottish team boss, Forsyth made his debut the following day with Graham in a friendly match against Hull City at Old Trafford, which United won 3–1.

Next, the Doc turned up in the Third Division for yet another Scot, signing centre half Jim Holton for £80,000 from Shrewsbury – without ever seeing him play! The Doc really was in a hurry. The club urgently needed a big strong stopper to fill the gap left by Bill Foulkes. Holton was 6ft 2in, lean and mean, very mean.

The Doc's reputation had been revived as manager of the Scottish national side, and he enjoyed an initial surge at United, a run of eight games that produced five wins and three draws for a life-saving thirteen points. Holton made his First Division debut in a 2–2 draw against West Ham on 20 January and then played in a goalless game with Everton. It was at Coventry, his third game, when he got himself booked.

It gave me little pleasure that the new United under Docherty had a reputation for being tough, perhaps too heavy-handed. Docherty was sensitive to such criticism. The new United centre half was sent off in a friendly in Portugal. He played three times more, including an Anglo-Italian cup tie in which he scored, before the disciplinary committee caught up with him. After three previous cautions with Shrewsbury, the booking against Coventry took him over the twelve-point limit and he was given an automatic two-match suspension. He returned against Newcastle United at Old Trafford and ran into more trouble: referee Tom Reynolds sent him off just before the end for butting Malcolm Macdonald, the England centre half at the time, in the back of the head. Macdonald claimed: "I felt a hell of a bang on top of my head. In my opinion United were crude, not only in their tactics but in the way they played. It is a terrible shame that a great club should resort to such methods." The Doc was typically bombastic in his response, suggesting that SuperMac hadn't got a kick out of Holton and was suitably peeved and that's why he made his derogatory observations. But it was papering over the cracks and he couldn't prevent a one-goal defeat in the third round of the FA Cup at Wolverhampton. Holton, The Bull, carried on regardless. In his first two months at Old Trafford his record read: played nine, sent off twice, booked once and scored three times.

The Doc couldn't rein in his spending either. After paying a modest £20,000 to Bohemians for Mick Martin, he splashed out £200,000 for Celtic's Scottish international striker Lou Macari, just hours after Shankly had failed to lure Macari to Liverpool. Macari made his debut at Old Trafford against West Ham in a 2–2 draw. When Holton spotted Birmingham's John Roberts giving little Lou Macari a hard time, Holton told him: "I'll break you in two when you come to Old Trafford for what you did to the wee dwarf today." Tough talking as well as tough tackling, but this was not the direction you wanted to see a great club like Manchester United taking.

Docherty's revival brought in a 3–1 home win against Bari in the Anglo-Italian Cup and a resounding 4–1 triumph in Verona. The Verona game was Bobby Charlton's last in Europe for the Reds after twenty years. But the club planned a proper send-off. The final televised league match of the season on 28 April came from Stamford Bridge, where Chelsea played Manchester United. It was a strange spectacle as the ground was undergoing a major refurbishment and the whole of one side of the ground, the one facing the cameras, was a building site. The players had to change in a series of Portakabins in the corner of the stadium. But it was Bobby Charlton's last chance to say farewell to United, the man who had played a club record 604 league games in seventeen seasons of first-team football, scoring 199 league goals. A fitting presentation took place before kick-off and everyone in the stadium gave him a deserved standing ovation as he left the field. As it turned out, Peter Osgood scored the only goal of the game.

Docherty beat the drop by just seven points. No one was more relieved than Matt Busby, who had been watching the empire he created begin to crumble. O'Farrell's demise caused Sir Matt much heartache. But Matt had got it wrong with his assessment of Docherty: "Things are going right now: there is a spirit about the club again and I feel the future looks reasonably good. Tommy Docherty and Tommy Cavanagh have this knack of human contact and have created a good relationship with the players. They have given them the spirit and the will to fight for results. They have all responded to him, playing to win and running about to win ... Now I feel we are over the hill. It is a tremendous feeling of relief."

With the arrival of Lou Macari, Docherty swiftly sold MacDougall to West Ham. But far more significantly, Bobby Charlton had retired and Law was given a free transfer. Charlton and Law were irreplaceable. The flying Scot scored 171 goals in 305 league appearances, 236 goals from 393 United matches. That distinctive style of pulling his long-sleeved shirt over his hands and raising one arm aloft whenever he scored is one of the great images of the era. Denis remains a Manchester United icon.

Sir Matt summed up the emotions of Bobby Charlton's retirement at the age of thirty-five: "The announcement is very sad. He has been at Old Trafford the best part of twenty years. Jimmy Murphy and I have seen him stride from being a whippersnapper of a schoolboy to greatness as a man. He will leave something at Old Trafford for young players to emulate. Every boy in the land can try to reach the standards he set in every respect of football. Tommy Docherty and the board tried to persuade him to play for another year but this was Bobby's decision and as such it is the wise and right one. It was reached in a happy spirit and he will leave Old Trafford in the right frame of mind. "

Sir Matt added later: "The name of Bobby Charlton will stand for ever. In fact we may be too close to his great playing career to appreciate the full significance of his contribution to professional football. Time will undoubtedly add to Charlton's stature rather than diminish it."

I am sometimes astonished that football clubs now hold press conferences at the drop of a hat. But at this time, a press conference was a pretty unusual event. Bobby pointed it out when he held his very own press conference: "I always thought press conferences were for prime ministers and other such people, certainly not professional footballers. But I have been under so much pressure recently that I thought it would be the easiest thing to do if I told you all together in an official manner. It was certainly not my intention to hold such a conference. I thought the simple thing to do would be to hand out a statement saying I was finishing at the end of the season. It hasn't quite worked out like that, however.

"I always recall Tom Finney, a player for whom I had a great deal of admiration, deciding to get out when he was on top. That's the proper way to do it although I don't class myself as another Tom Finney. I feel I could play for another year but couldn't really do the game justice. I have started to feel the training more."

Of course Bobby didn't want to dwell too much on the problems that existed and glossed over them, saying he felt the club was in good hands as he left, but I am sure he knew that wasn't really the case. Instead, he preferred to concentrate on a glorious career, quite rightly so, when he added: "Winning the

European Cup was the greatest moment the club has had but it has not been quite the same since. We strived so long to win this particular prize that any ambitions since have been an anti-climax. If the club had gone down I would most certainly have carried on."

For me, Bobby Charlton, who went on to be Sir Bobby, was the greatest ambassador for English football – and, of course, still is. He had thunder in his boots; he could play whatever attacking role was asked of him. For sustained longevity of excellence, it is unlikely we will see Charlton's equal at Old Trafford.

Manchester United retained their status as the most-watched team in the land, and more importantly they survived the drop, but with more than a million passing through the Old Trafford turnstiles, those loyal fans were now watching a team in decline and the big question was whether Docherty was the right man for the job.

## 1972–73 ROLL OF HONOUR

*Champions:* Liverpool

*FA Cup:* Sunderland

*League Cup:* Spurs

*European Cup:* Ajax

*European Cup-Winners' Cup:* AC Milan

*Footballer of the Year:* Pat Jennings

*European Footballer of the Year:* Johan Cruyff (Barcelona)

# 11

## 1973–74

Yes, I had retired not just once, not even twice, but three times. The third time was definitely it, or so I thought, but yes, I was persuaded to play again. First United chairman Louis Edwards spoke with me and announced that I would resume training and then the next day I publicly declared my intention of playing again after talks with Tommy Docherty.

I reported for training on 10 September, and a couple of weeks later I played for forty-five minutes in Eusebio's testimonial match in Lisbon as Benfica played the Rest of the World. Then on 3 October, I played in Denis Law's testimonial game for Manchester United against Ajax and three days later for Manchester United's reserves against Aston Villa reserves at Old Trafford in front of 7,126 spectators. Next came a friendly at Shamrock Rovers, and at last my first-team comeback, against Birmingham City at Old Trafford on 20 October. Four days later, I played in Tony Dunne's testimonial for Manchester United against Manchester City.

But it was not getting any better. In fact it was getting far worse. It just seemed incredible to me that Manchester United kicked off the season without Law or Charlton, and had been reduced to just a bit of Best now and again. Manchester United's golden era was coming to an ignominious end, and it says everything that the highlight of the season for me was opening the Slack Alice nightclub in Manchester.

I was particularly sad to see Denis go. For me he was The King, just as everyone described him, as the best goalscorer in the country. Denis was a raw and fiery talent that turned him into one of the great entertainers. Law's generation was old-fashioned; drinks were traditional, drugs unheard of for professional footballers, certainly not performance-enhancing. Bill Shankly signed him for Huddersfield Town in 1956, a sixteen-year-old fresh from school in Aberdeen, the hair sculpted into a Teddy Boy quiff. By the time he reached twenty, Law was at Manchester City for the first time and then off to Italy. He was one of the first British players to ply his trade abroad when he joined Torino in 1961. There he shared a flat with Joe Baker, and they used to sit at home quite often, miserably picking at the strange pasta. Spaghetti bolognese hadn't arrived in Aberdeen at that point. Law couldn't wait to get home and, fortunately, Matt Busby paid a record fee of £115,000 to sign him. For the next ten years, until Tommy Docherty gave him a free transfer, he was, with Jimmy Greaves, the most exciting goalscorer you'd ever seen. I can still visualise the sloping run away from a stricken goalie, one arm straight up in the air, shirt all over the place and, always, the hands clutching the sleeves. The Torino fans loved his wild side and it was in Italy that he developed the toughness and, perhaps, the temper that would see him through his glory days when everybody was trying to chop him down. He always loved a battle.

Now, he was battling for Manchester City in a season where everyone was simply blown away by the amazing consistency that Leeds showed right from the word go. Leeds led the table from the start, winning their first seven matches. They beat Sheffield United's all-time record of twenty-three opening games without defeat, and just failed to equal Burnley's undefeated run when they were beaten 3–2 at Stoke in their fiftieth match, on 23 February. Before that defeat, they had been nine points ahead of second-placed Liverpool, but out of nowhere the old Leeds self-doubts once again manifested themselves. They had been in this kind of position far too often for their liking, without actually bringing home the trophies, and it was the fear of finishing second best they needed to overcome because their talent was never in any doubt. Liverpool's refusal to give up saw the Leeds lead gradually eroded when they hit a run of three defeats in March: 1–0 at Anfield, amazingly 4–1 at home to Burnley, and 3–1 at West Ham. This left Liverpool only four points behind with three games left to play; but Liverpool involvement in the FA Cup, with a draining semi-final replay, proved too much and, as Leeds recovered, so Liverpool began to falter.

Leeds had been at the top of English football, or thereabouts, for the past decade, although they had not won the rewards they felt they deserved – five times league runners-up in those ten years. Most of the side who won the league for the first time in 1969 were still there, although Harvey was replaced by Gary Sprake in goal, Trevor Cherry had come in for Cooper and Gordon McQueen for Jack Charlton. Clarke and Jordan reinforced the front line, although Mick Jones led the league scorers with fourteen. Above all, Billy Bremner had been the inspirational driving force behind their success, a tremendous all-round footballer and an influential captain, apart, of course, from his constant whining at the referees and his unsavoury gamesmanship.

Leeds found themselves in the sweetest position of having long-time rivals Arsenal to thank for finally clinching them the league championship, as Ray Kennedy's goal for the Gunners at Anfield inflicted Liverpool's only home defeat of the season and meant they could no longer catch Leeds.

Ipswich Town silenced their "one-season wonder" critics by finishing fourth again, thrashing Southampton 7–0 en route. But in East Anglia this is the season best remembered for Ipswich's first UEFA Cup adventure, knocking out Real Madrid, Lazio and Twente Enschede before encountering East Germany's Lokomotive Leipzig at the quarter-final stage. With the score drawn at 1–1 on aggregate, Ipswich, not for the last time, lost the tie on a penalty shoot-out. Leipzig went on to contest the final. Several of Town's 1973 FA Youth Cup-winning side made a successful emergence to the first team, with outstanding full back George Burley amongst them. But the phenomenal Kevin Beattie was the gem developed at Portman

Road, nominated Player of the Year thanks to his dominance at the heart of the defence and the soul of the side. It was the launch pad for a shot at the title. The following season Ipswich's shock Boxing Day defeat at home to struggling (and eventually to be relegated) Luton was only the difference between winning and losing the league, with Bobby Robson's side eventually finishing third, just two points shy of eventual winners Derby County. Youth product Brian Talbot was the team's midfield powerhouse, with another home-grown player, tricky winger Clive Woods, supplying the ammunition for goal-machines David Johnson and Trevor Whymark.

It was ironic that Leeds should win their second title in six years by sitting on their backsides, after missing so many honours when their fate was in their own hands and they ballsed it up at the last minute. I knew as well as anyone in the country the kind of love-hate emotions that Leeds generated. Most of the country loathed them, but, of course, their fans loved the success Revie had brought to Elland Road. But none could deny their right to be called champions. Their midfield axis of Giles and Bremner had built a reputation for playing a hard game. No one relished messing with them. Although some tried and some succeeded, most failed.

As infamous as the Mackay-Bremner picture by Monte Fresco is – with the little fiery Scot finally meeting his match, being held by the scruff of the neck by the even harder Scot in the Tottenham team – there is another wonderful image from that era, when Giles clashed, fists flying, with Kevin Keegan in the 1974 Charity Shield at Wembley. Giles recalled: "Keegan was quite an emotional lad and he was in one of his moods that day. He'd been involved in a couple of tackles round the edge of the box. The ball broke loose between us, and I tried to shield it when he came in. And yeah, I admit it, I swung a punch and caught him. The referee let me off with it … me and Billy Bremner had this thing where we'd pass trouble on to each other. So Billy put in a few tackles on Keegan and was giving him a bit of the verbals. He must have hit a raw nerve because suddenly Keegan started punching him! Of course the two of them were sent off, but afterwards a lot of people said I should have gone before that. Which was a legitimate point."

Eddie Gray was one of the legends under Don Revie. Gray played for the Leeds first team from 1965 to 1984 as a truly gifted, old-fashioned left winger in the era that took them from Second Division stragglers to the very top of the pile, the old First Division. Gray insists he never talks about "the good old days" but the history of the club is in his very being. "This club has been my life. It's in my blood. People ask me if there is anything of Don Revie in my system. I don't really know, but I do know that when I first came to Leeds at the age of fifteen I absorbed his beliefs about how the game should be played. It is no coincidence that a huge percentage of the side went on playing until they were thirty-six or thirty-seven, because they loved the game. Many of them went into management and coaching – Jack Charlton, Norman Hunter, Allan Clarke, Billy Bremner, Johnny Giles, Willie Bell and so on. Revie always told the players when they were young and even when they were older, and it still stands today, about the three Cs. Courage to use your ability. Confidence to play in front of crowds. Concentration to be able to apply yourself for ninety minutes."

Bristol City were seventh in the Second Division when they succeeded where the First Division elite had failed on twenty-nine occasions – they beat hitherto unbeaten Leeds, the league leaders and cup favourites. In this hard-fought fifth-round FA Cup replay at Elland Road, Bristol City won 1–0 and richly deserved to do so. Full of confidence and effort, and with a touch of unexpected skill, Bristol City were full value for a victory that earned them their first quarter-final place for fifty-three years and a home tie with league champions Liverpool. The match winner came in the twenty-third minute from twenty-two-year-old Scottish striker Don Gillies.

The FA Cup was won by Liverpool by the handsome margin of 3–0 over Newcastle United. Since Shankly became manager in December 1959, Liverpool had won the Second Division title, three league championships, the UEFA Cup and now their second FA Cup. The third team Shankly patiently built at Anfield was far from being the ruthlessly efficient, finished article, yet it did bulge with real talent. Liverpool played so well that the much-admired Newcastle side were swept away. Kevin Keegan emerged as the hero with two beautifully taken goals, but it was a triumph for Liverpool's work ethic. Smith made the first goal in the fifty-seventh minute with a cross that Keegan chested down and then drove with a flourish into the net. With Hall, Callaghan and Cormack in control,

Liverpool went further ahead in the seventy-fourth minute when Toshack headed on a long pass and Heighway, bringing the ball under control, changed direction to place it wide of McFaul. The third goal, two minutes from time and scored by Keegan, was the culmination of nearly a dozen passes.

Following a row with Tommy Smith, Shankly replaced him as club captain with Emlyn Hughes. The change led to a long-running feud between Smith and Hughes that continued in print for decades after both had retired from the game. At the time, though, it had an impact as it led to tension in the dressing room, where the older players remained loyal to Smith and voiced their disapproval of Hughes.

Following Liverpool's victory over Newcastle in the final, several players urged Smith to the front of the celebrations, ahead of Hughes, but after Shankly's unexpected retirement in the close season, Hughes was confirmed in the post by his successor, Bob Paisley. Hughes never had the same personal bond with Paisley as he'd had with Shankly, but on the pitch he became the driving force for the side with his relentless passion for the club. His unflinching commitment to Liverpool's cause inevitably made him a great favourite with the fans. With Hughes now frequently playing in central midfield, Liverpool would embark on their great run of triumphs by winning another double of the league and UEFA Cup (this time defeating Bruges) in 1976, and then in 1977 coming close to a treble. They retained the championship, lost the FA Cup Final 2–1 to Manchester United, then four days later – in their sixty-first game of the season – outplayed Borussia Mönchengladbach again in Rome to claim their first European Cup. Hughes, newly voted the Football Writers' Footballer of the Year, lifted the trophy with what the commentator Barry Davies called "the smile of the season". That match was the last for Liverpool for both Smith and Keegan. But Liverpool, at this time, had the unnerving knack of finding even greater talents. Kenny Dalglish arrived as a forward, and his inspiring individual skills took the team to still greater heights.

Hughes' achievements at Anfield had not gone unnoticed by England managers. He won his first international cap against Holland at left back in 1969, and was a squad member during the 1970 World Cup in Mexico. Hughes went on to win sixty-two caps (twenty-three as captain), the last in 1980; the team failed to qualify for both the 1974 and 1978 tournaments. It cannot have helped that Hughes, who largely shared the captaincy with Keegan in the mid- and late-1970s, did so under four different managers.

After the FA Cup Final triumph this season, Liverpool fans had prostrated themselves at Shankly's feet on the pitch. Two months later he resigned, ending a fifteen-year reign at Anfield. His final act was a typically shrewd move. The Liverpool way was to strengthen well before it was necessary. Competition was so fierce that players dreaded being sidelined through injury for fear that they might not get back in the team. It was after Shankly unveiled his last signing, Arsenal's Ray Kennedy, that he bowed out. The Liverpool board may have been worried that the Shankly aura might continue to linger unhelpfully at Anfield in the way that Busby's had at Old Trafford. In the event, the break, though his decision, was final. Yet Shankly was said to have found it surprising the club didn't want to retain him in some capacity and was inevitably hurt by the experience. Although the final parting was painful there can be no doubting his legacy. He had transformed Liverpool from a struggling, unambitious club into one of the most formidable sides in world football. Though Shankly died in 1981, his name adorns the gates at the entrance to his beloved Anfield, and his spirit will linger for ever.

Another career with an everlasting, ever-lingering impact on the English game also came to an ignominious end.

Alf Ramsey was sacked as England manager after winning sixty-nine and losing just seventeen out of 113 games between 1963 and 1974. Ramsey had been an inauspicious player, although very much a cultured full back in that famous Spurs "push and run" side which won the championship in 1951. He was capped thirty-two times for England between 1949 and 1954.

But it was as a manager that Ramsey truly excelled. Ramsey was, in fact, the first full-time England manager and he insisted on being given sole responsibility for selection, a freedom that the country's managers now take for granted.

Early in his reign he predicted that England would win the World Cup, but that hardly looked likely when, in his first game in charge of the national side, England were hammered 5–2 by France, who were not highly rated during this period of evolution of the international game. But, as we all know, he was proved right. No one has ever won the World Cup since for England and, let's get real, not really looked like it, even though Bobby Robson took England to the semi-finals in Italia 90 before losing to the Germans on penalties. England had a better team in 1970 when they were defending the World Cup in Mexico, but were knocked out in the quarter-finals. Ramsey survived England's quarter-final exit in the 1972 European Championships when the Germans again proved to be a stumbling block.

But the FA lost confidence in Sir Alf after England failed to qualify for the 1974 World Cup finals. Sir Alf Ramsey's side needed a victory at Wembley against the Poles to qualify after losing 2–0 in Chorzow. Ramsey controversially omitted Bobby Moore in favour of Norman Hunter, but it was "Bite Yer Legs" Norman whose uncharacteristic mistake let in Jan Domarski for Poland's goal. England could only draw 1–1 with Poland at Wembley, largely thanks to the goalkeeping skills of Jan Tomaszewski. The fateful night was 17 October, 1973. England peppered Tomaszewski's goal for the entire ninety minutes in one of their most frustrating international fixtures. It took an Allan Clarke penalty to beat him, but by then Poland were one up, Domarski's shot squeezing under Peter Shilton's body. England had failed to get past Tomaszewski in twenty-one attempts, but the draw was not enough. Ramsey, whose watch had stopped during the match, delaying him bringing on striker Kevin Hector, was sacked as a result of such a bitter defeat. He said: "I lost track of time but I suppose we were fated not to win the match."

The fact that Poland went on to be one of the surprise teams of the tournament in Germany, playing some delightful football on their way to finishing third, was of little consolation to anyone in the country, least of all Sir Alf, whom the FA had sacked a month earlier.

The Polish keeper had been dubbed a clown by Brian Clough, but the cream of English strikers couldn't get past him. We should all have loved to have seen Cloughie in charge of England. He was eccentric. Had he been put in charge of England he would have lasted either forty-four days or turned them into world beaters – it is a mammoth regret that we will never know what he would have achieved. My gut feeling is that he would have been a huge success. "When I go," he told a friend, "God's going to have to give up his favourite chair."

Like Revie, Clough relied on day-to-day control over his players. He bought and sold them and set the wages of each. Unlike a national coach, he never had to fight another manager for the services of a player, or fight the press on several fronts at once, or prevent petty jealousies from dissipating the spirit of a squad from whom only half the members, all accustomed to star status at their clubs, could ever be picked to play. But somehow, I am convinced he would not have been worried by all these problems, and would have emerged as an England manager every bit as successful as Sir Alf. Yes, I am sure Cloughie would have delivered the World Cup for his country if he'd been given the opportunity.

Indeed, the sacking of Ramsey, shocking though it was, was

even overshadowed by the apparently more parochial drama that occurred between Clough and Derby. But such was Cloughie's profile that he commanded more media attention than even the England manager. A row with the board took place after an incident at United in October. Derby had won 1–0 at Old Trafford, and Clough and Taylor ventured into the club's boardroom where they were greeted by Louis Edwards with a bottle of champagne. This didn't go down too well with the Derby directors and Taylor was called in on the Monday morning to explain what they'd been up to. Clough was furious and he and Taylor decided to resign on a point of principle, though privately, he wasn't ready to leave and believed the board would reject his resignation.

You can imagine the reaction to Clough walking out – front- as well as back-page news and a players' revolt and the Baseball Ground virtually under siege from the fans. Leicester were due next at the Baseball Ground and the players were on a crusade to reinstate their beloved boss, even threatening to strike. I can't help but admire the man's cheek – he even turned up for that Leicester match. Of course, he said he wanted to say goodbye to the fans, but he had hoped that their reaction, after all the fuss the players made, would again force the board to reinstate him. Of course, they didn't. Cloughie didn't stay long; he nipped in through the players' entrance, made his way up to the directors' box, waved to the fans, headed back to his Rolls and shot down to London to appear on the Michael Parkinson show. Cloughie blamed himself and Taylor for quitting: "We were stupid, we were headstrong, we were stubborn and full of our own importance, but we were terribly, terribly wrong."

Next Clough and Taylor pitched up at Brighton, arriving at the Goldstone Ground late in 1973, while the protests were still raging back in Derby. I always expected the unexpected with Clough, but the Third Division! He was enticed to the unlikely south-coast destination by their charismatic, larger-than-life chairman Mike Bamber, a wealthy nightclub owner. Virtually from the moment he arrived, Cloughie hated it there. The highlight seemed to be meeting Les Dawson. But he didn't see the funny side. He recruited John Sheridan from the Derby coaching staff, but he felt lonely at the seaside with Taylor initially making infrequent visits until he moved down there into rented accommodation with a sea view. The sea air didn't agree with them and Clough and Taylor quickly sought a way out. He admitted: "We couldn't win a match at Brighton to save our lives." Less than a year before he'd been in a European Cup semi-final against Juventus, now all he had to look forward to was a first-round FA Cup tie against Walton & Hersham.

The managerial merry-go-round was not over. Cloughie later caused another sensation when he took up the reins at Leeds when Revie, equally sensationally, took over the England job. Leeds were champions and it was quite a shock when Revie jumped ship. I suspected at the time that his choice might also have had something to do with the fact that he now had an ageing side that would need a major overhaul sooner rather than later.

Joe Mercer acted as caretaker manager for seven matches

before Clough was appointed. Yet the signs were all wrong for Clough even before he set foot inside Elland Road. For a start, the break-up of his formidable partnership with Taylor occurred. Taylor did not want to leave Brighton, where the chairman offered him the opportunity, for the first time, to become a a manager in his own right.

For some it remains a mystery why Cloughie would want to join the club he detested but I felt Cloughie wanted to out-do Revie; he wanted to build a team capable of winning the European Cup. But as he put it himself, "I hardly lasted long enough to be given my own tea-cup at Leeds." A young Clough clashed with senior dressing-room personalities such as Billy Bremner and was on his way, complaining of excessive player power, after just forty-four days, barely long enough to make any profound mark on the team.

When he had his first players gathering, Cloughie was at his irrational, irrepressible peak, hardly out to ingratiate himself with his new charges: "I told Peter Lorimer he tried to con refer-ees, I told Norman Hunter and Johnny Giles they were such good players they didn't need to go around kicking people, and I told Scottish international winger Eddie Gray that, with his injury record, if he'd been a racehorse they'd have had him shot. I honestly thought that bit of friendly stick might have melted the ice, but I couldn't have been more wrong. They couldn't take it." Well, that's how to win friends and influence people the Brian Clough way! Yes – unique.

On that first day, the first five-a-side and Cloughie was whacked from behind by Allan Clarke, leaving the new boss on his backside, minus his watch; it was a week later before he got his watch back. There was no obvious laughter, but Cloughie knew what the reaction would be behind his back.

Clough needed familiar faces to back him up, and watch his flock, so he naturally returned to Derby to sign John McGovern and John O'Hare, and shortly afterwards took a gamble by splashing a quarter of a million on Duncan McKenzie from Nottingham Forest, the extrovert striker who smoked forty ciga-rettes a day and who could jump over Minis in the car park. The crunch came when Cloughie tried to sign Peter Shilton and Leeds' Scottish international David Harvey asked him outright if he was trying to replace him. Attitudes among the players hardened, a meeting was called and Clough was out. This time he didn't make the mistake of resigning, and ended up getting Leeds to pay his tax for the next three years as well as a pay-off which terminated his mortgage.

Although Allan Clarke was the one who kicked Cloughie on day one, Cloughie had kissed him when he scored the only goal of the only victory of his stay, and Clarke was the only player to see Cloughie when he left to say he was sorry he was going. That was typical of the kind of perverse nature of the unreal forty-four days in charge at Elland Road.

I followed Clough's career all the way down the line, who couldn't be fascinated by the man? It was interesting to see how it all panned out. Derby won another title in 1975 then eventu-ally plummeted down the divisions, heading for bankruptcy. Leeds reached their European Cup final but lost in Paris, and Clough went on to his greatest triumph: landing two European

Cups with Nottingham Forest. Who knows what Cloughie might have achieved with either Leeds or England, but, in my view, had he been given a fair chance with either he would have taken them to the very summit of the game.

After almost eighty years, new rules were introduced this season – three up and three down. Up came Middlesbrough, Luton Town and Carlisle United, and with Middlesbrough promoted, Jack Charlton arrived in the managerial big time and within one season of Big Jack taking charge the club was back in the First Division for the first time in nearly twenty years.

Charlton brought in Bobby Murdoch from Celtic, adopted a counter-attacking style and Boro ran away with the title. They won the Second Division with eight games to spare. "When Jack Charlton came to the club I thought it was the end for me," recalls Stuart Boam, "because he was also a centre half. Instead, he made me captain and we fought tooth and nail. I represented the players and he represented the club, and there was a lot of aggravation. He was a wind-up merchant and I fell for it, but it was my most successful spell as a player." Alan Foggon was Boro's top scorer with nineteen goals in the title-winning season, and was regarded by many as the most important player in the line-up. He signed for Newcastle at fifteen, then joined Cardiff. He played 141 games for Middlesbrough from 1972. Foggon was signed by Manchester United, but made only three substitute appearances. One of the stars of the Jack Charlton show was none other than Graeme Souness. Born in Edinburgh, he joined Boro in 1972. Souness, who won fifty-four Scotland caps, was a tough midfielder and was voted club Player of the Year in 1974. He moved to Liverpool in 1978 where he, of course, won three European Cups and five league titles.

I had never really given much thought to the relegation issues: I had always thought of Manchester United as glory hunters, winners of European cups in nights of high drama and passion, of cup triumphs, and challenges for the championship crown. It simply never dawned on me that Manchester United might be involved in a relegation scrape. No one in the game realised just how much fear would be generated by switching to three up and three down. That is something that has intensified over the years because so much more is at stake, with the financial gap grown into a chasm between the elite in the Premiership and the old Second Division.

George Burley loves to recall that on 29 December, when he was just seventeen, he made his debut for Ipswich Town, and his brief was to mark me. It turned out to be my last appearance for United at Old Trafford. Ipswich lost 2–0, but a month later Ipswich came back to Old Trafford in the fourth round of the FA Cup and won 1–0 courtesy of a Kevin Beattie winner. Again Burley played, though I was no longer in the side. I had played just twelve games for Docherty before he dropped me. Though at the time I didn't know it, 1 January, 1974 was my last game ever for United in an away fixture at QPR, which we lost 3–0. Stan Bowles scored against us for QPR, leaving defender Martin Buchan looking pretty fed up. Three days after the defeat, I failed to turn up for training.

Docherty was the kiss of death for me personally. He was plain deceitful in his dealings with me. And it was hard adjusting to dealing with such a man, when, previously, I had had such an honest manager in Matt Busby. The day after I had failed to turn up for training, Docherty had decided to leave me out of the team to play Plymouth Argyle in the FA Cup third-round tie at Old Trafford. Although I had missed the previous morning's training, I made up for it by training throughout the afternoon and travelled to the game with Paddy and Bill Foulkes, fully expecting to play. I asked Docherty for an explanation shortly afterwards. He told me that it was because I had turned up a quarter of an hour before the kick-off drunk and with a blonde lady on my arm. That was rubbish on both counts. For a start it couldn't have been a quarter of an hour before kick-off when I turned up because Docherty told me, an hour and a quarter before kick-off, in the referees' room, that I had been left out. Secondly, I have never turned up for a game drunk in my life: it's an insult to suggest that. It is also an insult to anyone's intelligence to believe it, because there is no way you could play if you turned up drunk and tried to perform in front of 60,000 people. I said at the time that if he left me out against Plymouth then I wouldn't play for him again.

On 12 January, I was suspended for two weeks and transfer listed by the club. Four days later Tonbridge were keen to sign me and offered United £100,000, which Docherty dismissed as a publicity stunt. Crewe Alexandra also made enquiries. By the middle of February I had been arrested in Manchester and later charged in London with stealing a fur coat, passport, cheque book and other items from the flat of Miss World, Marjorie Wallace, but was later released on bail of £6,000, and by 24 April was cleared of all charges. In May I went off to South Africa to play in five games for the Jewish Guild and have no doubt that I was sitting on a beach somewhere in the glorious sunshine when somebody told me that Manchester United were on the verge of being relegated.

It all came down to an incredible finale, *the* Manchester derby, with Denis Law playing for the "wrong" team. How ironic that it should be Denis Law's goal that would condemn United to the Second Division. His last-ever game before hanging up his boots. He turned away without the arm up and, for probably the first time, with his head down. He didn't kick another ball in this or any other club game. It was over.

In reality, it has nothing to do with that famous Law back heel. United were down long before that. But it weighed heavily on Denis's shoulders. It hurt him. There was a pitch invasion after Denis Law put City one up and that remained the score when the match was halted four minutes from time. "The way things are going, the FA and the league will have to be thinking in terms of fences," was the after-match judgement of Sir Matt Busby.

Everyone remembers the end with the Law goal, but of course there was a pointless final game of the season to play out, a 1–0 defeat at Stoke. Manchester United were relegated with just thirty-two points from forty-two games. In the final table United finished four points behind Southampton. Southampton finished twentieth in the league and became the first Division

One side to suffer the new three-up, three-down system. United were five points adrift of Birmingham, the team that just avoided the drop. Norwich were the other club relegated. Manchester United, European champions just six years earlier, found themselves in Division Two for the first time since 1938.

There were awful mixed emotions when I heard. I felt sad at United's demise, I felt for the players, the staff – apart from Docherty – the fans and everyone connected to the club. I was really a Manchester United fan myself. But funnily enough I wasn't distraught because I always knew that they would come back immediately: the club were simply too good for the Second Division. Manchester United and the top level go hand in hand, and I never doubted that it would only be a temporary demise.

## 1973–74 ROLL OF HONOUR

*Champions:* Leeds United

*FA Cup:* Liverpool

*League Cup:* Wolves

*European Cup:* Bayern Munich

*European Cup-Winners' Cup:* Magdeburg

*Footballer of the Year:* Ian Callaghan

*European Footballer of the Year:* Johan Cruyff (Ajax)

# EPILOGUE

Sir Stanley Rous was succeeded as president of FIFA by Brazil's Joao Havelange before the start of the 1974 World Cup, heralding the start of a new order in world football and a new era for the entire game. The game was never the same again. Rous was rooted in the ideals with which I was more comfortable, while Havelange was dangerously more materialistic. Johan Cruyff of Ajax signed for Barcelona in August for a world record £922,300, about £400,000 of which he pocketed himself. Player power was beginning to take a grip, and a number of traditionalists such as Bill Nicholson found the whole experience distasteful. When Nicholson found average players making extortionate demands from his club, he knew it was time to pack it in. He wasn't for bending his principles; he would rather get out, and he did. You have to admire him for that.

It might seem sentimental, or even arrogant, to equate my own personal decline and that of my beloved Manchester United with that of the game as a whole, but by 1974 there really was something in the air, and it was hard to avert it.

The giants who had transformed the game were moving on: Busby, Nicholson, Catterick, Mee, Ramsey, Greenwood, Revie. For a variety of reasons none of them were in tune with the demands of a new era. Shankly retired too, but such was the strength of the dynasty he had created at Anfield that his own chosen replacement from the boot room, Bob Paisley, and then Joe Fagan after him, were able to take the formula to even greater heights. The youngsters, Bobby Robson and Brian Clough, had further glories ahead of them still. Bobby was a great survivor and finally became England manager, while Clough never rose to the job he always coveted but was too controversial to attain. Like Herbert Chapman and Sir Alex Ferguson, Clough made history at not just one club but two. In tandem with Peter Taylor, he was up with the best of all time.

I went into exile for a while, seeking a new beginning in the glitzy birth of the game in the USA. And for a while it worked. I was in good company too, with old pals like Rodney Marsh and Charlie Cooke and senior stars of the world stage like Beckenbauer and Pele. We all laughed at the hype and the razza-matazz, little knowing that one day this would be par for the course in the English game and European competition. Though the money involved in football was still peanuts compared to today's sums, the changes were beginning. As I said at the outset, the breaking of the maximum wage and the coming of television were football's Pandora's box, changing the game financially for ever. Though it was yet to reach the saturation levels developed by Rupert Murdoch with Sky in the 90s, tele-vision coverage was becoming more important commercially in the 70s. Money was more and more of a factor and Trevor Francis, the first million-pound player (something unthinkable to us in the mid-60s) was just around the corner.

EPILOGUE

When Edward Heath took us into the EEC in 1973, Britain entered Europe and the early signs of something that would dominate British football was first visible. The traditional imports like myself from the working-class ship-building and coal-mining districts of Scotland and Northern Ireland, while not yet something of the past, had as a phenomenon definitely passed its peak. We were starting to notice new dimensions afoot in Europe: Ajax were in the middle of their three successive European Cup triumphs under the tactical guidance of Rinus Michels. There was an intelligence and skill at work that largely seemed lacking in the English game. Perhaps the first importation of this was seen at Ipswich with Robson's acquisition of Arnold Murhen and Frank Thyssen, who brought style, dignity and success to Ipswich's blend of home-grown talent and continental know-how. Italy and Spain had long welcomed foreign talent from other parts of Europe and South America. But little did we know then that European and world talent would come to dominate and, some would even say, smother the British game and its home-grown talent.

But what of the players of my era? My own journey is well documented. Others went into management and coaching with mixed results. Leadership on the pitch and talent with a ball don't always equate with managerial success. And what of those who didn't take the football management path? Financial insecurity, ill health, poorly equipped to deal with the end to fame. Many found solace at the bottom of a bottle, most found some sort of work elsewhere and, when times got really tough, there were always the medals to sell. We were the first generation to have to deal with the modern stardom of football. Some handled it better than others.

# GEORGE BEST

**Born** 22 May 1946

*Football League debut*:

Manchester United v West Bromwich Albion, 14.9.63

*Football League farewell:*

Bournemouth v Wigan Athletic 7.5.83

*Football League career:*

411 games, 147 goals

# SELECT
# BIBLIOGRAPHY

The following books have been invaluable to me in bringing the era back into focus and I can heartily recommend any one of them as further reading.

*Manchester United Football Book* (Seasons 1965–1974) by David Meek, Stanley Paul, 1965–1974

*Strange Kind of Glory: Life of Sir Matt Busby and Manchester United* by Eamon Dunphy, Heinemann, 1991

*The Official Manchester United Illustrated Encyclopedia*, Manchester United Books, 1998

*Manchester United in Europe: Tragedy, Destiny, History* by Ken Ferris, Mainstream, 2003

*Red Devils in Europe* by David Meek, Hutchinson, 1990

*Seventy-One Guns: The Year of the First Arsenal Double* by David Tossell, Mainstream, 2002

*Charlie George: My Story* by Charlie George, Century, 2005

*Chelsea's Century* by Harry Harris, John Blake, 2005

*Kings of the King's Road: The Great Chelsea Team of the 60s and 70s* by Clive Batty, Vision Sports, 2004

*Glory, Glory Nights: Complete History of Spurs in European Competition* by Colin Gibson and Harry Harris, Hutchinson, 1986

*Bill Shankly: 'It's Much More Important Than That'* by Stephen F. Kelly, Virgin Books, 1996

*The Shankly Years: Revolution in Football – Liverpool FC 1959-74* by Phil Thompson, Ebury Press, 1998

*Everton: School of Science* by James Corbett, Macmillan, 2003

*The Toffees: A Concise Post-War History of Everton* by Dean Hayes, Parrs Wood Press, 2000

*Football with a Smile: Authorised Biography of Joe Mercer* by Gary James, Polar Print, 1993

*Clough: The Autobiography* by Brian Clough, Corgi, 1995

*Clough* by Tony Francis, Stanley Paul, 1993

*Don Revie: Portrait of a Footballing Enigma* by Andrew Mourant, Mainstream, 1990

*The Unforgiven: The Story of Don Revie's Leeds United* by Rob Bagchi, Paul Rogerson, Aurum Press, 2002

*It is Now!: The Inside Story of England's 1966 World Cup Triumph* by Roger Hutchinson, Mainstream, 1995

# INDEX

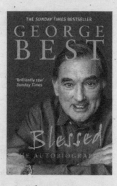